WORLD RELIGIONS

A SOURCE BOOK

1904   041426   1386   7B

This is a Flame Tree Book
First published in 2003

01 03 05 04 02

1 3 5 7 9 10 8 6 4 2

FLAME TREE PUBLISHING
Crabtree Hall, Crabtree Lane, Fulham,
London, SW6 6TY, United Kingdom
www.flametreepublishing.com

Flame Tree is part of
The Foundry Creative Media Company Limited

Copyright © 2003 Flame Tree Publishing

ISBN 1 904041 42 6 trade edition

A copy of the CIP data for this book is available from the British Library

Printed in China

Special thanks to Ray Barnett, Vicky Garrard, Elizabeth Huddlestone, Julia Rolf and Polly Willis

WORLD RELIGIONS

A SOURCE BOOK

INTRODUCTION BY DR SEÁN MCLOUGHLIN

FLAME TREE
PUBLISHING

CONTENTS

INTRODUCTION

World Religions: A Source Book is an informative and accessible reference
work intended for a general readership. A majority of the contributors
are scholars lecturing and researching in universities across three
continents. As anthropologists, geographers, historians, philosophers,
sociologists and theologians, their wide-ranging backgrounds reflect the
dynamic and multidisciplinary nature of the study of religions. Other
contributors are experienced freelance writers and professionals who
have encountered religions and engaged religious people in the course
of their work in the media, religious education, community development

and interfaith relations. Some are 'outsiders' to the religions they write about; others are 'insiders'. However, in the best traditions of the academic study of religion, all bring perspectives of both empathy and critical understanding to their accounts.

Unlike some books on religions, *World Religions* does not confine its interest to 'the usual suspects': Christianity, Islam, Hinduism, Buddhism, Sikhism and Judaism. Rather, it has a more inclusive conspectus and is divided into six sections organized by geographical area: Asia, Africa, the Americas, the Near East, Europe and Oceania/the Pacific. As one might expect, there are substantial chapters on the major world faiths mentioned above, all of which trace their origins to Asia or the Near East. However, often-ignored traditions such as Confucianism, Taoism and Shintoism, are also included. So too are the beliefs and practices to be found in more small-scale African, Native North American, Aboriginal and Maori 'tribal' religions. Moreover, as well as the living traditions that continue to prosper into the twenty-first century, there is room too for an account of the religions of ancient civilizations, from Greece and Rome to the Egyptians in Africa and the Incas of the Americas.

Organizing a study of religions by geographical area has certain advantages. Most obviously, it underlines the importance of locating a tradition in terms of its origins. Sometimes, there is a tendency to view religions as discrete and monolithic 'isms', abstracted from the contingencies of historical context. However, an emphasis on region provides an opportunity to reflect on the relationships between traditions, both in terms of the cross-fertilisation of ideas and the formation of identity through polemics. Certainly, what we know today as the distinctive religions of 'Jainism' and 'Buddhism', both began as

◀ *LEFT: A bas-relief from the Achaemenid necropolis*

developments related to the complex weave of 'Hindu' traditions in India. At the same time, it is impossible to study the monotheism of Judaism without understanding its reaction against the polytheism of Canaanite religion. In the contemporary period, too, the now independent religion of Baha'ism first emerged in the context of messianic Shi'ism in Muslim Iran and Iraq.

While considering religions in terms of their geographical and historical origins is extremely valuable, many of the accounts contained in World Religions also recognise that traditions develop and change not only through time but also across space. Therefore, while in the past some religions have been associated with particular peoples or places, others have always had more 'universalising' ambitions, truly anticipating the notion of 'world' religions. For good or ill, proselytising faiths of Near Eastern origin such as Christianity and Islam have spread successfully to many parts of Asia, Africa, the Americas, Europe and Oceania/the Pacific. Of course, some 'ethnic' religions, such as Judaism, have formed a diaspora for many centuries, while, in an age of globalization, there are few cultures that have not been affected by international migration and pluralism. In any case, whether historically or in the contemporary period, as people have moved from one social, cultural, political and economic context to another, they have had to reconstruct their religious beliefs and practices anew. Therefore some scholars have argued that we can only properly speak of Christianities, Judaisms, Hinduisms and so on, both in terms of diverse and competing denominations and traditions, but also in terms of the adaptation of religions to localised cultures.

Finally, the organization of World Religions requires a little further explanation. In each chapter the text is divided into manageable entries of one or two pages under appropriate subheadings. At the end of each

◄ *LEFT: A statue of the Hawai'ian war god Lu*

entry there are helpful references to related entries within the chapter or elsewhere in the book. Other reference tools to help the reader compare material across traditions include an Index and a Glossary, as well as dedicated sections on Festivals and Sacred Texts. *World Religions* also contains short bibliographies for each of the chapters as a guide to further reading. These bibliographies include a selection of essential titles in each field of study, as well as examples of more recent research. Last but not least, the text is also generously illustrated with an impressive collection of fascinating pictures. Complementing the contributors' texts, they serve to document the many dimensions of religion as one of the most significant and varied aspects of human history and culture: sacred texts, objects, places and personalities; experiences of the transcendent; rituals, festivals and rites of passage; communities, political leaders and social institutions; myths, histories and the development of traditions; theologians and philosophers, law-givers and moral exemplars; art, architecture, music and drama. Enjoy!

Dr. Seán McLoughlin
School of Theology and Religious Studies
University of Leeds

ASIA

c.1450 BC	Development of Brahma worship; composition of the Vedas begins; probable beginnings of Hinduism
605–520 BC	Life of Lao Zi (traditional founder of Taoism)
599–527 BC	Life of Vardhamana Mahavira, the last tirthankaras (founder of Jainism)
566 BC	Buddha born
551–479 BC	Life of Confucius
528 BC	Buddha achieves Nirvana and preaches first sermon
526 BC	Buddha founds Sangha
500 BC	Beginnings of Shinto, Japan
c.500 BC	Zen Buddhism founded by the Historical Buddha as the Dhyana (meditation) tradition
483 BC	Buddha achieves Parinirvana (dies)
50 BC	Jainism spreads to Southern India
AD 125	Third Buddhist Council; acceptance of the Buddha image
2nd century AD	Confucianism becomes official ideology and cult of the state
2nd century AD	Taoism developed into a full-blown religion
7th century AD	Japanese government chooses Shinto to distinguish traditional worship from Buddhism
AD 900	Large-scale construction of Hindu temples, India
AD 960–1279	Sung Dynasty revival of Confucianism
c.1200	Zen Buddhism founded in Japan
1469–1539	Life of Guru Nanak (founder of Sikhism)
1604	The Guru Granth Sahib (Sikh Holy Scripture) was compiled by Guru Arjun
1945	The Rehat Maryada (Sikh Code of Conduct) published

SHAMANISM

Shamanism is recognized as the world's oldest religious tradition, evolving before the Neolithic period (c. 8000–3000 BC) and the Bronze Age (2000–500 BC). It was originally practised among hunting and gathering societies of Siberia and Central Asia.

SAMAN

Shamanism is believed to have been present in most parts of the world, but is known to have originated in Siberia. The word *saman* is derived from the Tungus people of Siberia, becoming shaman in Russian, and has been interpreted to mean 'he who knows' or 'one who is excited, moved, raised.' References to these figures include medicine men, sorcerers, magicians, necromancers, ascetics, healers, ecstatics, acrobats and Brahmans, but essentially the shaman is an indigenous practitioner whose expertise lies in entering a trance which enables his or her soul to travel to the upper and lower worlds of the spirits and demons. Alternatively, in mastering the spirits, the shaman will invite the spirits into him or herself. The shaman's journey through this altered state of consciousness is conducted in order to pass into the world of the spirits as a mediator for his tribe or people.

Siberian shamans have distinguished between the realms of the cosmos, according it upper, middle and lower realms. Shamans can rescue souls from the lower realm of the cosmos, whilst attaining council from those in the heavens. Siberians also distinguish shamans as being 'black shamans' or 'white shamans'. The black shaman calls upon a wicked deity and the wicked spirit whilst shamanizing, whereas the white shaman applies to a benevolent deity and to good spirits.

◘ *see* THE SHAMAN p. 140

▲ *ABOVE: A shaman in Nepal enters a trance aided by the sound of flutes*

SHAMANS

Shamans come into their roles for a variety of reasons. Often it is a question of inheritance, or they are something of a social misfit, or else they undergo an alteration in character. They may appear possessed and experience remarkable behavioural changes and neurosis. This is referred to as the Initiation Crisis. Generally, once initiated, these symptoms disappear and the shaman abandons his or her former life in submission to a new path. Women are as likely as men to be shamans. Essentially the shamans are in possession of a supernatural gift that is received from the spirit realm and the donor becomes the spiritual guide or spiritual 'spouse'. Shamans know initiation when they have an apparition of their guide, who will seemingly steal the soul and travel to another realm of the cosmos where the soul will perish, only to be reproduced and, in a sense, reborn into a new vocation.

🔄 see SAMAN p. 12

▼ BELOW: A shaman's soul catcher from British Columbia

SHAMANIC RITUALS AND PROPS

Shamanic rituals differ in all traditions, yet all share certain characteristics. These are associated with the trance-like state attained by the shaman in order to journey to the outer realms or to submit to possession by the otherworldly spirits. To coax the shaman into trance certain props are used. The most common of these is the shaman's costume which, when examined, reveals the core beliefs of shamanism, as any doctrine or myth might. The Siberian costume consists of a caftan adorned with mythical animals and iron discs, used for protection whilst in combat with the spirits. A mask is a very common feature sported by the shaman. Often grotesque and extraordinary, with extravagant colour and awesome designs, it allows the shamans to be transported, disguising them from their peers. Often the shaman is blindfolded and so journeys by an inner light, isolated from the outer reality. Animal skin, fur, feathers, bones, bells, a staff, a crown or cap and staves make up the shaman's regalia. During the ritual, the shaman will induce violent breathing, may shake or sweat furiously, and may dance in a wild, frenetic manner, aided always by the constant and climactic beating of the drum.

◗ see SHAMANS p. 14

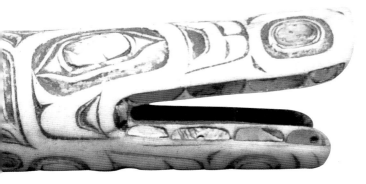

HINDUISM

The word Hindu is derived from the name given to the people who settled on the banks of the river Sindhu (Indus in northern India). Hinduism is regarded as the most ancient living world religion, being over 5,000 years old. It originated on the subcontinent of India but its uniqueness lies in the fact that it was not based upon or started by any one single individual, and its origins cannot be traced back to any particular historical period. Hinduism is regarded as a way of life, not just a religion.

SHRUTI AND SMIRITI

Hinduism has as its basis an enormous collection of texts which were conceived many thousands of years ago by various authors in the Sanskrit language – the root of all modern Indian languages. These were not actually written down until relatively modern times but were passed down by many learned *rishis* or sages who realized these teachings.

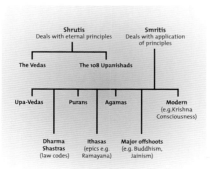

These Hindu scriptures contain systematic explanations on various subjects including science, religion, metaphysics (first principles), philosophy and spiritual knowledge. They are not limited to a few books because Hinduism is not confined to a single set of ideas

◄ *LEFT: Hindu Scriptures*

and so the scriptures have become a home for many different schools of thought. They are divided into two main categories: *Shruti* ('that which is heard') and *Smriti* ('that which is remembered').

The *Shrutis* deal with the never-changing, eternal principles of Hinduism. *Shrutis* consist of the *Vedas*, which are the root of the Hindu religion and are possibly the oldest books in the world. There are four *Vedas*:

- *Rig Veda* – deals with general knowledge, and is the longest of the Vedas.
- *Sama Veda* – deals with knowledge of worship (upasana) and is also the originator of Indian Classical Music.
- *Yajur Veda* – deals with knowledge of action (karma).
- *Atharva Veda* – deals with knowledge of science, and other miscellaneous subjects.

▶ *RIGHT: The* Sri Bhagavata Purana

There are also the *Upanishads*, of which there are approximately 108. These are known as *Vedanta* ('the end of the *Vedas*') They were written to make understanding of the *Vedas* easier. They contain the essence of the *Vedas* and also conclusions from them (hence the name *Vedanta*).

The *Smritis* explain the practical applications of the eternal principles described in the *Shrutis*. They detail social and moral codes in the 18 *Smritis*, the most famous of which was written by the great *rishi* Manu which explains the four stages of life and the division of labour through a class system. The *Smritis* also contain the *Puranas*, of which there are 18 major ones. These are a series of myths and legends, as well as the stories of great men which were designed to simplify religious teaching for the benefit of the people. However what is most famous about the *Smritis* is the two great epic poems, the *Ramayana* and the *Mahabharata*. The characters described in these epics give a set of ideals to which a person can aspire and so they display the perfect examples of kindness, nobility and faithfulness which are intended to inspire the reader.

The *Mahabharata* contains the famous section known as the *Bhagavad Gita*, which is the essence of the *Vedas* and the *Upanishads*, which have been beautifully condensed into 700 concise *shlokas* (verses). It is renowned as the jewel of ancient India's spiritual wisdom, and was spoken by Lord Krishna (an incarnation of Vishnu) on the great battlefield of the Mahabharata.

◆ *see* HINDU GODS AND GODDESSES p. 23

BRAHMAN

It is a commonly held belief that Hindus worship many gods. However, God in Hinduism is thought of as Brahman – the Absolute. This is to say a being without form who pervades everything, is present everywhere, is

▶ RIGHT: A statue of the god
Ganesh from Sri Lanka

all-knowing, is all-powerful and who transcends time and space. This is the Nirguna (attributeless) Brahman. There is another aspect of God, and this is Saguna (with attributes) Brahman.

There are different schools of thought about the nature of Brahman. Among these are three main ones. *Shankara charya* is the upholder of attributeless Brahman i.e. there is only one Brahman and the individual soul is also Brahman, with *maya* (the material world) being an illusion or a dreamworld of Brahman. This philosophy is termed absolute non-dualism. *Ramanuja charya* stood for Brahman as being full of attributes: He is the ocean of wisdom, bliss and grace. *Maya* is a power of Brahman and is a part of him. The individual soul is also a small part of Brahman, and when experiencing bliss can be said to be the same as Brahman. This is qualified non-dualism. *Madhava charya* said that in Brahman there are both aspects. He is attributeless as well as full of attributes.

Also, the individual soul is limited and is under the influence of *maya*; while Brahman is all powerful, all pervading and all knowing, and *maya* is subject to Him. Therefore the individual soul should always try to seek God. This philosophy is termed dualism. There are all these different views, which may cause confusion, but the *Upanishads* also declare that self-realization is the supreme unity, and in it alone all differences are harmonized.

◖ *see* HINDU GODS AND GODDESSES p. 23

KARMA

Life is a long journey back to the creator, 'interrupted' by death for the person's own good, to continue the journey in another body. This concept of rebirth is explained simply by Lord Krishna in the *Bhagavad Gita* as follows: 'As a man leaves an old garment and puts on one that is new, the spirit leaves his mortal body and then puts on one that is new.'

The law of *karma* is the concept that 'As you sow, so shall you reap.' Therefore action and reaction (on a physical, mental and spiritual level) are equal and opposite. *Karma* is what a person does, what a person thinks, and even what a person does not do. The results of one's actions in one life can also be carried over to the next, which can affect one's fortunes depending on the individual's past actions.

◖ *see* THE FOUR NOBLE TRUTHS p. 45

MOKSHA

Meaning total freedom from all pain and suffering, *Moksha* is the goal of life for all Hindus. It is the mind which is said to be the cause of suffering, or freedom from suffering. If a state of mind is reached when

▶ *RIGHT: A preacher gives a sermon in a Hindu temple*

one is able to transcend the pains and the pleasures of life, when one's will merges with the will of God, then that person has attained *Moksha* and is free from the cycle of births and deaths. This joining of oneself with God is called *yoga*.

⬦ see YOGA p. 22

YOGA

Skilfulness and excellence in action is *yoga*; all activities performed with God-consciousness is the supreme yoga. The science of *yoga* consists of different paths and the subdivisions are as follows:

Karma Yoga (the Path of Action) is that if a person acts with his or her mind fixed on Brahman (God) he or she will become free and at peace. The results of one's actions should be offered up to God in order to become one with Him.

Jnana Yoga (the Way of Knowledge) is achieved through study, meditation and contemplation.
Bhakti Yoga (the Way of Devotion) is worshipping God through a particular image or form, and keeping one's mind constantly upon God by prayer and devotion.
Mantra Yoga uses chants of the all-pervading sound 'Aum' with the name of one's chosen deity.
Raja Yoga (the Path of Dedication) focuses on

◀ LEFT: Shabari is considered to be a perfect example of devotion to god in the yogic tradition

control of the mind, often through meditation, or pranic (life-force breathing), which allows one to commune with God. Most seekers practise some or a combination of all these paths to succeed. However it is *Hatha Yoga* (physical postures and breathing exercises, regarded as the first stage to reach God) which is practised with considerable interest in the West.

see BRAHMAN p. 18

HINDU GODS AND GODDESSES

Those who are beginning on a path of spirituality cannot immediately embrace the concept of the Absolute or Brahman. It is much easier to contemplate a physical manifestation of God, and use that as a means to concentrate and focus one's mind.

▶ *RIGHT: The god Shiva*

The many manifestations of God give the different aspects of the Absolute through which He can be reached. The Absolute controls the universe through three major qualities, regarded as the Trinity or *Trimurti* of Hinduism: Brahma – The Creator, Vishnu – The Preserver and Shiva – The Destroyer. All three of these are inseparable and operate simultaneously. The function of Brahma is to create through the will of God. Vishnu in turn preserves what is created, and to that end he is said to have incarnated on earth during various stages of humanity's evolution to destroy evil and re-establish righteousness. Shiva is regarded as the destroyer, for he is believed to periodically destroy the world when evil has prevailed, so that it might be recreated in its pure form. In temples he is worshipped in the phallic form of a Shiva lingam which represents the indefinable nature of the Absolute. His physical form is that of an ascetic (one who has given up the world and its pleasures); and his ash-covered body serves to remind all that the body eventually ends up as ash.

The female aspect of God is a fundamental part of Hinduism and the all-compassionate form of the Divine Mother is very dear to all Hindus. There are many different female deities. Saraswati, the consort of Brahma, represents the power of knowledge, best utilized to find God. The symbols used for gaining knowledge are rosary beads, books and music. Her white sari signifies purity of motive to gain knowledge.

The consort of Vishnu, Lakshmi, is the goddess of wealth. She is said to have accompanied Vishnu in his *avatars* (e.g. as Sita when he incarnated as Rama). She is seen standing on a lotus flower. The lotus grows in muddy waters yet is beautiful; similarly humanity needs to learn to live in this harsh world with detachment from its surroundings.

◄ LEFT: *Mother Parvati, revered as a protector of good and destroyer of evil*

Parvati, the consort of Shiva, is more commonly worshipped as the destructive form of the Mother Goddess, called Durga or Kali. She is called upon to destroy evil in times of need and to give protection to good people. Her form, riding upon a tiger and holding symbols of power in her eight hands emphasizes this purpose.

Hindus can worship the deity of their choice. In the path of devotion, those who see God as the Divine Mother and worship all the female forms as one, are called *Shaktas*. Those who worship Shiva as the all-pervading God are known as *Saivas* and those who worship Vishnu (usually as Lord Krishna) are *Vaishnavas*. The *Agamas* are the writings which deal with all aspects of these philosophies.

◆ *see* BRAHMAN p. 18

THE AVATARS OF VISHNU

Vishnu is thought to have incarnated nine times already upon the earth, in various different forms, to save humanity from evil. His most famous incarnations for Hindus are as Rama and Krishna, the central characters in the epics *Ramayana* and *Mahabharata* respectively. They have a rich cultural significance and provide models for society. Therefore Vishnu is worshipped mainly through the forms of these incarnations. The Buddha, progenitor of Buddhism, and Mahavira, founder of Jainism, are also believed to be his incarnations who came at times when society needed rejuvenation. There is a tenth *Avatar* of Vishnu called Kalki who will come at a future time to save mankind and to promote righteousness.

◆ *see* HINDU GODS AND GODDESSES p. 23

SANTS (SAINTS)

All Hindus look upon saints as a reflection of God. The saint would have many of the qualities that one would associate with God. India has produced many saints or masters who would fit this description. Among them are Guru Nanak, the founder of Sikhism, Ramakrishna

◀ LEFT: The avatars of Vishnu

Paramahansa, Sai Baba and Chaitanya Mahaprabhu. Shree Chaitanya Mahaprabhu was a great saint born in 1542. He propounded the message of devotion to Lord Krishna. According to him, glorifying the divine names and attributes of Lord Krishna through chanting is the supreme

means of salvation. Swami Prabhupada, the founder of the Hare Krishna movement, was a follower of Chaitanya Mahaprabhu.

💠 *see* THE ULTIMATE SPIRITUAL REALITY p. 86

ASHRAMAS

Human life is considered a journey to meet with the creator, yet human desires need to be fulfilled along the way. The Hindu way of life combines both these needs in the four stages (*ashramas*) of life.

- The first, or student, stage (*Brahmacharya*) is for good education, self discipline, learning about one's *dharma* (a person's rightful duty to self, family and society) and laying a good foundation to life for being physically and mentally strong for the future.

- Entering the family life (*Grihasta*) is the second stage. Life is not complete without marriage and children. A loving, caring family environment enables one to serve others, including the community and the nation. This stage of life allows the acquiring of material possessions for comfortable living and enjoyment of worldly happiness through the satisfaction of man's natural desires.

- The third stage is retirement (*Vanaprastha*). Once the children are all settled one can start withdrawing oneself from worldly desires and attachments to devote more time to spiritual pursuits.

- The final stage is *Sanyasa* (preparing for *moksha*) when one renounces all desires, possessions and needs, spending every moment in meditation. There are some who take up this stage from a young age, even before marriage, to spend the rest of their lives in pursuit of self-realization. It is the duty of the *Grihasta* to provide for the day-to-day needs of the *Sanyasi*.

◀ *LEFT: A woman prays in the river Ganges, India*

SAMSKARAS

Within the above-mentioned four stages (from birth to death) there are 16 *Samskaras* (sacraments). Apart from the funeral sacraments all the others are causes for celebration. Friends and relations are invited, fed and entertained with dance and music. While some of the 16 are rarely practised nowadays, the main ones are as follows:

- The birth ceremony.
- The sacred thread ceremony, where the child is 'initiated' and given a sacred mantra or name of God to chant regularly.
- The Hindu marriage.
- The final *Samskara* after death.

◖ *see* FESTIVALS p. 34

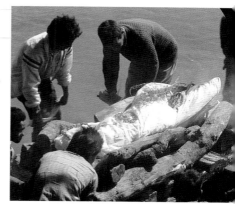

▶ RIGHT: A body is prepared for cremation in Varanassi, India

THE CASTE SYSTEM

Thousands of years ago a *Varna*, or class, system was introduced into Hindu society, in order to give it a strong infrastructure. Each person was put into one of the four classes according to the role in society they could best perform.

- *Brahmins*: those who took to learning and imparted knowledge and spiritual guidance to others.
- *Kshatriyas*: those who were to defend and protect society (as warriors and lawmakers).
- *Vaishyas*: those who provided for the material needs of the people, especially food.
- *Sudras*: those who served the community.

Originally all the classes were equal, but the system slowly became corrupt as the class began to be determined by birth, or caste, rather than personal qualities. This caused discrimination and created divisions in society. However, in modern times, through the efforts of Mahatma Gandhi and many other Hindus, the system has been outlawed, and although its influence is still strong, Hindu society is being reoriented.

◆ see ASHRAMS p. 29

◀ LEFT: A marriage ceremony in Kerala, India

MANDIR AND PUJA

A *mandir* or temple is a Hindu place of worship. While most Hindus have a shrine in their own home to worship the deity of their choice, a purpose-built temple for the whole community has great importance. It serves as a centre where God is worshipped in the presence of a congregation. Many festivals, religious events and regular ceremonies are held with great enthusiasm, to create a religious atmosphere which encourages the mind to turn towards God for real peace. The temple is meant to reflect the human body. It has an outer structure with shrines, inside which the deities reside. The human body is an outer casing inside which God resides, in the form of the *atman* or soul.

The deities in a temple are regarded as living entities after installation ceremonies, and the resident priest has to look after them as such (i.e. wake them, bathe them, put clothes on them, offer them food and put them to sleep). Some devotees visit the temple regularly, others when they have the time or on special occasions. They offer *puja* (worship) collectively with the priest during the daily service and also partly by themselves individually in a number of different ways including the offering of food.

◆ see FESTIVALS p. 34

◀ *LEFT: Radha and Krishna*

▲ *ABOVE: The* arti *ceremony*

THE SACRED COW

The cow was perhaps the first animal to be domesticated by Hindus in India. It was a real blessing to the ancient rural community because it provided milk, from which many other common food products could be made. Cow dung would also be used as a fuel and could be mixed with mud for plastering walls and floors. On farms, bulls were used to plough the fields as well as being used for travel and transport of goods. It is hardly surprising that soon the cow occupied in the life of man the same position as a mother in the life of a child. It became unthinkable to kill and eat the flesh of one. In Vedic literature the cow is a symbol of the divine bounty of the earth and the scriptures prohibit the slaughter of cows. This is the reason for the Hindu reverence for cows, and why Hindus refrain from eating beef. This belief is also designed to encourage people not to harm or kill any creature, and so many Hindus are vegetarians.

see PARASPAROPAGRAHOJIVAANAM p. 42

FESTIVALS

The Hindu Calendar is full of festivals, religious, cultural and social. The festivals are varied and colourful and temples get crowded at these times as people always come (for *darshan*) to offer their prayers. Some of the most important festivals are *Diwali*, *Navratri*, *Janmashtami* (birth of Lord Krishna) and *Holi*.

Diwali is a rich and exciting tradition and heritage left by the great teachers of the past. It is a five-day festival. The first three days are dedicated to the female deities Mahalaxmi, Mahakali and Mahasaraswati, the goddesses of wealth, strength and knowledge (the

word maha means 'the purest'). Prayers are offered to use these gifts for the highest good of humanity. The fourth day is the Hindu New Year's Day – a day of forgetting, forgiving and conveying good wishes to one and all for a happy and prosperous new year. The fifth day is a demonstration of love between the brother and the sister with partaking of food together and a sharing of gifts.

Navratri, or the 'Nine Nights', festival takes the form of celebrating by dancing to music around images of the Divine Mother. The devotees dance by clapping their hands (*garba*) or by using small sticks (*raas*). The festival takes place to celebrate the victory of the Divine Mother over the demon Mahishasur. The more devout devotees of the Divine Mother fast and devote as much time as possible during the nine days and nights to praying and receiving blessings.

The birthday of Lord Krishna during August is celebrated at midnight (Indian Time). Devotees come to do *darshan* and receive the privilege of rocking the cradle of baby Krishna.

Guru Purnima is celebrated on the full moon day in around June or July. Puja is first offered to Veda Vyasa, the compiler of the *Vedas* and the writer of the *Mahabharata*. *Puja* is then offered to one's own *guru* or spiritual guide (or Lord Krishna if one does not have a *guru*.). This is the only day when the followers are allowed to give whatever they want to the *guru*, who usually accepts it.

Raksha Bandhan occurs on the next full moon (during July or August). The sister ties a multicoloured string, *rakhi*, on the right wrist of the brother. This symbolizes the affection between the sister and brother who in return promises to protect her throughout the year.

⬧ see HINDU GODS AND GODDESSES p. 23

◀ LEFT: A man draws a rangoli pattern during Diwali

PILGRIMAGE

India is thought of as the holy land of all Hindus. Temples, rivers, mountains, cities and other holy places are reminders of historical events from the scriptures or of saints and sages who lived up to the teachings of the scriptures. During pilgrimage, whatever one's status, the simplest living and highest thinking are of the essence. Any difficulties encountered are considered as a test of one's strength of will for the success of the pilgrimage. Pilgrimage may be for the fulfilment of a vow or as a result of a birth or death in a family.

The River Ganges is revered as 'Mother Ganga' and the devotees have faith that bathing in the holy river will wash away their sins. The river's forceful and destructive flow from the heavens is believed to be halted through flowing first into the matted locks of Lord Shiva and then letting it flow more gently for the benefit of mankind. The *Kumbha Mela*, a gathering of all Hindus, at Allahabad on the banks of the Ganges is held every 12 years, and is the biggest gathering of people that takes place in the world.

see PILGRIMAGE p. 147

▶ *RIGHT: Devotees make the pilgrimage to the river Ganges*

JAINISM

The name Jainism comes from Jina, meaning 'victor' over the passions and the self. Jinas, whom Jains call *tirthankaras* attained omniscience by shedding destructive *karma* and taught the spiritual path of happiness and perfection to all humans. Jainism is centred around the Indian subcontinent, and is one of the oldest religions in that region.

TIRTHANKARAS

Jains believe that time rotates in a cycle, descending and ascending. In each half of the cycle 24 *tirthankaras* establish the fourfold order (*sangha*) consisting of monks, nuns, laymen and laywomen, and revive the teachings of the previous *tirthankaras*. The first *tirthankara* in this descending cycle was Risabhdeva, who is traditionally believed to have lived thousands of centuries ago. The twenty-third was Parsvanatha (c. 870–770 BC) and the twenty-fourth and last was Vardhamana Mahavira (599–527 BC).

see MAHAVIRA p. 37

◀ LEFT: Jain temple near Jaisalmer, Rajastan province, India

MAHAVIRA

Mahavira became a Jina at the age of 42. He attracted a large number of people, both men and women, to his teachings. Those who accepted vows totally (*mahaavrata*) became ascetics. He taught his followers to observe:

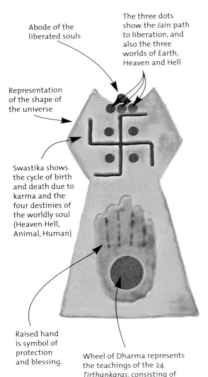

The three dots show the Jain path to liberation, and also the three worlds of Earth, Heaven and Hell

Abode of the liberated souls

Representation of the shape of the universe

Swastika shows the cycle of birth and death due to karma and the four destinies of the worldly soul (Heaven Hell, Animal, Human)

Raised hand is symbol of protection and blessing.

Wheel of Dharma represents the teachings of the 24 *Tirthankaras*, consisting of non-violence and other virtuals

- *Ahimsaa*: non-violence and reverence for all life
- *Satya*: truthfulness; communication in a pleasant and non-hurtful manner that is free from falsehood
- *Asteya*: not stealing or taking anything which belongs to others without their permission
- *Brahmacharya*: chastity and control over senses, for the ascetics total celibacy and for the laity faithfulness to one's spouse
- *Aparigraha*: non-attachment to material things

Mahavira was a great reformer and addressed the various problems of the day, such as the caste system, slavery, equality of women, carnal desires, killing or harming life for religious rituals or pleasure of the senses. He taught acceptance of

◀ LEFT: The symbol for Jainism

multiple views (*anekaantaavada*) and qualifying dogmatic assertions (*syaadavaada*), a spiritual democracy that made Jains tolerant to others.

▶ *see* TIRTHANKARAS p. 37

JIVA AND AJIVA

The universe as conceived by Jains has two parts, occupied and unoccupied, and it consists of six substances: the soul, matter, medium of motion, medium of rest, space and time. All except the matter are formless.

The soul is the living being (*jiva*) and the others are non-living substances (*ajiva*). Both *jiva* and *ajiva* are interdependent and everlasting. It is the attachment of non-living substance (*karma*) to the soul that causes apparent injustices of life, and an unending cycle of birth, death and rebirth in any destiny: heavenly, human, animal and plants or infernal as a mobile being with two to five senses or as an immobile being with one sense. The celestial beings live in the 'upper world' of the occupied universe. Humans, animals and plants, astral bodies and lower kinds of heavenly beings occupy the 'middle world'. The infernal beings live in the lower world.

The Jain way of life aims to shed *karma* attached to the soul and manifest the soul's true characteristics: infinite bliss, infinite knowledge, amity and equanimity. It consists of the coordinated path of the 'Three Jewels': Right Faith, Right Knowledge and Right Conduct. Right Faith is belief in the nine 'real entities' (living being, non-living being, merit, demerit, influx of *karma*, *karmic* bondage, stoppage of *karma*, shedding of *karma* and liberation); Right Knowledge is a proper grasp of the nine 'real entities'; and Right Conduct is the ethical code, behaviour and actions taught by the Jinas.

▶ *see* KARMA p. 40

KARMA

Jainism describes *karma* as a subtle matter, not perceptible to the senses, found everywhere in the cosmos and having the property of penetrating the soul and clouding its characteristics. The soul's activities cause vibrations in its structure and cause *karmic* particles to be attracted (influx) to it. If there is *karmic* matter around the soul, these particles will stick to it, but if it is absent as in liberated souls it will not stick. Benevolent acts cause good *karma* (merit), while sinful acts cause bad *karma* (demerit). Both merit and demerit keep the soul in the worldly cycle, they do not cancel each other out.

The quantity, size, type and density of *karmic* particles determine the severity of *karmic* bondage and the form that the soul will assume in forthcoming births and its inherent passions. Of course, external environments affect these passions, increasing their severity in a complementary way, but Right Conduct can influence the *karmic* result and reduce suffering. On maturity *karmic* particles attached to the soul discharge continuously, but as replenishment also takes place, the soul remains in bondage.

Liberation of the soul from the *karmic* bondage is a two-stage process: stoppage of *karmic* flow (blocking of all channels through which *karma* flows by ethical behaviour and control over desires); and shedding the attached *karma* by austerities. When all *karmic* particles are shed, which may occur after long spiritual development, the soul attains liberation and reverts to its natural state. It ascends to the apex of the universe where it dwells in *siddha silaa*, a liberated soul without material body, enjoying infinite bliss, infinite knowledge, amity and equanimity.

see KARMA p. 20

▶ ***RIGHT: Jain temples in Gujurat, India***

PARASPAROPAGRAHOJIVAANAM

The guiding principle of the Jain practice is their conviction in the phrase *parasparopagrahojivaanam*, meaning interdependence of life on each other. Jains are vegetarians; they care for the environment and are involved in human and animal welfare. They have built beautiful

temples all over India and observe many festivals; most are spiritual in nature such as *paryushana* (sacred days of fasting and forgiveness).

They observe six essential duties: equanimity, veneration of the 24 *tirthankaras*, veneration of ascetics, penitential retreat, renunciation and meditation with bodily detachment, which are meant to enhance their quality of life, physically, mentally and spiritually.

Jainism, though restricted to a minority, continues to be a living tradition. The Jain way of life is not at odds with normal everyday life. It is an ethical doctrine with self-discipline as its core. It does not recognize an Almighty God or a Supreme Being as creator God, but believes in godhood that can be attained by any of us, provided we follow the teachings of the Jina and liberate our souls through self-effort. Jains worship *tirthankaras* as examples and do not ask for any favours.

 see THE SACRED COW p. 33

PRATIKRAMANA AND PARYUSHANA

Jains perform penitential retreat (*pratikramana*) daily in the morning and evening to shed the *karma* that is

◀ *LEFT: Devotees at a statue of the Jain saint Lord Bahubali*

◀ LEFT: The Ranakpur Temple in Rajastan

attracted due to the transgressions of Right Conduct, knowingly or unknowingly. They ask for forgiveness for their transgressions, perform penance, and see that such aberrations are not repeated. Jains observe *paryushana*, an annual period of atonement and repentance for the acts of the previous year, and of austerities to shed accumulated karma. Listening to the *Kalpa Sutra* (sacred text), taking positive steps to ensure that living beings are not killed, showing amity to fellow Jains, forgiveness to all, austerity and visiting neighbouring temples, these are important activities undertaken during this festival. On the final day (*samvatsari*), Jains seek forgiveness from all for any harm which they have caused and forgive those who have harmed them, saying '*micchami dukkadam*'.

◆ *see* KARMA p. 40

DIGAMBRA AND SVETAMBRA

In the fourth century AD, Jainism developed two major divisions: *Digambara* (sky-clad ascetics) and *Svetambara* (white-robed ascetics). With the passage of time, both *Digambara* and *Svetambara* communities have continued to develop, almost independently of each other, into different sects.

◆ *see* JIVA AND AJIVA p. 39

▶ *RIGHT: A 14 m (46 ft) long reclining Buddha at Vihara in Sri Lanka*

BUDDHISM

The Buddha was born, lived and died a human being. He is not a god. The special thing about him was that he realized the state of sublime wisdom and compassion called *Nirvana*. He discovered the causes of all suffering, and the way by which all beings could reach the same state.

THE FOUR NOBLE TRUTHS

The heart of the Buddha's teaching are the Four Noble Truths. They are:

- The fact of suffering;
- The cause of suffering;
- The fact that there is a way out of suffering;
- The way itself.

The Buddha observed that all beings suffered. The cause of this suffering is selfish desire, and a misunderstanding of the nature of 'self', which is not the fixed, separate and enduring entity that it appears to be. What we call 'self' is actually a collection of *skandhas* (heaps or particles) which are constantly changing. These are form, feelings, perception, mind-contents and consciousness. The relationship of these constitutes our 'self' at any moment, and creates *karma* (action and reaction) which influences our birth, life and rebirth. One of the *skandhas* is form, so rebirth is always in some form, which need not be human.

Having discovered for himself that there is a way out of suffering, the Buddha proceeded to outline it. This is the final Truth, The Noble Eightfold Path of the way out of suffering:

- Right view (understanding, attitude);
- Right aim (intention, resolve, motive or thought);
- Right speech (not lying, slandering or gossiping);
- Right action (or conduct);
- Right livelihood (means of living);
- Right effort;
- Right mindfulness (awareness of things as they are);
- Right concentration (contemplation, meditation).

The Buddha summed up this path as: 'Cease to do evil; learn to do good, and purify your heart.'

see THE LIFE OF THE BUDDHA p. 46

THE LIFE OF THE BUDDHA

Gautama Siddhartha, the historical Buddha, was born in the year 566 BC, the son of the king of the Sakya people in present-day Nepal. At his birth it was prophesied that he would either become a world ruler or a great sage. His father wanted the former, so he arranged for his son to be brought up without seeing the troubles of the world. Gautama grew up to be a handsome youth, who excelled in all kinds of activities. He lived a happy and contented life within the walls of the palace, and married a princess, Yasodhara, who bore him a son, Rahula.

One day, Gautama persuaded his groom to take him outside the city walls. There he encountered four things which changed his life. First he saw an old man, then a sick man, and a corpse. Gautama was shocked, and asked for an explanation. The groom told him that these conditions were normal, and happened to everyone. Gautama then met a wandering holy man, who had given up everything to practise the religious life and seek the answer to suffering. He radiated a sense of serenity which Gautama knew he had to find.

Soon afterwards, Gautama shaved his head, and slipped out of the palace. He wandered far and wide, begging for his food, and subjecting himself to all kinds of austerities. Eventually, almost dying with hunger, he decided such practices would not achieve his goal. He resolved to practise a middle way between austerity and luxury. He took a little food, and sat beneath a tree at a place called Bodh Gaya in present-day Bihar, vowing not to move until he had achieved his goal.

At the age of 35, on the night of the full moon in May, he realized *Nirvana*,

▶ RIGHT: *Solid gold Buddha from Thailand*

(awakening, enlightenment) entering into deep meditation and becoming the Buddha, the Enlightened One. The Buddha would never explain *Nirvana*, saying that it is essentially beyond words and thoughts, and so Buddhists also refrain from speculating about it.

see THE FOUR NOBLE TRUTHS p. 45

THE DHARMA

In his lifetime, the Buddha taught all who wanted to listen, men and women, rich and poor. His message was always the same: 'suffering, the causes of suffering and the way out of suffering'. He did not talk about God or the soul, or encourage speculation in matters that could not be proved. Rather, he specifically told people to believe and practise only those things which were helpful and led to freedom and peace of mind. It was a combination of profound wisdom and deep compassion, and a practical way which could be followed by those who wished. This teaching he called the *Dharma*. Many of his disciples chose to follow the Buddha into the homeless life, and thus was born the *Sangha*, or community.

🔹 *see* THE LIFE OF THE BUDDHA p. 46

SANGHA

Following the death of the Buddha in 483 BC, the concept of the *Sangha*, or community, of monks grew ever more important. The Buddha had ordained monks in his lifetime, calling them to follow the homeless life and practise the *Dharma*, and their number continued to grow after his passing.

The first monks were considered to be arahats, beings enlightened by the Buddha's teaching. They in turn ordained others. The Buddha had charged his followers to 'travel for the welfare and happiness of people, and out of compassion for the world', and this they did. Some 200 years after the Buddha's death the movement had spread throughout India. They depended on lay people for food and other necessities, and the relationship grew whereby the monks were fed in

◀ *LEFT: The symbol of the Buddha's eyes, painted on a temple wall in Kathmandu, Nepal*

return for teaching. The Buddha's teaching embraced all classes, as he rejected the caste system and taught that all could attain enlightenment.

Soon after the Buddha's death (in approximately 483 BC), the First Great Council of 500 senior monks was held. These monks were all *arahats* who had known the Buddha. They met to recite the teaching as they remembered it, and to agree a definitive version.

The teaching was preserved in oral tradition, and it was not until many years later that it was written down. It was grouped into three *pitakas* or baskets. *Vinaya* consisted of the rules for monks (*bhikkhus*)

▼ BELOW: Four young monks at the Bodnath Stupa, Kathmandu valley, Nepal

◄ LEFT: Nuns pray at Anuradhapura, Sri Lanka

and nuns (*bhikkhunis*). These not only provide guidelines for the monastic life, but allow for settling of disputes and imposing discipline. *Sutta* is the collection of the Buddha's sermons, while *abhidamma* (higher *Dharma*) consists largely of philosophical analysis of the Buddha's teachings. It was the differing interpretations in this section which caused most of the disputes between the various emerging schools.

A second Great Council took place around 383 BC. By this time, several schools had come into existence. Part of the controversy was over whether Buddhists should only try to gain their own enlightenment (*arahats*) or whether they should seek the freedom from suffering of all beings (*bodhisattvas*). In fact, as compassion is an essential aspect of Buddhist practice, this is largely a question of semantics. Today, there are two main traditions, the *Theravada* or Teaching of the Elders, and the *Mahayana* or Greater Vehicle, which contains a number of different traditions such as *Zen*, *Vajrayana* and Pure Land.

see THE CASTE SYSTEM p. 31

THERAVADA BUDDHISM

Theravada – the Way of the Elders – is the oldest form of Buddhism, being largely unchanged from the third century BC. It is found throughout Southeast Asia. Its teachings come from the *Pali* Scriptures, interpreted in a conservative manner which gives prime importance to the *Sangha* of ordained monks and the liberation of the individual.

The essence of the *Theravadin* way is based on the monastic life. This is the way to attain *Nirvana*, and, for most lay people, the goal is to be reborn in a life where they can become a monk or nun. Many laymen become monks for a few months, either in their teens or after their families have been cared for.

The *Sangha* is supported by lay people, and monks are not allowed to work or handle money. Their main activities are meditation, study and teaching the *Dharma*. Their only possessions are their robes, and a few articles for daily use such as a toothbrush and begging bowl. The *Theravadin Sangha* claims unbroken succession from the Buddha, as each ordination has to be conducted by a number of fully ordained monks.

The teachings of the *Theravada* are the basic ones of Buddhism. They are the Signs of Being, (*dukkha*, that life is essentially unsatisfactory, *annica*, that all things are impermanent or constantly changing, and *anatta*, that we do not have a permanent unchanging self); the Four Noble Truths and the Noble Eightfold Path. The practise of morality is very important, based on the Precepts or rule of life. The five basic precepts are:

- Not to kill or harm living beings;
- Not to take what is not freely given;
- Not to indulge in sexual impropriety;
- Not to use slanderous or lying speech;
- Not to become intoxicated by using substances which cloud the mind.

▶ *RIGHT: A monk at Angkor Wat, Cambodia*

People become Buddhists by announcing, usually before a monk, that they, 'Take refuge in the Buddha, *Dharma* and *Sangha*', and by agreeing to follow these five precepts.

An important practice is meditation, which is the way the Buddha achieved his goal. There are many kinds of meditation, and the basic forms practised in *Theravada* Buddhism are also found in other traditions.

◇ *see* SANGHA p. 49

◀ *LEFT: Borobodur, Java. Each dome contains a statue of the Buddha*

MAHAYANA BUDDHISM

Mahayana is the form of Buddhism found in Tibet, China, Mongolia, Vietnam, Korea and Japan. It recognizes the *Theravadin* scriptures and adds many more, some of which were composed after Buddha's lifetime. Some were based on remembered teaching, others are mythological, and some are said to have been recorded and hidden until the time came to reveal them.

In *Mahayana* Buddhism, Buddha is not limited to the historical Gautama. There are other Buddhas recognized who are not historical figures, but who represent different aspects of his enlightenment. Two

▶ *RIGHT: Statues guard the tomb of Emperor Tu Doc in Vietnam*

of the principle ones are Amitabha (the Buddha of Infinite Light) and Bhaisajya (The Medicine Buddha), but there are many more. Their lives and teachings were revealed by Shakyamuni Buddha, and are recorded in the *Mahayana* scriptures to help disciples understand various practices.

There are also *bodhisattvas* such as the Chinese Guan Yin or the Tibetan Tara, who represent the personification of active compassion, and Manjusri, the manifestation of wisdom. *Bodhisattvas* are often spiritualized beings who were disciples of the historical Buddha, but who delayed their own enlightenment, choosing to remain on earth, until all beings are freed from suffering. Their power can help practitioners who know the correct way of invoking it.

▲ *ABOVE: A sculpture of the Bhudda at Daoding Hill, China*

Mahayana practices include all the forms of meditation, as well as the practise of morality. However, it also includes a number of other practices not found in the *Theravada*. One of these is the *Bodhisattva* Vow, through which practitioners dedicate their practice to the release of all beings from suffering, and vow to master all the teachings and practices of the Buddha Way. Further, they vow not to attain their own enlightenment until all beings are freed from suffering. For *Mahayana* practitioners, it is the removal of suffering from the world that is more important than personal release. In general, *Mahayana* Buddhism is more ritualistic, although the ritual is seen as being a form of conscious *yoga* in which there is visualization of spiritual beings and an acceptance of the power of their help.

◪ *see* YOGA p. 22

TIBETAN BUDDHISM

Tibetan Buddhism, with its mysterious practices and colourful art, is becoming better known in the West, partly due to the influence of His Holiness the Dalai Lama. The Tibetan tradition is subdivided into a number of different schools which contain the whole range of Buddhist practices.

The principle teaching is the *Lam Rim* or graduated path, the first part of which consists of taking refuge in the Triple Jewel (Buddha, *Dharma* and *Sangha*), the practice of ethical behaviour and basic

▶ RIGHT: *Amitabha, Buddha of Infinite Light*

meditation. The second stage empowers meditations which help to overcome the limitations of greed, anger and ignorance, and an understanding of the interdependence of all existing things. The final stage is the *Bodhisattva* Path, in which the practitioner seeks full enlightenment for the benefit of all beings, through the development of Great Compassion and Perfect Wisdom. The *Vajrayana* or Diamond Way is the highest practice, which aims at achieving Buddhahood in this lifetime.

The Tibetan tradition encourages the use of grand ceremonies, music, dancing, chanting, and colourful paintings of various deities, the production of which is itself a spiritual practice. Many of its foremost lamas or teachers are rimpoches, or rebirths of famous lamas of the past, the discovery of whom is rigorously tested. Tibetan Buddhism also has a tradition of silent meditation without symbols called *Dzogchen*, which is in many ways close to Japanese *Zen*.

see ZEN BUDDHISM p. 58

ZEN BUDDHISM

Zen is the Japanese form of the Chinese *Chan*, which is the phonetic pronunciation of the Sanskrit *dhyana* or meditation. The practice of meditation – sitting or moving – is the basis for *Zen* activity of all kinds, whether in the temple, tea-room, the home or the martial arts practice hall.

It is said that *Zen* started one day when the Buddha silently twirled a flower instead of speaking. None of his disciples understood, except Mahakasyapa, who smiled. The Buddha then explained that the essential truth of his teaching is beyond words, and that he had given it to Mahakasyapa.

▶ *RIGHT: The tea ceremony*

The tradition passed down through a number of Indian patriarchs to Bodhidharma, who brought it to China in the early sixth century AD. *Zen* extended throughout China and spread to Japan, Korea and Vietnam. When *Zen* reached Japan, it became at the same time more organized and more iconoclastic. Three major streams emerged, as well as many charismatic figures.

• *Soto Zen* was founded by Dogen (1200–53). It emphasized *zazen* or sitting meditation, through which the sitter's Buddha Nature is revealed.

• *Rinzai Zen* was founded by Eisai (1141–1215). It emphasizes meditation on *koans*, riddles that have no logical answer. This creates a 'great ball of doubt', the shattering of which brings about sudden *satori* or enlightenment.

• *Obaku Zen*, the smallest of the schools, was founded in China, and maintained Chinese traditions in its chanting, ceremonies and other practices, retaining aspects such as the Pure Land teaching.

Zen had an impact on all aspects of Japanese life. Millions of people who never practised religious *Zen* were influenced by it through arts such as calligraphy, painting, tea ceremony, flower arranging and music. In all the arts, the *Zen* way of teaching includes mindfulness, which is a form of meditation. The potter pauses before putting the clay on the wheel, the musician practises 'Blowing *Zen*' as he plays his bamboo flute. The *Zen* influence on the tea ceremony emphasizes being in the moment, and caring for the guests. It has evolved it into a religious ritual, a moving meditation of hospitality. And, above all, the *Zen* ideal of the natural garden inspires visitors the world over with its peace and tranquillity.

◆ *see* TIBETAN BUDDHISM p. 57

BUDDHIST FESTIVALS AND CELEBRATIONS

One major feast, *Vesak*, is celebrated by Buddhists the world over. It brings together Buddhists from *Theravadin* and the various *Mahayana* schools. This is the Buddha's birthday, which is celebrated on the day of the full moon in May. *Theravadin* Buddhists also celebrate the Buddha's enlightenment and death on the same day. Others celebrate his *Nirvana* in December and his death in February.

Special ceremonies are used to celebrate the Buddha's birthday. In Chinese and Japanese traditions, a statue of the baby Buddha is bathed with sweet tea by all present, and there are street processions with elaborate floats commemorating events from the Buddha's life.

▶ *RIGHT: A Zen garden in Kyoto, Japan*

Another festival that is celebrated by Buddhists everywhere is that of the New Year, although the date varies from country to country. New Year celebrations are often mixed up with local traditions providing lavish festivities with music and dancing in which everybody can join. The *Sangha* are invited to bring a blessing to the New Year by chanting and making offerings to the Buddha. It is also a time when individual Buddhists will seek to forgive those who may have harmed them, and make reparation to those they have injured in any way.

see THE LIFE OF THE BUDDHA p. 46

CONFUCIANISM

Confucius (551–479 BC) was a teacher and political reformer who lived in China at a time when the power of the Zhou Dynasty (c.1027–256 BC) was in decline. Though Confucius thought of himself as a transmitter rather than an innovator he was nonetheless the originator of many of the basic ideas which have sustained Chinese civilization for well over 2,000 years.

THE RU SCHOOL OF PHILOSOPHY

Confucius deplored what he regarded as a decline in moral standards in the states of the Zhou domains. His study of ancient books led him to believe that this decline had come about through a failure by the rulers of his time to maintain the standards of a supposed golden age of antiquity. In a bid to halt this decline he developed a system of moral philosophy for the guidance of his contemporaries.

◀ LEFT: The founders of China's three belief systems

The school of philosophy which Confucius founded is known in China as the *Ru* school, the word *ru* coming to mean scholars or moralists. He transmitted his ideas mainly through word of mouth to his students. His words were compiled by his followers not long after his death into a book entitled *Lun Yu*, or *The Analects of Confucius*, which became one of the most influential books of East Asia, including China, Japan, Korea and Vietnam.

Confucius admired the founders of the Zhou Dynasty, who had ordered the feudal hierarchy and devised the ritual and music which he considered of key importance in maintaining social harmony and stability. He had special praise for the Duke of Zhou, brother of King Wu of Zhou, founder of the Dynasty. He believed the Duke's rule embodied the qualities of humanity and moral order which were dear to him.

But in drawing lessons from the past, Confucius was primarily concerned with the society of his own time. For example, he extolled the virtues of the *junzi*, which originally meant 'prince' or 'ruler', and contrasted it with those of the *xiao ren*, meaning 'small men' or 'common people'. But he used these terms in a new sense, namely with reference to people who exhibited superior or inferior moral qualities regardless of which class they belonged to. The term *junzi* is sometimes translated into English as 'gentleman' or 'superior man'. Thus: 'The gentleman is calm and at ease, the small man is anxious and ill at ease.'

◆ *see* MASTER KONG p. 65

▲ ABOVE: An early nineteenth century Chinese illustration of Confucius

REN, SHU AND YI

According to Confucius, the supreme virtue of a gentleman was *ren*. This term, which has been variously translated as goodness, benevolence and human-heartedness, is the sum total of all virtues. Confucius said that fortitude, simplicity and reticence are all close to the meaning of *ren*. When one of his followers asked him how to practice *ren* Confucius said: 'Love people'. He believed that the sage rulers of antiquity were men of *ren*, but he denied that he himself had attained *ren*: 'How dare I say that I am a sage or a man of *ren*? But I delight in striving toward *ren* and never tire of teaching what I believe.'

Ren is closely connected with *shu* (reciprocity), in that a man of *ren*

judges others by the same standards that he sets for himself. Confucius said: 'Do not do to others what you do not wish to be done to you.' and 'The good man is one who, wishing to sustain himself, sustains others, and, wishing to develop himself, develops others. To be able to use one's own needs as an example for the treatment of others is the way to practice *ren*.'

Confucius also placed great emphasis on *yi* (righteousness). This meant

◀ *LEFT: A late nineteenth century painting of Confucius teaching* doing what is morally right and proper in any situation, having regard for the five cardinal relationships upon which the family and society in general was said to be based: those between sovereign and subject, father and son, husband and wife, elder and younger brother, and friend and friend. While *ren* is the inner quality of goodness in the gentleman, *yi* is its outward manifestation in action, by which his character may be judged.

◆ *see* THE TAO p. 70

MASTER KONG

Confucius's surname was Kong and his personal name Qiu. In later life he came to be known as Kong Fuzi (Master Kong). This was Latinized in the sixteenth century by Jesuit missionaries as Confucius. Very little is known about Confucius's life, though legends abound. He was born and spent most of his life in Lu, which was one of the smaller states situated in present-day Shandong Province in East China. He belonged to a relatively small educated class of civil and military functionaries who were schooled in the Six Arts, which comprised ceremonies, music, archery, chariot driving, writing and arithmetic. He also became conversant with the ancient classical books on poetry, history and divination. Although he claimed that his best subjects were archery and chariot driving, his education and upbringing prepared him for public service, and this remained his ambition all his life.

In 497 BC he was appointed Minister of Justice in Lu where he hoped to put his ideas into practice, but he soon fell out of favour and spent the next 13 years travelling from state to state attempting to find a ruler willing to accept his advice. In this endeavour he was unsuccessful and he finally returned to Lu where he spent his remaining days teaching.

◆ *see* THE RU SCHOOL OF PHILOSOPHY p. 62

THE SPREAD OF CONFUCIANISM

Following the death of Confucius his disciples continued to expound his teaching. The followers of Confucius, notably Mencius and Xun Zi, expanded the scope of Confucius' teaching, touching on issues, such as human nature, which were contentious in their day.

Mencius (fourth century BC) considered that man was inherently good, and it behoved the ruler to liberate this goodness by setting a good example which the people would follow. Xun Zi (third century BC), on the other hand, believed that man naturally tended toward evil and that this tendency had to be curbed through education. In spite of these differences both Mencius and Xun Zi believed that men had the potential to become sages.

▲ ABOVE: The entrance to Confucius' tomb in his hometown, Qufu

Other schools of thought had emerged to challenge Confucianism, such as the Mohist school, who rejected its emphasis on a hierarchical society and advocated universal love, and later Taoism. China was unified under the Qin in 221 BC and another school, the Legalists, who believed that loyalty to the emperor and the state was the highest virtue, then became dominant. Many Confucians were put to death and their writings were banned. But the Qin was overthrown and the Legalists discredited. The Han Dynasty rulers, anxious to rebuild their bureaucracy on a firm ideological foundation, turned to Confucianism to provide it, and Confucianism became the orthodox school of thought supported by the majority of Chinese rulers for two thousand years.

The philosopher and politician Dong Zhongshu provided the theoretical basis for the ascendancy of Confucianism when he recommended to Emperor Wudi in 136 BC that Confucianism should be the means by which the rulers should effect general unification, and that 'All not within the field of the Six Classics should be cut short and not allowed to progress further.' The Six Classics were the ancient books on which Confucius based his teaching. Dong Zhongshu's intention was to discourage all other schools and promote Confucianism as an ideological basis for the education of officials. At the same time a cult of Confucius was encouraged, Confucian temples were erected in all towns and for a while Confucius was widely regarded as a god, but from the first century onwards this period of glorification ended.

The downfall of the Han Dynasty at the beginning of the third century ad was a great blow to Confucianism. During the following four centuries China was divided politically and the new religions of Buddhism and Taoism spread throughout China. Buddhism, in particular, became popular among all strata of society, right up to the imperial court. By the ninth century ad it was regarded as a menace to Confucian supremacy and severe measures were taken to restrict the number of Buddhist monasteries and temples.

In the eleventh century an intellectual movement within Confucianism sought to counter both Buddhism and Taoism. The most influential figure in the movement was Zhu Xi (1130–1200), also known as Zhu Zi (Master Zhu), who wrote commentaries on the Four Books of Confucianism: *The Analects of Confucius*, *The Book of Mencius*, *The Doctrine of the Mean* and *The Great Learning*. In 1313 the Emperor ordered that these four books should be the main texts used in the state examinations and that their official interpretation should follow Zhu Xi's commentaries.

Zhu Xi developed a theory which is known as Li Xue (The Doctrine of Li). According to this theory every object in the world, whether animate or inanimate, possesses an innate principle or

◀ LEFT: *Statue of a Confucian official*

68

li, which differentiates it from other things. But not only animate and inanimate objects had their *li*, but also government and social institutions. Although it was not intended by Zhu Xi, this was taken by some to mean that current institutions were immutable. Generally speaking the imposition of Neo-Confucian orthodoxy during the Yuan, Ming and Qing dynasty had the effect of obstructing political and intellectual change from the fourteenth to the nineteenth centuries.

Because of its idealization of the past and espousal by those in society opposed to change, Confucianism lost its status as a state orthodoxy early in the twentieth century, though it continues to exert an influence on the minds and social mores of the Chinese and other East Asian peoples. The concepts of loyalty and filial piety, which Confucians have promoted through the centuries, are still very much alive.

 see SANGHA p. 49

▶ *RIGHT: Celebrating Confucius' birth*

TAOISM

Taoism is the main surviving religion native to China. Its roots
lie far back in Chinese shamanism and in philosophy and its
name comes from the Chinese word for the way, meaning
'the Way, the very essence, of nature'. It developed into a full-
blown religion from the second century AD.

THE TAO

The essence of Taoism is maintaining the balance of nature of the *Tao*,
through controlling and influencing the forces of *yin* and *yang*,
exorcising evil spirits and seeking immortality.

Taoism teaches that the world, indeed the entire cosmos is finely
tuned and balanced and that the role of humanity is to maintain this
balance. The *Tao* is the primal source of all unity and existence – the One.
From this one comes the twin forces of *yin* and *yang*, polar opposites
that are locked in a struggle for supremacy, which can never be achieved
because they each contain the seed of the other within them. Thus, for
example, autumn and winter are *yin* but inexorably give way to spring
and summer, which are *yang*, which in turn give way to autumn and
winter.

In Taoism, the *Tao* (the Way) moves from being a descriptive term for
the relentless cycle of the natural world to being to all intents and
purposes the ultimate 'divine' force. The *Tao* is classically represented in
Taoist temples by three statues. These statues of male figures represent
the *Tao* as the Origin, the *Tao* as manifest in the human form of the sage
Lao Zi and the *Tao* as Word, as found in the *Dao De Jing*.

▶ *RIGHT: A seventeenth century painting showing the* yin *and* yang *symbols*

The two forces of *yin* and *yang* dominate all existence and from their dynamic, eternal struggle they produce the three of Heaven, earth and humanity. Heaven is *yang* while earth is *yin* and their interaction gives rise to the forces which enliven all life. Humanity is the pivot upon which this all hinges. We have the power to throw the cosmos out of kilter by creating too much *yin* or too much *yang*, or to balance the cosmos.

Taoism embodies this in many of its liturgies and rituals.

Taoism also offers the individual the chance to slough off sins and misdemeanours through rituals of repentance and of exorcism. It also seeks to control the forces of the spirit world, which can break through to harm this world. For example, it exorcises or placates ghosts of those whose descendants have not offered the correct rituals to ensure they pass to the spirit world.

● *see* LAO ZI AND ZHAUNG ZI p. 72

IMMORTALITY

One of the most important areas of teaching is the possibility of achieving longevity and even immortality. Taoism teaches that immortality is about ensuring the physical body is transformed into an eternal body through rituals and even diet. The quest for immortality and the supernatural powers which this involves, has been a major facet of the mythology of China and manifests itself today in serious practitioners on sacred mountains and in the extravagant antics, such as flight, of certain figures in popular Chinese movies and stories. The quest for immortality takes many forms. For some it is the literal quest for certain foods and substances which if eaten will transform the body. For others it is daily meditational practices which encourage the growth of a spiritual body. For yet others it is a life of abstinence and devotion, undertaken as a hermit in the wild, by which the body becomes simply a part of the cosmic *Tao* and thus can never die.

◐ *see* THE TAO p. 70

LAO ZI AND ZHUANG ZI

The two most formative figures in Taoist philosophy never saw themselves as belonging to a religion called Taoism. Lao Zi lived in the sixth century and Zhuang Zi in the fourth century BC. In their books, the *Dao De Jing* and the eponymous *Zhuang Zi* they explored the understanding of reality through exploring the meaning of the *Tao*.

Lao Zi was a philosopher who lived sometime in the sixth century BC and to whom a book of sayings *Dao De Jing* (meaning The Virtue of the Way) about the *Tao* is credited. It is likely that the bulk of the *Dao De Jing* are wisdom sayings and commentaries which were originally passed down orally and then came to be associated with the wisdom of Lao Zi. Virtually nothing is known about Lao Zi – the very name just means Old

Master. He was one of many hundreds of key philosophers who, from the sixth to fourth centuries BC, explored concepts of the *Tao*. The Way had originally been used as a moral term; Confucians saw the *Tao* as the moral path, which the world had to follow to remain balanced. But Lao Zi took this further and explored the *Tao* as the very origin of nature, the source of the origin, the very foundation of all reality.

Zhuang Zi was a rumbustuous character who lived in the fourth century BC and in his book of the same name we find one of the most entertaining, moving and complex characters of ancient philosophy. An inveterate arguer, joker and wit, he takes language to its limits and explores it through stories and ridicule. For Zhuang Zi, the *Tao* is about being natural, about being true to your 'innate nature'. He sees the innate nature as something good and given which becomes distorted when people try to reform others, make them conform to their ideas or do what they think is right. He is anarchic in his approach to authority and dismisses all attempts to control as attacks on the innate and essential goodness of human nature. This strand of optimism about the nature of life runs throughout Taoism

For both Lao Zi and Zhuang Zi, words and knowledge are secondary to experience and reflection. This is at the heart of the philosophy of Taoism.

◆ *see* TAOIST RITUALS p. 75

SHAMANISM AND TAOISM

The rise of Taoism as a religion in China from the second century AD onwards was essentially the resurfacing of the spirit of shamanism in a more 'respectable' form. In the second century AD a number of shamanic-type charismatic figures developed a new semi-philosophical framework,

within which shamanic practices such as exorcism, combined with the quest for immortality, were expressed anew within a religious philosophy of the *Tao*. One of the key moments in the origin of Taoism as a religious movement is usually taken to be an experience of Zhang Dao Ling at some time in the first half of the second century AD when this charismatic healer/preacher (very much within the shamanic tradition) had a vision. In the vision Lao Zi gave Zhang the power to use his teachings to bind evil forces and heal those who repented of their sins.

When Zhang Dao Ling claimed that Lao Zi had given him authority over spiritual forces, the key to immortality and the power of the *Dao De Jing* to combate evil, Zhang fused elements of the officially discredited shamanism of the ordinary folk with the quest for longevity and immortality and the philosophical and quintessentially anti-Confucian/elite teachings of philosophers such as Lao Zi. From this strange conglomeration came Taoism – the Way of the *Tao*, the religion of following Nature's Path, of seeking immortality and of combating the forces of evil spirits.

◐ *see* IMMORTALITY p. 72

TAOIST RITUALS

Taoism offers many rituals, charms, prayers and prescriptions for dealing with physical ailments and psychological troubles. It is possible to find a charm to be cited, burnt or ingested for almost any problem. As such it plays the role of priest, psychologist and counsellor for many people.

Taoist rituals are only tangentially related to the major rites of passage such as birth, marriage and death. A traditional Chinese wedding will involve elements of Buddhism, Confucianism and Taoism. Taoism's role is

◀ LEFT: *Shamans perform a ritual dance at Ichon, South Korea* more to do with establishing a relationship between the community and the spirit world, in the way that shamans link the spirit world with the physical. Taoism claims the power to control and shape the behaviour of the spirit world in order to enhance the life of those here on earth. There is still, nevertheless, an element of dealing with unpredictable forces in the Taoist rituals of invoking the spirit world. All of this is seen as part and parcel of maintaining the balance of nature of the *Tao*.

● *see* SHAMANS p. 14

▲ *ABOVE: A crowd watches as the Dragon dance is performed in the Chinatown area of Manchester, UK*

SHINTO

The traditional belief system of Japan, Shinto has no
fundamental creeds or written teachings, and is not
particularly evangelical. However it resonates with a
veneration for Japanese tradition and the invisible presence of
innumerable spiritual powers, or *kami*. Shinto is essentially a
body of ritual to relate with *kami* in a way that is respectful,
warm, open, positive and vibrant.

THE KAMI

The name 'Shinto' combines the Chinese characters for *kami* and way,
(implying the way to, from and of the *kami*). It was originally chosen by
government in the seventh century to distinguish 'traditional' worship
from Buddhism. Shinto reflects much of the ancient shamanic traditions
common to its Asian neighbours. Most Japanese people, have always
spoken simply of 'the *kami*', (never 'Shinto') and moreover practise a
mixture of Buddhism and Shinto, without any sense of contradiction.
Furthermore, few Japanese would refer to either Buddhism or Shinto as
'religion', or *shukyou*.

Japan's earliest histories, the Kojiki and Nihonshoki, were compiled on
the orders of the imperial family in AD 712 and AD 720 respectively, for the
purpose of justifying the royal lineage, and describe many of the most
important *kami*. Although there was a political aim to unite all the
regional and clan deities under the authority of the imperial, Yamato,
clan-deity Amaterasu O-mikami, the *kami* of the sun, these legends
provide an explanation for most Shinto rituals and the starting point for
any official, Shinto 'theology'.

Some basic concepts that emerge are:

- *Kami* are not necessarily the same as 'gods'. They can die like mortals. Some are human. There is no easy divide between what is animate and inanimate, cultural and natural, human and divine. Rather, all creation is the expression of spiritual powers. All things are bound together in a kind of spiritual family, and it is natural therefore to try and relate with the world emotionally, as well as materially and scientifically. Spiritual power is not spread equally, but can be recognized as especially powerful in particular phenomena and these are the *kami*.

- The *kami* are invisible and countless. Shinto focuses upon those that reveal their importance to people. Particular *kami* are identified with the kitchen, safety on the roads, education etc. Others are identified with places, especially forests, mountains or waterfalls, that seem especially numinous, or natural phenomena that are especially awesome, such as winds and thunder. Individuals too, who seem possessed of a special charisma or just very successful, might be called *kami*. Other, less important, spiritual forces are recognized, such as mischievous elements like fox-spirits, *kitsune*, or tree-spirits, *tengu*. These may be called on to communicate with us through mediums, to explain their behaviour. On special occasions, the *kami* may also possess a medium to send an important message.

- Individuals should venerate and entertain the *kami* most important to them, not only because their good will is required but also because they appreciate that individual's concern. They are not all-knowing, and want to be informed about significant events. They love most to see individuals enjoying themselves in a happy community.

- There is no teaching about the original creation of the universe, or about any future end or final judgement. Likewise, there is no clear description of any after-life. After a person dies, they simply merge with their ancestral *kami* and have no individual soul.

- Purity is essential to a right relationship with the *kami* and the avoidance of failure or disease. Many rituals feature the exorcism of sins in order to be restored to original purity. Cleanliness, sincerity (*makoto*) and politeness in particular signify freedom from bad external influences, and reliability. The *kami* are especially repelled by blood and by death. Traditionally, women were banned from shrine events during menstruation; those who worked with dead bodies, such as tanners, were not tolerated and soldiers required special purification after battle.

◆ *see* SAMANS p. 12

◄ LEFT: A woman visits a Shinto shrine

JINJA (SHINTO SHRINES)

Shinto shrines and ritual very carefully mark entry into a special world. Even in a bustling city, shrines express a different atmosphere. Surrounded by evergreen trees, and approached on a noisy gravel path, they still everyday conversation. There is a special silence, broken only by ritual hand-claps, or the sound of crows and seasonal insects. Shinto ritual, including music (*gakaku*) and dance (*kagura*), is characterized by a special slow, measured pace, appropriate to the timeless *kami* and quite different from daily life outside. On special occasions (*matsuri*) a mass of local people will be crowded together in noisy festivity, letting themselves go in front of the *kami* in ways they would never dream of doing outside the shrine.

It is important that the shrines blend into the environment chosen by the *kami*. Traditionally built from wood and generally left untreated, they need regular repair or rebuilding, and the work of the local community is thus bound to the life of the local shrine. This is still the tradition of Japan's most celebrated shrine, the Grand Shrine of Ise, dedicated to Amaterasu and reconstructed in ancient style every generation. Worship is done primarily in the open air, and the key buildings enshrine the tokens that are the focus of veneration.

The *kami* do not 'live' in the shrines, and must be summoned politely. The approach to each shrine is marked by one or several great gateways, or *torii*, and there will be a basin to rinse hands and mouth. A shrine is usually dedicated to one particular *kami*, but may host any number of smaller shrines, representing other *kami* that local people should also venerate. Sacred points, such as entrances or particular trees and rocks, will be marked off by ropes of elaborately plaited straw, or streamers of plain paper.

▶ *RIGHT: Heinin-Jingu in Kyoto, Japan*

The *kami* are usually summoned by pulling a bell-rope outside the shrine, making a small (money) offering followed by two hand-claps, a short silent prayer, and two bows, but variation is tolerated and this procedure is longer at the most important shrines. The primary audience is always the *kami*. Matsuri, for example, seem great fun but always begin with an invitation by priests facing away from the people, towards the *kami*, and inviting them to attend, and end with priestly farewells on their departure.

Traditionally, the professional priesthood was limited to the great shrines, and local people took it in turns to be the priest. But recently the professional priesthood has grown to about 20,000, including 2,000 women priests. All except the smallest shrines will be the responsibility of a team of priests (*guji*) of various ranks, assisted by a team of local (unmarried) girls (*miko*) who perform ceremonial dances (*kagura*) and other services. Most new priests are now university graduates, usually from Shinto universities, and are often from priestly families. There is no equivalent to a Pope or leader of Shinto, and each shrine is independent. But most shrines are linked together through the national shrine organization (*jinja honcho*) which provides information and administrative services, and helps represent Shinto overseas.

see SHRINE FESTIVALS p. 83

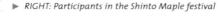

▶ *RIGHT: Participants in the Shinto Maple festival*

SHRINE FESTIVALS

Shinto shrine festivals were traditionally held to celebrate seasonal events in the calendar. The four major seasonal events are: New Year, Rice-Planting (spring), *O-Bon* (a visit by the ancestors in mid-July or

▲ *ABOVE: The outer gate to the Tobakushi Shrine in Nagaho, Japan*

August) and Harvest Thanksgiving (autumn). In addition there will be the festival days of the local *kami*. There will also be special events to mark rites of passage, such as presenting a new-born baby to be recognized and protected by the *kami*, followed by further presentations during childhood (boys aged five, girls aged three and seven), then a coming-of-age ceremony when 20. Within the last 100 years, marriage has also begun to be celebrated at the local shrine. Funerals are left to Buddhist priests, since shrines must avoid pollution.

◄ *see* JINJA (SHINTO SHRINES) p. 80

▲ ABOVE: Shinto priests perform part of a fire ceremony in Osaka, Japan

SIKHISM

Founded only 500 years ago by Guru Nanak (1469–1539), Sikhism is one of the youngest of the world religions. Nanak was succeeded by nine *Gurus*, a common term in all Indian traditions for a spiritual guide or teacher. A Sikh (disciple, or seeker of truth) believes in One God and the teachings of the Ten Gurus, enshrined in the holy book, *Guru Granth Sahib*.

HAUMAI

In Sikhism, time is cyclical, not linear. Time is seen as repeated sequences of creation and destruction, and individual existence is believed to be a repeated sequence of birth, death, and rebirth as the soul seeks spiritual enlightenment. Sikhs believe that greed, lust, pride, anger, and any attachment to the passing values of earthly existence constitute *haumai* (selfcentredness). This is the source of all evil. It is a person's inclination

to evil that produces the *karma* that leads to endless rebirth. *Haumai* separates human beings from God. Sikhism teaches that human life is the opportunity for spiritual union with the Supreme Being; and for release from the cycle of death and rebirth.

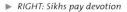 *see* ENLIGHTENMENT p. 87

▶ *RIGHT: Sikhs pay devotion*

THE ULTIMATE SPIRITUAL REALITY

Guru Nanak defined God as the Ultimate Spiritual Reality and he rejected the idea of exclusiveness of any prophets, gods, race, or religion. To Sikhs, religion in its true sense, is a search for the Ultimate Spiritual Reality and an effort to harmonize with it. The primary purpose of human life is to merge with God under the guidance of true *Guru*. Enlightenment, not redemption, is the Sikh concept of salvation.

The material universe is God's creation. Its origin was in God and its end is in God; and it operates within God's *hukam* (God's Order). One of the basic hymns in the Sikh Scripture describes the indeterminate void before the existence of this universe. Guru Nanak spoke of innumerable galaxies, of a limitless universe, the boundaries of which are beyond human ability to comprehend.

The nature of God is not to be understood through one's intellect, but

through personal spiritual experience. A believer has to meditate upon this belief, in order to experience the existence of God. The emphasis is on mastery over the self and the discovery of the self; not mastery over nature, external forms and beings.

God is Omnipotent, Omniscient and Omnipresent in Sikhism. He is present in all relationships, directs all events within the universe, and watches over them in the manner of a kind and compassionate parent.

◖ *see* GURU NANAK p. 89

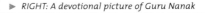

▶ *RIGHT: A devotional picture of Guru Nanak*

ENLIGHTENMENT

Guru Nanak's ethics of truthful living were directed towards enlightenment rather than redemption. To him enlightenment not salvation was of primary importance, which happens only through God's grace. Enlightenment leads to spirituality, which inspires humans to dedicate his or her life to the service of humanity.

Humans, practising a highly disciplined life are capable of further spiritual progression. It is important that Sikhs retain the primacy of spirit over material matter, but it is not required that they renounce the world. However, they should reject conspicuous consumption and maintain a simple life, respecting the dignity in all life, whether human or not. Such a respect for life can only be fostered where one can first recognize the Divine spark within oneself, see it in others, and cherish it, and nurture it.

Humans have the capability to further their spiritual progression through conscious choice. The method suggested by Guru Nanak is one of spiritual discipline, meditation and prayer, and sharing. Sikhism emphasizes mastering *Haumai*. This is achieved by developing five positive forces: Compassion, Humility, Contemplation, Contentment and Service (*seva*) without expecting any material or spiritual reward. Sikhism also preaches strong family involvement, in which a person pursuing this spiritual discipline also works to create an atmosphere for other members of the family to progress spiritually.

The true end of the human beings is in their emergence as God-conscious beings, who operate in the material world, with the object of transforming and spiritualising it into a higher plane of existence. In this spiritual state individuals are motivated by an intense desire to do good, transforming their surroundings. Enlightened spirits become benefactors of humanity and the world around them. Such individuals would not exploit another human or sentient being, as each is a manifestation of the eternal and the supreme. In this God-conscious state they see God in all and everything, and a Sikh life is one of harmony with other individuals, beings and forms.

◆ *see* HAUMAI p. 85

▲ ABOVE: *An elder leads the congregation in prayer at a* gurdwara *in London, UK*

EQUALITY

The cornerstone of Guru Nanak's teachings was equality. He said that in the eyes of God everyone is equal and God's grace may come to the scholar as well as to the unlettered, high or low, the rich or poor. It does not depend on caste, knowledge or penance. Guru Nanak denounced the idea that spirituality was only for men and not for women. He perceived that there can be no enduring democratic culture unless grounded in recognition of full gender equality. In a society deeply divided by religion, gender and caste, and with widespread intolerance and exploitation, Guru Nanak instituted three practices to promote equality and alleviate suffering. *Sangat* was an invitation to people of all castes and backgrounds to meditate together. Before or after the meditation, he asked people to sit and eat together irrespective of their social background to create a sense equality, called *pangat*. He also started a tradition of free distribution of food to the rich and poor alike at places of worship, named *langar*. These three institutions still exist in Sikh society today.

◆ *see* THE CASTE SYSTEM p. 31

GURU NANAK

Guru Nanak founded the Sikh religion after a revelatory experience at the age of about 38. He began to teach that true faith consisted of being ever-mindful of God, meditating on God's Name, and reflecting it in all activities of daily life. Travelling throughout India, Sri Lanka, Tibet and parts of the Arab world he discussed his revelation with people he met, and attracted followers of both Hindu and Muslim faiths. Guru Nanak's teachings of service, humility, meditation and truthful living became the foundation of Sikhism.

◆ *see* THE ULTIMATE SPIRITUAL REALITY p. 86

THE GURU GRANTH SAHIB

Guru Nanak appointed his successor who was known as Guru Angad and he was followed by eight subsequent *Gurus*. The last living *guru*, Guru Gobind Singh, who died in 1708, pronounced the end of the line of succession and ordained the *Guru Granth Sahib*, the Sikh Holy Scripture, to be the ultimate spiritual authority for Sikhs. The *Guru Granth Sahib* was compiled and edited by the Fifth Guru, Guru Arjun, in 1604. It occupies the same place in Sikh veneration that was given to the living *gurus*, and its presence lends sanctity to the Sikh place of worship, the *gurdwara*.

The *Guru Granth Sahib* contains the writings and hymns of saints and preachers with different religious backgrounds but whose philosophy conformed to the spirit of Sikhism. The entire Sikh holy book is composed in music and poetry. It contains 5,894 hymns, of which Guru Nanak contributed 974, composed in 19 *ragas* (musical modes). The singing of these hymns from *Guru Granth Sahib* is an integral part of Sikh service.

◖ *see* SHRUTI AND SMIRITI p. 16

REHAT MARYADA

The *Rehat Maryada* (Sikh Code of Conduct) published in 1945, regulates individual and corporate Sikh life. Life-cycle events are recognized in Sikhism by naming of the newborn in the *gurdwara*, the marriage ceremony, and the funeral, following which the body is cremated. Funeral monuments are prohibited. Guru Gobind Singh, the Tenth Guru, instructed his followers to drop their last names, which in India indicate one's caste. All Sikh men, therefore, take the additional name Singh (lion) and women take the name Kaur (princess) to show their acceptance of the equality of all people regardless of caste or gender.

◖ *see* GURU NANAK p. 89

THE GRANTHI

Sikhs do not have a priestly order, monks, or nuns. The Sikh 'clergyman' is the *granthi*, who is encouraged to marry. Sikh congregations are autonomous. There is no ecclesiastical hierarchy. The Akal Takhat heads the five temporal seats of Sikh religious authority in India which debates matters of concern to the Sikh community worldwide and issues edicts which are morally binding on Sikhs. These decisions are coordinated by the SGPC (the Shiromini Gurdwara Parbandhak Committee) which also manages Sikh shrines in India. Formal Sikh worship consists mainly of

singing passages of the Guru Granth Sahib to the accompaniment of music. A passage of the holy book is read aloud and expounded upon by the *granthi* at the conclusion of the religious service. The central prayer of Sikhs, *Ardas*, is recited by the *granthi* and the assembled congregation. This prayer gives a synopsis of Sikh history as well as being a supplication to God. Any Sikh with sufficient religious knowledge is permitted to conduct *gurdwara* worship in the absence of a *granthi*. All are welcome to attend Sikh religious services and to participate in the *langar* served afterwards.

◆ see EQUALITY p. 89

◀ *LEFT: A Sikh marriage ceremony*

INITIATION FOR BAPTISM

The tenth and the last *Guru*, Guru Gobind Singh (1666–1708) initiated the Sikh Baptism ceremony in 1699, giving distinctive identity to the Sikhs. The first five baptized Sikhs were named 'Panj Pyare' ('Five Beloved Ones'), and they in turn baptized the *Guru* on his request. At the *Amrit Pahul* ceremony, the initiate promises to follow the Sikh code of conduct as an integral part of the path toward God-realization. He or she vows at that time to abstain from the use of tobacco and other intoxicants; never to cut the hair on any part of the body; not to eat the meat of animals killed in a religious or sacrificial manner; to refrain from any sexual contact outside of marriage; and to wear the five symbols of Sikhs.

After this ceremony, the initiate is considered a part of the *Khalsa* (Belonging to God) brotherhood. *Khalsa* means a spiritually integrated person alive to his duties both to God and society, and is enjoined to tithe both time and income and to pray and meditate daily. He or she

▲ ABOVE: A temple leader in India prepares the temple flag pole for New Year

93

must live a moral life of service to mankind, in humility and honesty. The five symbolic 'K's' worn by the initiated Sikh are: unshorn hair, over which men wear a turban; comb; a steel bracelet; a short sword; and a garment that is usually worn under a Sikh's outer clothes.

◆ see EQUALITY p. 89

◀ LEFT: Sikh merchandise

SIKHISM AND OTHER FAITHS

Interfaith dialogue and cooperation have been a part of Sikhism since Guru Nanak founded the faith. He did not attempt to convert the followers of other religions but, rather, urged them to rediscover the internal significance of their beliefs and rituals, without forsaking their chosen paths. He indicated that because of human limitations, each group grasps only a narrow aspect of God's revelation. The Sikh *Gurus* were opposed to any exclusive claim on truth, which a particular religion might make. Just as this indicates a pluralistic acceptance of the legitimacy of all faiths, and all that are valid, it indicates an acceptance of all groups and individuals. Guru Arjun said: 'All are co-equal partners in the Commonwealth with none treated as alien.' (*Guru Granth Sahib*). Numerous examples suffice to show how this attitude has evidence itself in Sikh history. When compiling the manuscripts that would make up the *Guru Granth Sahib*, Guru Arjun included hymns written by both Hindu and Muslim religious thinkers. There are, in the *Guru Granth Sahib*, hymns written by persons considered by Hindus to be untouchables. The holiest of Sikh shrines, the Golden Temple at Amritsar has four doors, each facing a cardinal direction. This was done to indicate that all are welcome. The cornerstone of the Golden Temple was laid by a Muslim holy man. The ninth *guru*, Guru Tegh Bahadur, died championing the rights of Hindus to practise their own religion.

◗ *see* HINDU GODS AND GODDESSES p. 23

▶ RIGHT: *The Golden Temple at Amritsar, in the Punjab, India*

AFRICA

ANCIENT EGYPT

Documented Egyptian history, from the unification of the country to the acceptance of Christianity as the official religion, lasted some 3,500 years. This huge expanse of time saw periods of confidence, prosperity and empire, separated by times of economic trouble and political fragmentation. But throughout, the fundamentals of Egyptian religion appear to have remained constant.

THE KINGDOMS OF EGYPT

Egypt enjoyed several major periods of prosperity, with the state strongly centralized under the pharaoh who was regarded as a god-king. The first of these 'high points' was the Old Kingdom (Dynasties 3–6, c. 2650–2150 BC). At this time the resources of the state were concentrated on the building of massive royal tombs in the form of pyramids. The pyramids were symbols of the sun, and of the primeval mound on which the sun first appeared. The pharaoh was the intermediary between the gods and people and was their provider. It was through the pharoahs that the aloof gods provided sustenance and justice to the people.

Troubled times followed the end of the Old Kingdom. There was no single ruling dynasty in control of the whole country and rival families competed for power. Egypt was reunited and enjoyed another period of prosperity under the Middle Kingdom (Dynasties 11–13 c. 2007–1700 BC).

A second period of breakdown was followed by the reunification under the New Kingdom (Dynasties 18–20, c. 1539–1069 BC). The temples of the kings and gods now replaced pyramids as the focus of the state's building operations. The temples became vast structures serving as the theatre for elaborate festival processions. They were also the storehouses for the wealth of the empire.

Following the end of the New Kingdom there was another period of fragmentation. Despite the loss of empire and periods of foreign rule, the Late Period (Dynasties 26–30, 664–323 BC) did see many huge temples constructed. This was also the time when the cults of sacred animals were most popular.

In 332 BC Alexander the Great of Macedon took Egypt from the Persians, and for the three centuries following his death the Ptolemaic

◀ LEFT: The pyramids at Giza

Dynasty ruled the country. This period brought many Greek settlers to Egypt and saw the identification of Greek with Egyptian gods (so Re, the sun god, was identified with Helios, and the goddess Hathor with Aphrodite), and also the spread of some Egyptian cults around the Mediterranean. This process continued when Egypt fell under Roman rule, and the cult of Isis became one of the major religions of the Roman Empire. Christianity found a home in Egypt very early and monasticism flourished in the deserts. During the first centuries AD, Christianity co-existed with traditional Egyptian Gods.

◆ *see* THE LIFE OF JESUS p. 189

DEITIES

Egyptian religion developed in the Predynastic Period (c. 5000–2900 BC) before the unification of Egypt into one kingdom. The Egyptians were polytheistic: they accepted the existence of numerous gods, some with very specific functions, and others who were only vaguely defined. They also created many new gods as occasion demanded. Some Egyptologists have claimed that – certainly by the later periods – all gods were aspects of one, and that Egyptian religion was moving towards monotheism.

◄ *LEFT: The god Horus, Lord of the Sky*

One of the most striking features of Egyptian religious imagery is the way that animal and bird heads are combined with a human body. Gods can often be associated with more than one animal, representing different characteristics or phases of their existence. The scarab beetle was a symbol of the creator god Khepri because it lays its eggs in a ball of dung. The scarab rolling the ball of dung was associated with the sun god pushing the sun disk across the sky; but more important, the small scarabs emerged from the dung as if they had created themselves. Emerging as the new-born sun, Khepri rose into the sky and was transformed into the falcon-headed god at the sun's zenith. After sunset he assumed the head of a ram to travel through the night towards his rebirth next dawn.

Many of the goddesses had an ambivalent nature, so Hathor could appear as the wild cow of the Delta marshes which had to be calmed, and in doing so became the domestic cow. Although calmed, such goddesses always had the potential to become violent again. This appeasing of violent aspects of the world is at the heart of Egyptian cult practices.

There were numerous minor deities who had specific functions in relation to the underworld, or protection in this life. The major

▶ RIGHT: A stylized head of Hathor the cow

deities tended to be rather less specific, although many appeared as creator or solar gods. Falcon-headed gods were common, and associated with the sky. Many of the goddesses could appear as both vulture and rearing cobra, the *uraeus*, which spits fire at the pharaoh's enemies. Nekhbet, and other goddesses such as Isis, were thought of as the mother of the pharaoh, therefore they could assume vulture form and queens wore a headdress in the form of a vulture with extended wings; they could also be shown with vulture wings enfolding their bodies. In Egyptian hieroglyphis the word 'mother' uses the symbol for a vulture.

◆ *see* TEMPLES p. 104

OSIRIS AND THE AFTERLIFE

The Egyptians believed that it was the pharaoh who ensured the afterlife of the ordinary people: he cared and provided for them in the afterlife as he had on earth. Even so, during the Predynastic period, the dead were buried with food and other equipment to assist them. Towards the end of the Old Kingdom, with a decline in royal power, there was a change, and everyone expected to enjoy the afterlife. The cult of Osiris developed

at the same time and rose to ever-greater prominence in the Middle and New Kingdoms. Osiris was a mythical pharaoh murdered by his brother, who cut his body into pieces and scattered them across the globe. These pieces were collected by his sister-wife Isis and mummified by Anubis, the dog- or jackal-headed god

◆ *LEFT: Osiris judges the dead*

of the cemeteries, who invented embalming. Briefly restored to life he was able to father Horus (the pharaoh) before becoming ruler of the underworld. Every Egyptian could look forward to becoming 'an Osiris'. To this end elaborate preparations were made: mummification to preserve the body so that the soul (the *ba*) could return to it (the *ba* is shown as a human-headed bird, and is thought of as leaving the tomb and flying around), and a tomb and grave goods. Complex religious texts (the 'Book of the Dead') aided the passage of the soul through the gates of the underworld, to the judgement hall of Osiris, where the heart was weighed in the balance against 'truth'. It was only after vindication that the deceased could go on to enjoy the afterlife.

🔁 *see* DEITIES p. 100

▲ *ABOVE: The pharoah with Anubis, the jackal-headed god of the dead*

TEMPLES

In Egypt the priests performed rituals in the temples on behalf of the pharaoh, to ensure the preservation of the cosmos. Egyptian temples were a significant part of the state machine. Few temples from the early periods survive, and those that do are quite small. The major focus of state building in the Old Kingdom was the pyramid and its associated temple, emphasizing the role of the pharaoh as god on earth. In the New Kingdom (c.1539–1069 BC) temples were major land-holders and employers throughout the country. The temples became the repositories of the wealth of Egypt's empire, and they were the focus of the largest state building operations. However, the temples and the priesthood remained under the direct authority of the pharaoh: there was no division between Church and State.

In the New Kingdom festival processions became an important feature of religion and this, too, played its part in the development of temples and the religious landscape of the cities. The gods now travelled between temples, along the river, canals or sphinx-lined avenues. Carried in the sacred barks (portable boats with a shrine for the statue of the god), the veiled images were still invisible to the ordinary people, but their presence was indicated by the head of the god which adorned the prow and stern of the bark.

In form, the Egyptian temple combined the attributes of a house, with an image of the moment of creation. Protected by high towers (a pylon), the entrance led into a public open court, where people could come to make their offerings and prayers to the gods. Beyond this court, access was increasingly restricted. One or more columned offering halls, flanked with rooms for the storage of cult objects, led to the sanctuary, where only the highest priests could go. This sanctuary represented the world at the moment of creation and here the god's image resided in a shrine, the focus of the daily ritual. The temple precinct included other chapels, a sacred lake that supplied water for the temple rituals, houses for the priests when on duty, storage areas and workshops, and 'hospitals' in which the ill were treated, combining medicines and 'magic'. The roof of the temple was used for observations of the stars, and for the New Year festival when the statue of the god was taken to receive the rays of the rising sun.

◆ *see* WORSHIP p. 106

▲ *ABOVE: Luxor Temple*

WORSHIP

The Egyptians made offerings to their household gods, and perhaps to their ancestors, at shrines in the main rooms of their homes. These gods protected against the hazards of daily life, such as snakes and scorpions, illness and disease, and during the dangerous times of pregnancy and childbirth.

The other major focus of religious activity was the tomb. Egyptian tombs were family vaults, focused on a decorated tomb chapel built by the leading member. Here, at certain times of the year, families would gather to celebrate rituals of renewal with their ancestors, bringing the statues out from the chapel to receive the rays of the rising sun. They would also enact the elaborate burial rituals to ensure the journey of soul into the afterlife.

◆ *see* TEMPLES p. 104

AKHENATEN

The most striking episode in Egypt's religious history is the 17-year reign of the pharaoh Akhenaten (c. 1352–36 BC) at the height of the New Kingdom. This is still one of the most controversial subjects in Egyptology. Ascending the throne as Amenhotep IV, the new pharaoh soon abandoned the major state cults, notably that of the god Amun, in favour of a solar cult which

▶ *RIGHT: Akhenaten*

emphasized the visible disk of the sun, the *Aten*. At some point in the reign there was an iconoclastic phase when the images of gods, particularly Amun, were destroyed. The extraordinary style of art adopted at this time, allied with the poetry and content of the sun hymns, led early Egyptologists to present a false impression of the pharaoh as a true monotheist, and a pacifist. They also suggested that Akhenaten was the pharaoh who had befriended Joseph, and that his hymns to the sun were an influence on the biblical Psalms. Egyptologists now think that in many ways Akhenaten's religious ideas were reactionary, attempting to reinstate the sun cult of the Old Kingdom pyramid builders, with its emphasis upon the pharaoh as the sole intermediary between the divine and human realms. The experiment proved unacceptable and following Akhenaten's death the traditional cults were rapidly restored.

◆ *see* DEITIES p. 100

▶ *RIGHT: Amenhotep IV*

AFRICAN TRADITIONAL RELIGION

Africa has a rich cultural and spiritual heritage, expressed in complex and historically diverse religious traditions. Amidst the tremendous diversity there are a number of common features; above all, a concern for community and the expression of common humanity.

THE CELEBRATION OF LIFE

Focusing on fertility and the defence of civilization against nature, African traditional religion is centrally concerned with the establishment and building up of human society, with human flourishing and the celebration of life. But it is also intensely aware of the fragility of life. Existence and wellbeing are constantly threatened. Much of African religious practice is devoted to coping with the eruption of evil and its persistence in the world.

African approaches to religion may be characterized as the glorification of everyday life, imagined and enacted through ritual. Religion is not enshrined in books, in scriptures or written liturgies, but in customs and ritual performance, in folk tales and proverbs, creation myths, prayer and invocation, music and dance. The spirit world is mediated through sacred sites and persons: priests and diviners, kings and elders, musical performers and official 'remembrancers'. They

▶ RIGHT: Rain festival in Nok, Nigeria

108

function as guardians and transmitters of that corporate sense of community; they define a society's place in the natural world and its relation to the spiritual world.

◆ see CELEBRATIONS AND DANGER p. 113

GODS AND ANCESTORS

Ancestors (the 'living dead'), nature spirits and gods are guardians of the community. These beings are refractions of spirit, the High God, the dynamic principle of life. The African cosmos is populated by spirits who occupy a realm which is outside normal reality, but which impinges at many points on human society. There are nature spirits who typically inhabit the uncultivated places and wilderness which stand over against the abode of people. Such spirits are by their nature fickle and best

avoided; their potential for harm to human society is great. The ancestors are more directly involved in the life of the community; they are also more benign, though they can be offended. In many African societies the dead are buried near the homestead, and the ancestors of the family have a tangible presence. In some societies, there is a class of ancestors who assume wider significance, as heroic figures, who achieve divinity, and whose cults spread far and wide.

◘ see CULTS OF AFFLICTION p. 115

◀ LEFT: Shango, the god of thunder from culture in present day Benin

▲ ABOVE: Eguguns (resurrected ancestors) return to their descendants at a festival in Benin

ORIGIN OF DEATH

African cosmologies have in common a tendency to attempt to explain the loss of immediacy between the two worlds of humans and spirits, and to account for the fragility and disharmony of existence.

According to the Moru in Sudan, when God created the world, heaven and earth were close together, connected by a leather ladder. People were constantly moving to and fro. They loved to attend the dances and feasts of heaven, and returned to earth rejuvenated. One day a girl was grinding some *sorghum* (*sorghum* is a grain used for food and to make beer). She delayed and was late for the dance. In her haste she started to climb the ladder without washing her hands. The trail of *sorghum* on the ladder attracted the hyena. He began licking the ladder. That set him to gnawing at the leather, until the ladder broke. So the communication between earth and heaven has been broken. People cannot be rejuvenated and death has come into the world. In Zulu mythology the chameleon was entrusted with a message to take to earth – immortality for humankind. But he loitered on the way and was beaten to earth by the lizard. The lizard also had a message – death for humankind. Thus death came into the world.

■ see CULTS OF AFFLICTION p. 115

◀ LEFT: A fertility statue from the Baoule culture of Ivory Coast

CELEBRATIONS AND DANGER

Rites of passage are important stages for the affirmation of life, times of celebration but also of danger. They are liminal experiences when people stand on the threshold of the spirit world. Fertility and procreation are celebrated, but they too are surrounded by danger. The birth of twins illustrates the combination of vitality and danger. In some parts of Africa, twins are regarded as an anomaly: by mischance the spirit counterpart of the child has also been born, an offence to the spirits and a danger for all. In parts of East Africa, by contrast, twins are regarded as a special blessing, a sign of the super abundance of the spirit world. Special twin names are given not only to the children, but to those who are born after them, and to the parents themselves. Such names are held in great honour. Naming is of great importance and often has strong religious connotations. Children are given the names of divinities. If the birth has been difficult, or occurs after a history of trouble within the family, the name might have a somewhat derogatory implication, in the hope that the vengeful spirit may overlook the rejoicing and not inflict further punishment.

see THE CELEBRATION OF LIFE p. 108

INITIATION

The most important communal rites are often at adolescence when boys are initiated through circumcision. They are sent away from normal human society and for a time live beyond its rules. In the circumcision camp, on the boundary between civilization and wilderness, humanity and the spirits, initiates learn important new skills appropriate to the adult world, gender and sexual roles, the history and ethics of the group as transmitted from one generation to the next. Not all African societies perform circumcision. The Zulu are said to have abandoned circumcision during the time of Shaka, when it would have compromised the fighting effectiveness of the *impi*. Female 'circumcision' is less common than male circumcision. But where it does occur it is meant to have the same socializing role. Missionaries strongly condemned female circumcision in the 1920s and were in turn attacked for wanting to destroy African culture. More recently human rights and women's groups have renewed the opposition to the practice, insisting that it is, in effect, female genital mutilation.

◆ see INITIATION p. 283

▲ ABOVE: A boy from the Samburu tribe in Kenya prepares for his circumcision

MASKS AND MASQUERADES

The great communal celebrations of rites of passage or harvest festivals, as well as initiation into healing or status cults, are often accompanied by pageants and masquerades, dramatic performances, song and dance in which the relationship between the spirit world and human society are enacted and re-enacted. In donning a mask the performer loses his own individuality and entirely becomes the entry point for communication with the realm of spirit.

▶ *see* GODS AND ANCESTORS p. 110

▶ *RIGHT: A Kuba mask from the Congo*

CULTS OF AFFLICTION

Only the death of the very old can easily be accepted as part of the natural flow of events. The death of younger people needs explanation, as does illness and bad luck, particularly if they are recurrent. There may be proximate explanations, such as a specific symptom or event, but what is the enduring, determining cause? The problem may be located in a failure to respect ancestors or other spirits, or the accidental or deliberate failure to comply with certain norms. It may be caused by jealousy on the part of kinsfolk or neighbours, or be due to the malice of

115

▶ RIGHT: *Carvings at the sacred shrines of Oshogbo, Nigeria*

witchcraft. A number of religious professionals can be consulted. There are healers who are skilled in herbal medicines. Diviners use a variety of paraphernalia – bones, cowry shells, animal sacrifice – to discover the reasons. Mediums are possessed by spirits and act as their mouthpiece in diagnosing the problem and offering solutions. Witches and sorcerers also have access to spiritual powers, but do not admit freely to such deeply anti-social activity. Morever their covert activity is frequently a cause of alarm and anxiety, as spiritual powers can be used for both good and evil.

The search for relief and therapy is often embodied in 'cults of affliction'. In Bantu-speaking areas these often go under the general name of *Ngoma* ('drum': referring to the music and dance which may be part and parcel of membership of the group). Such groups have a public existence and (unlike witchcraft activities) have respect from society. But initiates enter into a secret world, which may involve learning an arcane language and the symbolic performance of acts normally taboo. Women are often the majority. They may begin their

involvement by consulting a diviner for some particular problem during pregnancy and be gradually drawn into membership. By becoming adept at healing or divination, women have opportunities to gain a status otherwise denied them.

◆ *see* ORIGIN OF DEATH p. 112

AMERICAS

THE AMAZONIANS

Not only is the longhouse the centre of the everyday lives of the Amazonian people but, during ritual, their house becomes the cosmos. With the assistance of the shaman, space and time become one as the participants experience the invisible world which is essential to their continuing wellbeing.

◄ LEFT: A Yanomamo Indian family in the rainforest

COSMOLOGY

The peoples who inhabit the Amazonian forest, located predominantly in Brazil but also Venezuela, Colombia and Peru, live by shifting agriculture, hunting, fishing and gathering.

For them the cosmos is animate. According to their cosmologies, the universe has three layers, each peopled by different beings. In the underworld live aquatic creatures, the most important of which are the anaconda or caiman. In the sky live the birds, of which the vulture or harpy eagle are the most significant for myth and beliefs generally. On the earth live people and forest-dwelling creatures, of which the jaguar is the most powerful. All creatures are believed to be controlled by the 'master of animals' who is sometimes the group's shaman.

For the Barasana, who live in the upper Vaupes region in Colombia, the anaconda is the first ancestor and is associated with the sacred. He plays flutes and trumpets which are kept under water and represent its bones. He refers to a timeless generating force, known also as *Yurupary*. In myth, Yurupary was the culture hero who established order in nature and taught the first men rules and ritual conduct. These instruments must never be seen by women and girls, and only by boys who have been initiated. During ritual, as those involved dance and chant, ancestral time is recreated; the house is seen to become the cosmos.

◆ *see* COSMOLOGY p. 125

THE SHAMAN

Often the only individual with a specialized role in the community, the Shaman is able to see the invisible world, which co-exists with the visible. Shamans communicate with it and are responsible, for example, for releasing game animals for which the souls of new-born babies have to be exchanged. They can also travel to the different layers of the cosmos or send others there in trance or by means of hallucinogenic drugs. In many groups, the son of a shaman is apprenticed to his father, but in others, men become shamans by means of a severe illness, by revelation or simply ambition.

The latter pay for their initiation and accumulate power in the forest through direct experience. It is a hard training, involving sexual

abstinence, fasting, vomiting and other dietary prohibitions. The shaman
enters into a relationship with one or more ancestral spirits, and is given
his spirit weapons. Potency lies in the invisible world which is viewed
with ambiguity (as is the self-made shaman). All shamans have access to
considerable power which they can use for good or evil: the most

▶ RIGHT: A Manuka shaman inhales hallucinogenic snuff

◄ *LEFT: A sixteenth century print depicting Brazilian Tupinamba shamans*

powerful can turn themselves into jaguars. Mostly, however, a
does good in his own community but wards off mystical attacks sent by
shamans from elsewhere.

Shamans can cure both physiological illness and social disorder; they
may blow tobacco smoke over the patient, suck out spirit weapons or go
into a trance to fight the spirits causing the problem. More powerful is
water-throwing carried out in the midday sun. For this water scented
with aromatic leaves is thrown over the patient's body which is thought
to 'trawl' through it removing spines, bundles of fur or feathers which
the shaman throws away amid much blowing, clapping of hands and

flicking of fingers. The shaman makes a performance out of such rituals: for he has not only to know all the myths, rites and other esoteric knowledge (of plants, animals and the stars) but also to add something of himself in order to become highly respected.

◗ see SHAMANIC RITUALS AND PROPS p. 15

THE BARANSA HOUSE AS COSMOS

During ritual, the floor of the house becomes the earth and the roof the sky, supported by the house posts which become the mountains. The horizontal roof beams represent the sun's path. Any grave under the house is seen as being in the underworld, and the ritual ornaments hanging from the ceiling beams, collectively known as 'macaw fe act as the mediator between the earth and the sky. The *cassava*

used by the women is like the cosmos, and said to be the one dropped by the female maker of the world (Roumi Kumu), when there were only sky people and the Primal Sun. She was the originator of domestic fire, and it was her sacred beeswax gourd that gave men their shamanic power.

◗ see THE
SHAMAN p. 121

THE MAYA

In what is now Mexico, the Maya dominated the lowland peninsula of the Yucatan highlands, Chiapas and most of Guatemala. There was never one unified theocracy but a number of aggressive city-states. The Maya favoured the arts and learning and pushed knowledge of astronomy and mathematics much further than any previous civilization in the Americas.

COSMOLOGY

In Maya cosmology, seven layers extended above the earth ruled by the 13 deities of the heavens: six marked the sun's ascent, six its descent and one its position at midday. Below the earth was Xibalba, the realm of the dead, consisting of four layers and ruled by the nine deities of the underworld, an unpleasant place of putrefaction and strong smells from which illnesses came. Each night, the sun passed through the underworld in the guise of a jaguar, descending through four layers before midnight, to ascend again (through four) to rise in the east. The underworld was linked to the heavens by a huge tree, the ceiba, which is still considered to be sacred in Mayan communities today. The tree marked the centre of the earth, distinguishing where the sun rose (our east and linked to the colour red) from where the sun set (west and linked to black). The north and south (or up and down) were simply known as sides of heaven and associated with white and yellow respectively.

◆ see THE COSMOS p. 128

◀ *LEFT: A shaman distributes coca during the Bransa chanting ceremony*

THE MAYAN CALENDARS

The effects on the Mayan people of their huge pantheon of supernatural forces – deities, spiritual beings and essences, could in part be discerned or predicted by the use of their Calendars. The Mayans, like other Mesoamerican peoples such as the later Aztecs, had a sophisticated calendar. The divinatory, 260-day calendar intermeshed with the 365-day calendar (rather like interlocking cog wheels) to give each day its distinct character.

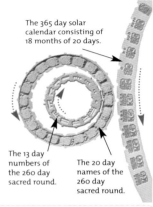

The 365 day solar calendar consisting of 18 months of 20 days.

The 13 day numbers of the 260 day sacred round.

The 20 day names of the 260 day sacred round.

▲ ABOVE: The Mayan calendar

The *Tzolkin* or divinatory calendar, consisted of 13 numbers linked to 20 day names, each of which was a divine force: the first, Imix was linked to the earth monster. All gods were endowed with a calendrical presence, some more directly than others: the Pahuatuns or wind deities (Ik in the calendar); the Chicchans, a giant snake (Chicchan); and the four Balams, jaguars who protected the cultivated fields (Ix). Also important were Exchel, the moon and the four Chacs or rain gods.

The other, 365-day calendar was important for determining the dates of ritual. It consisted of 18 named months linked to 20 numbers (360) and a month of five days known as the Uayeb, whose days were considered particularly unpropitious. The 365-day calendar was based on astronomical calculations and intermeshed with the 260-day divinatory calendar. With the two calendars combined, an identically named day only occurred every 52 years, after which a new cycle began.

◆ *see* CALENDAR FESTIVALS p. 130

RITUALS AND SACRIFICE

Rituals were huge affairs, preceded by fasting, abstinence and ceremonial steam baths, accompanied by music, dancing and incense and attended by many. Autosacrifice was an important means of contacting the deities. By drawing a cord or piece of grass through the

▼ BELOW: Jade serpent from Chichen Itza

penis or the nose, and letting blood, visions could be induced, personified by the Vision Serpent. This was performed particularly by the king and his wife. Human sacrifice did occur, especially of war captives and occasionally of children, but not on a scale comparable to the Aztecs. Animals and birds, such as armadillos and parrots, were also offered, and plants or plant products: copal, flowers, cacao, honey and chichle, from which chewing gum is made.

 see HUMAN SACRIFICES p. 131

see HUMAN SACRIFICES p. 131

▶ RIGHT: Mayan deities

127

THE AZTECS

The Aztecs settled in the Valley of Mexico between AD 1200 and 1300. Daily life was dominated by the sun, Tonatiuh, who at the height of the Aztec civilization (1350–1525) was often equated with Huitzilopochtli, their principal deity and also a god of war. He demanded to be fed by blood in order to keep rising, necessitating human sacrifice.

THE COSMOS

The Aztecs had made Tenochtitlan (today Mexico City) their home in around AD 1325, after a long journey south from Aztlan during the fifth and final Sun, which was to bring earthquakes and famine. According to myth, there had already been four previous Suns, each of which had been destroyed. But the last was a Sun of movement, such that some of the gods had even sacrificed themselves in order to keep it in motion. The world was believed to consist of a disc surrounded by water with 13 layers above and nine layers below. In the highest lived Ometeotl, the omnipotent supreme being, deity of duality, both masculine and feminine, but who also lived in Mictlan, the underworld and peopled all the other layers. Ometeotl had four sons, the four Tezcatlipocas, (a name usually translated as 'Smoking Mirror') two of whom are sometimes known as Quetzalcoatl ('Plumed Serpent') and Huitzilopochtli ('Hummingbird on the Left').

▶ *RIGHT: The building of the great Aztec capital of Tenochtitlán*

Associated with the four early Suns, they were responsible for creating fire, a half sun and moon, water, other divine beings and the calendar. But it was the fifth Sun that completed the cosmos.

see THE COSMOS p. 132

CALENDAR FESTIVALS

The Aztecs had two calendars, the *Haab* and the *Tonalpohualli*, but most of the large monthly religious festivals were related to the former, the 365-day cycle. Many were for agricultural matters and dedicated to Tlaloc and the Tlaloque (the deities of water and fertility), while others propitiated Huitzilopochtli, Tezcatlipoca or Xiuhtecuhtli (deity of fire), or female deities, such as the goddess of love, Xochiquetzal ('Precious Flower') or Coatlicue ('She of the Serpent Skirt').

Festivals were lavish and costly affairs, at least in Tenochtitlan which was a large and sophisticated city, with 30 distinct classes of priests and priestesses, education for women, and slaves. The ceremonies were held in the open air and were attended by thousands, including the common people. During the preparatory days, the priests fasted (one meal per day) and observed prohibitions on bathing and sex. An all-night vigil preceded the festival itself, which was usually of several days' duration. Shrines were embowered and decorated with flowers, and offerings of food, clothing and rubber-spattered papers were made, accompanied by burning incense and libations.

◄ *LEFT: Coatlicue, a goddess of life, death and the earth*

Throughout the festivities sacred songs were sung, music played and there was dancing.

Festivities in the countryside were simpler, more benign and often dedicated to local and feminine deities (such as Tonantzin, who represented the power of the earth). For although the Aztecs conquered a huge area and brought all the foreign deities into their pantheon in Tenochtitlan, they were unable to obliterate local customs.

🔹 see THE MAYAN CALENDARS p. 126

HUMAN SACRIFICES

Each festival had one or more processions which included those to be sacrificed, sometimes dressed up as deities (*ixiptla*), whom they impersonated for a day or two, living in luxury, before their hearts were cut out with an obsidian knife and offered up in ceremonial vessels and their flayed skins worn by male dancers. These were theatrical occasions with dramatic appeal and a compelling political message: that the Aztecs were the servants of their deities.

Often thousands of men and women were sacrificed, captives from neighbouring groups, their bodies allowed to fall down the steps from the top of the ceremonial pyramids, after which their heads were placed on the skull rack and their flesh cooked.

🔹 see RITUAL SACRIFICES p. 127

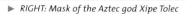

▶ RIGHT: Mask of the Aztec god Xipe Tolec

131

THE INCAS

The Incas were brought to the Cuzco Valley by legendary leader Manco Capac in 1200. At the head of the empire was a divine monarch, who demanded a loyalty akin to slavery, but provided for all the needs of the people in return. Religion was organized in a similar fashion, with Viracocha, the supreme immanent deity, responsible for all the others. The most important religious ceremonies took place in Cuzco, the centre of the empire, for the Sun (Inti), his consort the Moon (Mama Qiya) and Ilyap'a (the thunder and weather deity).

THE COSMOS

At the beginning of the cosmic cycle, Viracocha was associated with Lake Titicaca, out of which the sun, moon and stars emerged and ascended as gods. The numerous lesser deities were believed to have emanated from the caves, hills, springs and mountains, many taking animal (zoomorphic) or bird (avian) forms. The Quechua-speaking indigenous people today still associate their deities with these sacred locations known as *huacas*. Considered to be animate, they are imbued with supernatural power and mythic significance, and are usually marked by stones. Some are the tombs of ancestors, which contained their mummies during the time of the Inca empire. It was to the *huacas* that sacrifices of alpacas and llamas and sometimes children were made, linked to divination by ritual specialists. Mostly of regional significance, nonetheless travellers made and still make offerings of coca, chicha (beer), pieces of clothing or an additional stone, particularly during pilgrimages. The earth itself, known as Pachamama (the earth mother), has not only to be consulted, but also assuaged.

◆ *see* COSMOLOGY p. 147

▲ ABOVE: Macchu Picchu

133

SACRED GEOGRAPHY

Conceptually, the Inca cosmos was divided into spheres linked together by Viracocha (as the cosmic river). This earth (*kaypacha*) was seen as an almost vertical domain, probably because of the immense physical diversity that characterizes the region – rising from sea level to high mountains in a very short distance.

Only east and west, where the sun rose and set, were named, while the country was seen to consist of four unequal ritual quarters, as was Cuzco itself. Radiating out from the Coricancha (the temple of the Sun in Cuzco) were *ceques* – a series of some 41 conceptual lines along which still lie some 328 *huacas*.

◆ *see* THE BARANSA HOUSE AS COSMOS p 124

DIVINE ANCESTORS

The first Inca (king) was Manco Capac, who was also seen as an androgynous founder ancestor. All subsequent Incas and their wives, (the Coyas) were also considered to be of divine descent: the Inca, the son of the sun; the Coya, the daughter of the moon.

◆ *see* THE COSMOS p. 132

FESTIVALS

Inca festivals were ordered according to a calendar based on the moon and stars and consisting of 12 months. They gave particular importance to the Milky Way, two of whose constellations were named as a baby and an adult llama. The Pleiades, known as *Qolqa* ('the granary'), were particularly important for prognostication of agricultural fertility and many of the bigger ceremonies centred around the growth cycle.

Important rituals were also held at solstices. During the festival of *Qapaq Raymi* in December, as held in Cuzco, boys of royal descent were initiated and llamas sacrificed to the sun. The llama was sacred to the royal lineage. So, for the *Ayriwa* celebrations, in April, a perfect white llama was dressed in red with gold ear ornaments and taught to ingest coca and chicha and allowed to live. For other festivals, the llamas were less lucky and were usually sacrificed, sometimes in large numbers and usually accompanied by prayer, music, dancing and drinking.

◆ *see* CALENDAR FESTIVALS p. 130

▲ *ABOVE: Tiahuanaco, the solar deity*

NATIVE NORTH AMERICANS

Over many thousands of years successive migrations of peoples had filled every inhabitable region of North America, from the Arctic tundra to the interior plains, and from the sea coasts to the desert plateaux of the arid south-west. Speaking over 300 distinct languages, each tribal group had developed its own distinctive culture, mythology and rituals, specific to living in harmony within their local environment.

RECLAIMING TRADITIONS

Scholarly estimates, based upon both oral tradition and archeological evidence, suggest that the population of the Americas prior to the arrival of Christopher Columbus in 1492 exceeded 100 million. When, from the end of the fifteenth century, Europeans began to explore North America, they found a large and culturally diverse population. However, epidemics, genocide and frequent warfare – coupled with the loss of land and resources to an increasing flood of immigrants – decimated the scattered populations. Many ancient traditions were lost in the process and it was only in the 1960s that a resurgence to reclaim them began.

Gradually the old religious traditions and ceremonies are returning. Often elders can still remember how sacred dances and rituals were conducted. Museums and public art galleries have been ordered to repatriate sacred artefacts, dance masks, etc. to the tribes to which they belong and to return ancestral bones for re-burial. Native languages and spirituality now form established courses in many universities, while some elders work as chaplains in many hospitals, universities and prisons.

◖ see CEREMONIES AND SWEAT LODGE RITUALS p. 141

SPIRITUALITY

The recent resurgence of native spirituality provides the self-respect and cultural identity essential to the ongoing struggle to regain treaty lands and achieve political independence. Despite wide variations in mythologies, ceremonies and rituals, it is possible to generalize. Native spirituality expresses the close relationship between people, nature and the spirit world.

Native tribal culture and self-image are based upon the continuous habitation of place. People and place together form a social, cultural and spiritual unit. Prominent landscape elements are the sacred sites – places where the spiritual world is manifest. They may mark the place of the emergence of a people from the underworld, or of its creation by mythological spirit powers. Here the ancestral bones rest.

Oral histories, stories of origin and of ancient mythological creatures vary across the continent, but all serve the function of culturally

▶ *RIGHT: An Native American reserve for the Blackfoot tribe*

bonding a people together. They all stress the interaction between people and the natural and spiritual world. Story-telling, chanting, dancing and role-playing wearing elaborate dance masks enable people to participate actively in addressing issues of ultimate concern, and expressing the unity and spiritual origin of all things.

◆ *see* NATURE p. 138

NATURE

Nature is experienced as hierophanic, that is, manifesting the spiritual. It is said that nature itself is the cathedral, the site where the spiritual may be encountered. For each tribal group, certain specific places (a high mountain or a spring, for example) and specific creatures will assume special significance, and can and do become vehicles for revelation. A bear, a buffalo, a raven, and so on will, on occasion become, or body forth, the power of the spirit world to protect, teach, warn or heal tribal members.

◆ *see* ANIMAL SPIRITS p. 140

MEDICINE WHEEL

The focus upon spatiality may be expressed in the medicine wheel, a circular form, frequently marked out in rock patterns on the land. The medicine wheel is a symbol of inclusiveness, of the four directions (north, south, east and west), of the whole people (children, youth, adult and elderly), of the circle of the *teepee*, inside the circle of the tribe, inside the circle of the world. Prayers can be addressed to and blessings sought from the four directions.

◆ *see* POWWOW CIRCUIT p. 144

▶ *RIGHT: A Native American medicine man in costume*

ANIMAL SPIRITS

Spirituality is pervasive throughout all life and, therefore, all animals are part of the sacred creation. They contain a spiritual essence no significant than our own and so must be treated with respect. It is often possible to be in spiritual communication with an animal spirit. A hunter may 'call' animals towards himself. On killing an animal for food, the hunter should make a reciprocal offering, possibly of tobacco, to the animal spirit and to the Creator, expressing thanksgiving, respect and acknowledgement of the hunter's reliance upon the animal for survival.

◐ *see* NATURE p. 138

THE SHAMAN

Shamanism is found throughout Native North America. The shaman (usually a tribal elder or holy man) has, by fasting and prayer, established a close relationship with his specific guardian animal spirit. He undertakes journeys into the spirit world where he may be given wisdom to prophesy, to give warnings to his people, or inform people why certain animals are scarce and where they should hunt. He has extensive knowledge of herbal remedies and may be called upon (instead of, or in addition to, modern medical facilities) to provide both physical and spiritual healing.

Shamans, with their healing powers, are highly respected. Their activities are extremely diverse, ranging from knowing the movements of Arctic fish, to healing with sand paintings and traditional chants in the south-western deserts. Today, some undertake work as counsellors, advisors or chaplains in hospitals and colleges. Their clients increasingly include non-native followers.

◐ *see* SAMAN p. 12

CEREMONIES AND SWEAT LODGE RITUALS

Ceremonies and rituals reinforce a reciprocal relationship between people, nature and the spirit world. Spiritual power or *Orenda* (Iroquois), *Manitou* (Algonquin), *Wakan-Tanka* (Sioux) or *Kachina* (Hopi), ensures the abundance of nature, and people play an essential role in this by offering gifts, rituals and gratitude.

Before most ceremonies a sweat lodge is built for purification from sin, addiction and brokenness. Constructed of saplings bent together to form a half sphere, with the entrance facing east, it is covered with cedar boughs and tarpaulins to ensure darkness. Very hot rocks are placed in the central fire-pit and, accompanied by prayer and chanting, cold water is sprinkled on them. The lodge combines earth, air, water and fire. Aromatic herbs, drums and rattles may also be used.

◐ *see* THE SUN DANCE p. 145

> ▶ *RIGHT: A Hopi* Kachina *doll representing a divine ancestral spirit*

VISION SEEKING

Another widespread tradition is that of vision seeking. After receiving instruction from a shaman, and after making offerings and receiving purification in a sweat lodge, the vision seeker goes to a wilderness location to spend several days in solitude, fasting and prayer. The seeker may have dreams and see beyond the physical world into the spiritual. Many receive a visit from an animal who will reveal itself as being the person's spiritual guardian.

◐ *see* ANIMAL SPIRITS p. 140

PUEBLO TRADITIONS

In south-west USA, pueblo traditions are based upon a cosmology of the emergence of people from underground worlds. The stonewalled, underground *kiva* chambers symbolize emergence from the womb of the earth up a vertical axis. Located in the centre of the village, the *kiva* is the domain of the men and is where the *Kachina* masks and costumes are stored.

The annual ritual cycle follows the seasonal cycle of nature: cultivation of crops in the summer and harvest in the fall being followed by the dance and ceremonial cycles, generally lasting from the winter to the

summer solstice. For the complex cycle of masked dances and ceremonies, the sacred masks are brought out of storage in the *kivas* and may be repainted and decorated. The dances form a liturgical cycle in which both mask and dancer become the embodiment of the spirit power that is represented. Dolls are made for the children as small replicas of the *Kachinas*, so that they can learn to recognize each of the masks and its associated spirit powers.

◆ *see* MASKS AND MASQUERADES p. 115

▼ *BELOW: Ruins of a Native American village dating from 1050-1300*

THE POTLATCH

The nations of the Pacific north-west acknowledge the profound spiritual relationship that exists between people and nature, by carving the story of the family relationship with both real and mythological creatures into house posts, mortuary poles and *totem* (or family crest) poles.

The most important ceremony is the *potlatch* (prohibited from 1884 until 1951). In large and wonderfully carved assembly halls, feasting is followed by elaborate dances in which the dancers wear huge, fabulously carved masks to depict ancestral legends honouring a particular chief or clan. Dancing is followed by a lavish 'give-away', in which the giver of the *potlatch* gains status by his generosity. *Potlatches* may be held to

celebrate any major event such as a birth, wedding, anniversary or appointment of a new chief.

◆ *see* SPIRITUALITY p. 137

THE POWWOW CIRCUIT

The recent resurgence in national pride and culture has led almost every tribal group and reservation to hold a regular summer celebration (homecoming), during which *powwow* dances form an essential part of the celebration. The *powwow* is a series of dances in which participants circle the dance arena to the rhythm of different drum groups. It may last anywhere from a few hours to

◀ *LEFT: A powwow ceremony*

several days. There are different categories of dancing; some for men, or for women, or children, and some open for everyone present to join in. There are different categories of the very elaborate types of dance costume. Prizes may be awarded for dancing and for costumes. Notable performers, a skilled hoop dancer, for example, may be invited to come a considerable distance to give a solo performance. Many younger band members spend their summer months on the *powwow* trail, moving from one celebration to another. They carry with them not only costumes and drums, but also new cultural, political and economic ideas and cement friendship bonds between native peoples of many different cultures.

💠 *see* PEYOTE p. 149

THE SUN DANCE

For so long declared illegal, it is only since the 1970s that a slow revival of the Sun Dance has been possible. It is held annually by an increasing number of bands in the central plains. A dance arena is selected and surrounded by an arbour of poles and evergreen branches. A central pole is erected, representing the axial centre of existence, linking dancers to both the circle of earth and the celestial circle of the spirit world.

Following weeks of preparation, the dancers begin each day with a sweat lodge, and fast throughout the four or more days of the ceremony. They circle the arena continuously during daylight hours, accompanied by groups of drummers who maintain a steady rhythm, like the heartbeat of the earth. It is also a test of endurance and bravery. Some of the young men choose to have skewers placed through their back or chest muscles, attached by ropes to heavy buffalo skulls. They compete to drag the skulls the furthest, and can win prestigious awards.

💠 *see* CEREMONIES AND SWEAT LODGE RITUALS p. 141

THE HUICHOL

The Huichol live high up in the inaccessible Sierra mountains in the state of Sinaloa, Mexico. The Huichol believe that their ancestors gave them the task of looking after not only their community but the whole cosmos. Every year they perform rituals for the earth led by their shamans. But these can only be performed after they have made a pilgrimage to the sacred land of Wiricuta, the birth place of the sun.

▲ *ABOVE: A depiction of Tatewari*

COSMOLOGY

All aspects of their cosmos are imbued with supernatural significance. The most important deity is Tatawarei (Grandfather Fire), made manifest long ago by the Animal People (specifically Deer Person and Ant Person), while Tayaupa (Our Father Sun) was subsequently created when a Huichol boy was thrown into the water to become the sun. He travelled down through five levels to the underworld and eventually emerged in the east in a burst of volcanic activity. The Huichol feel ambivalent about Tayaupa: he is potent and can be dangerous. The pilgrimage into the desert to Wiricuta, 480 km (300 miles) away, is partly to make offerings to him but it is also to hunt for *peyote*, a hallucinogenic cactus, which today has close associations with corn: both considered to be aspects of Tateima (Our Mothers or Mother Earth).

🔾 *see* THE COSMOS p. 132

PILGRIMAGE

In spring, before the start of the ceremonies to bring rain, up to 12 men and women make the pilgrimage led by their *mara'akame* (or shaman who is also priest, healer and community leader, and can be either male of female). The shaman wears deer antlers attached to his hat and becomes Tatewari accompanied by the mythical Kauyumari (the sacred Deer Person and culture hero). This is a tough journey requiring abstinence from salt, sex, washing, full meals and sufficient sleep for its duration, not just for those who go but for those who stay behind too. *Peyote* is believed to have been given to them by the deer and is 'hunted' until it reveals its whereabouts. Once gathered, it is treated with the greatest respect and carefully brought back.

Tatewari, having guided their quest, is equally important on their return; the Huichol circle the fire to thank him for their successful quest.

Before any ritual, Tatewari prepares them. They 'confess' their misdoings to the fire which cleanses them and Tatewarei is fed a small portion of all food and drink. Collected also in Wiricuta is a yellow root whose sap is used to decorate the faces of the entire community with designs showing their respect for Tayaupa.

◗ see PILGRIMAGE p. 36

◀ LEFT: A shaman during a ritual wearing a feathered hat

CEREMONIES AND RITUALS

The main rituals are to Tateima and Nakawe (Grandmother Growth) whom they believe they must nurture before the rains will come and the corn ripen, accompanied by music, song, prayers and chants. Amidst many candles and flowers decorated with ribbons, a cow is sacrificed (in the past this would have been a deer, but today the Huichoi do not hunt much). The blood not only feeds Tateima but unites everyone and everything, as each in turn has a little daubed on his or her forehead and on all their possessions.

Rain is believed to come from the sea and so, to ensure its continuance, the Huichol also make pilgrimages, not to the nearest ocean (the Pacific) but to the Atlantic. Entire families travel with their children, who are blindfolded as they approach. After keeping vigil on the beach all night, the children are ritually presented to the sea at dawn.

◗ see CEREMONIES AND SWEAT LODGE RITUALS p. 141

PEYOTE

During the dry season, the Huichols use *peyote* for many of their rituals, thereby increasing their knowledge of their cosmology. Children are introduced to it little by little when still quite young. During one whole day, they are taken on a metaphorical journey to Wiricuta by the shaman, by means of chants and songs accompanied by drumming.

When initiated, they stay up all night to dance and sing with everyone else and experience the full sensory complexity of their cosmos. It is not unusual for Huichols not to sleep for three to four nights in a row; a female shaman, sitting in her sacred chair in the *tuki* (sacred house), has been known to chant for up to 36 hours non-stop. However, only the shaman reveals to others what he or she has learnt from *peyote*.

◆ *see* COSMOLOGY p. 147

▶ RIGHT: Men dressed for a festival

RASTAFARIANISM

Rastafarianism is a loosely organized religio-political movement inspired by the 'black power' teachings of the Jamaican Marcus Garvey (1870–1940). Garvey taught that black Caribbeans were the lost tribes of Israel and that all black people in the Western world should shake off the oppression of the white man and return to Africa, the promised land.

HAILE SELASSIE

According to Garvey, the Bible showed that an African king would be crowned as the Messiah; Ethiopia was of special significance. A belief in Ethiopia as the cradle of civilization and site of a future utopia was popularized among black Jamaicans in the nineteenth century, taking inspiration from the biblical prophecy that 'Ethiopia shall soon stretch forth her hands unto God'.

With Garvey, Ethiopianism achieved its fullest development. Many blacks saw the 1930 coronation of Prince Ras Tafari Makonnen as Emperor of Ethiopia as the fulfilment of Garvey's prophecy. The Emperor, who took the name Haile Selassie (Power of the Trinity), was hailed as God or Jah, the divine saviour of the black people, and the Rastafarian movement began.

see RASTA BELIEFS p. 151

◀ LEFT: Marcus Garvey

RASTA BELIEFS

The Rasta belief system is very loosely defined. Emphasis is placed on a natural, straightforward lifestyle, on coming to know Jah (God) in every aspect of life, and on the individual's subjective interpretation of core themes: the belief that repatriation to Africa is the key to overcoming white oppression, non-violence, a belief in the divinity of Haile Selassie and a condemnation of Babylon (the white power structure). Ethiopia is sometimes understood literally as an earthly paradise, sometimes as a symbol of a time when black oppression will cease. The concept of 'I and I' is central to the movement and expresses the concept of oneness – God within all of us, and all of us as one people. The movement rejects Christianity although a majority of first generation Rastas were Christians or came from Christian homes.

There are two highly organized sects within Rastafarianism, the Bobos and the Twelve Tribes of Israel (to which Bob Marley belonged). However,

▲ ABOVE: An Ethiopian banknote bearing the face of Ras Tafari Makonnen

most Rastas prefer to live their own individual Rasta philosophy without belonging to an organization.

Haile Selassie's death in 1975 caused a crisis of faith. Some Rastafarians thought his death was a fabrication, others that it was part of a Babylonian (white man's) conspiracy. For Rastafarians, Babylon is the antithesis of Ethiopia and refers to the biblical kingdom that enslaved the nation of Israel. Some Rastas believe their saviour remains present in spirit, others that he will be resurrected.

■ see HAILE SELASSIE p. 150

▶ RIGHT: Prince Emmanuel, a Rastafarian community leader

SYMBOLS

The wearing of dreadlocks (hair grown long, matted and twisted into coils) sets Rastas apart from Babylon and is supported in the Bible: 'They shall not make baldness upon their head, neither shall they shave off the corner of their beard, nor make any cuttings in the flesh' (Leviticus 21:5). Rastafarians can also be recognized by wearing the colours of their religion: red, gold and green. Red symbolizes the blood of martyrs, gold the wealth of the homeland, and green the beauty and vegetation of Ethiopia. Sometimes black is used to represent the colour of Africans. The lion is also a prominent symbol. It represents Haile Selassie, the conquering Lion of Judah.

◆ *see* THE CHRISTIAN BIBLE p. 195

REASONINGS AND THE BINGHI

There are two main Rastafarian rituals: reasonings and the *binghi*. The reasoning is an informal gathering at which a small group of brethren generally smoke the holy weed, *ganja* (marijuana), and engage in discussion. Whoever lights the pipe says a short prayer and then the pipe is passed around the circle until everyone has smoked. The reasoning ends when the participants have all, one by one, departed. The *ganga* or 'wisdom weed' is smoked for religious reasons or to aid meditation; some do not use it at all.

The *nyabinghi* or *binghi* ritual includes drumming (believed to be the voice of Jah), chanting, dancing and praise to Jah Rastafari. *Binghi* rhythms inspired reggae and Bob Marley incorporated its drumming and chants into his music. Considered the most inspirational meeting of Rastafarians, the *binghi* is held on special occasions including the coronation of Haile Selassie (2 November), his ceremonial birthday (6 January), his 1966 visit to Jamaica (25 April), his personal birthday (23 July), emancipation from slavery (1 August), and Marcus Garvey's birthday (17 August). *Binghis* can last for several days and in Jamaica bring together hundreds of Rastafarians from all over the country.

◆ *see* THE CELEBRATION OF LIFE p. 108

NEAR EAST

2200 BC	Ziggurats built in Sumeria
2000 BC	Myths of Gilgamesh, King of Uruk, written in the Sumerian language on clay tablets
c. 2000 BC	Abraham born
c. 1360 BC	Canaanite Sacred Texts recorded on clay tablets at King Niqmad II's request
c. 1200 BC	Israelites reach Canaan; beginning of Jewish religion (worship of Yahweh)
c. 950 BC	Solomon, king of Israel, breaks Canaanite idols and alters; First temple built, Jerusalem
c. 628–551 BC	Life of Zoroaster (founder of Zoroastrianism)
c. 588 BC	Zoroastrianism becomes official religion in Persia
586 BC	Destruction of the First Temple. Jerusalem captured by Babylonians
44 BC	Jerusalem under control of the Roman Empire
c. 6 BC–AD 32	Life of Jesus of Nazareth
AD 48–95	New Testament written
AD 70	Destruction of the Second Temple, Jerusalem; Jewish diaspora begins
AD 404	Latin version of the Bible completed
AD 570–632	Muhammad the Prophet born in Mecca
AD 610	Qur'anic verses revealed to Muhammad
AD 661–750	First Dynasty of Islam formed (the Umayyads)
AD 750–1258	Second Dynasty of Islam (the Abbasids)
AD 935	Qur'an finalised
1483–1546	Life of Martin Luther ('father of the reformation')
1509–64	Life of Jean Calvin (reformer)
Late 16th century	Baptist movement arises
1624–91	Life of George Fox (founder of Quaker movement)
1703–91	Life of John Wesley (founder of Methodist movement)
1844	Baha'i faith founded by the Bab ('the Gate')
1844–1921	Life of Abdu'l-Baha
1861	Salvation Army founded by William Booth (1829–1912)
1863	Baha'u'llah announced that He was the figure foretold by the Bab and the Baha'i community was born
1948	Establishment of state of Israel

THE SUMERIANS

Sumeria, the earliest known city civilization, set the religious tone for the rest of Mesopotamia. Sumeria seemed to be saturated with divine presence and a concept of myriad gods and goddesses, each controlling their own aspect of life, together with the sacrifices required to humour them.

BELIEFS

Religion and rituals were all-pervasive in the Sumerian civilization. Their purpose was to deflect the anger of the gods by constant prayers and sacrifices. Sumeria, like the rest of Mesopotamia, was not an easy place to live and divine fury was thought to reveal itself through disasters such as drought, floods, pestilence, crop failure or the silting up of rivers. The Sumerians believed that humans had been created out of clay in order to relieve the gods of their workload. It followed that humans were the servants of the gods. Nevertheless, the gods were envisaged as much like humans, with similar physical form, needs, appetites and characteristics. This was why food became the most frequent form of sacrificial offering.

◆ see PRIESTS p. 158

▶ RIGHT: Gilgamesh

GODS AND GHOSTS

The vast Sumerian pantheon represented aspects of the world – the harvest, the wind or the sun – in divine form. The principal deity was Anu, ruler of heaven, who was later replaced by Enlil, lord of the winds. There were also some 3,000 other deities in Sumeria. In addition, individual villages had their own local gods, as did inanimate objects. Enlil, for instance, was god of the hoe through his connection with the moist spring wind and the planting season. Enlil's son, Ninurta, was god of the plough. Concepts of reincarnation and the afterlife were alien to Sumerian theology. The dead, Sumerians believed, had no specific place in which to continue in the same style they had known while living. Consequently, the living were thought to be constantly at risk from their presence and only by regular offerings of food and drink could these ghosts be dissuaded from haunting them.

◆ *see* THE FOUR SECTORS p. 161

▲ *ABOVE: Sumerian mosaic depicting a sacrifice*

PRIESTS

Priests in the Sumerian temples acted as conduits between the gods and human beings. They conducted the daily services and presided over festivals, such as *Akitu*, the festival of the new year, which fell approximately at the time of the spring equinox. They interpreted the entrails of sacrificed animals, usually sheep, in order to learn the divine will. They performed the public sacrifices which usually consisted of goats, cattle, birds and sheep. The divine portion of an animal sacrifice comprised the right leg, the kidneys and a piece of meat for roasting. The rest of the animal sacrifices were consumed at the temple feast. In addition, libations of water were poured over sheaves of grain or bunches of dates so that the gods of fertility would grant rain for healthy crops. All manner of offerings were brought to the priests in the temples for use by the gods:

clothing, beds, chairs, drinking vessels, jewels, ornaments or weapons. All these were classed as divine property and were placed in the temple treasuries. Clothing was first offered to the gods, then distributed among the priests and other officials who staffed the temples. The high priest had first pick, and the last went to the lowly sweepers of the temple courtyards.

◖ *see* BELIEFS p. 156

ZIGGURATS

The high temple towers known as *ziggurats*, which were topped by a small temple dedicated to one of the Mesopotamian deities, were a feature of religious architecture around 2200 BC and 500 BC. The practice of building *ziggurats* began in Sumeria, spreading later to Babylonia and Assyria. The step-sided *ziggurat* bore little resemblance to the later pyramids of Ancient Egypt. There were no internal rooms or passageways and the core was made of mud brick, with baked brick covering the exterior. The shape was either square or rectangular, with measurements averaging 40 or 50 sq m (130 or 165 sq ft) at the base. The most complete extant *ziggurat*, now named Tall al-Muqayyar, was built at Ur in south-west Sumeria (present-day southern Iraq). The most famous was the Tower of Babel, which is popularly believed to have had links with the *ziggurat* at the temple of Marduk, the national god of Babylonia. The Tower of Babel, having been built in the vicinity of Babylon, is regarded by some archaeologists and anthropologists as an extension of the worship of Marduk at his *ziggurat* temple in the city.

◖ *see* GODS AND GHOSTS p. 157

◀ *LEFT: A Sumerian harp from Ur*

THE BABYLONIANS

There were two empires of Babylonia – the Old Empire (c. 2200–1750 BC) and the Neo-Babylonian Empire (625–539 BC). The Babylonian religion originally derived from that of Sumeria. It stressed goodness, truth, law and order, justice and freedom, wisdom and learning, courage and loyalty. The chief Babylonian god was Marduk, 'king over the universe entire'.

BELIEF

The ethos of Babylonia was essentially philanthropic. Compassion and mercy were prime virtues. The poor and unfortunate, widows and orphans, were accorded special protection. No one, however virtuous, was considered to be faultless so that suffering, where it occurred, was never entirely undeserved. The gods handed out punishment for unethical or immoral behaviour. To obtain the help of the gods in solving problems, it was necessary first of all to confess sin and admit to failings. Only then would an individual's personal god intercede for them with the greater Babylonian deities. There was no comfortable afterlife in Babylonian belief. After death, the spirit parted from the body and all that awaited it was descent into the dark underworld. There was no protection from a wretched existence after death, not even for those who had led righteous and ethical lives.

◄ see WORSHIP AND RITUALS p. 162

▶ RIGHT: A relief showing a Babylonian map of the world

THE FOUR SECTORS

Babylonian faith encompassed the whole universe and each sector of it was under the rule of a particular deity. Heaven, earth, sea and air comprised one sector, the sun, the moon and the planets another. Nature, as manifested in rivers, mountains, plains and other geographical features was a further sector and the fourth was the city state of Babylon. Marduk, the chief god, presided over the pantheon. Like the Sumerians, the Babylonians believed that tools and implements – bricks, ploughs, axes, hoes – had their own particular deities. In addition, individuals had their own personal gods to whom they prayed and looked for salvation.

Magic was prominent in Babylonian religion and Ea, god of wisdom, was also god of spells and incantations. The sun and the moon had their own gods, Shamash and Sin respectively. Shamash was also the god of justice. Adad was the god of wind, storm and flood and Ishtar, a dynamic, but cruel deity, was goddess of love and war. Although the general tenor of Babylonian religion was beneficent, there was also a negative, fearful side to it. This was represented by underworld gods, demons, devils and monsters who posed an ongoing threat to the wellbeing of humanity.

🔄 see GODS AND GHOSTS p. 157

WORSHIP AND RITUALS

Worship and ritual at the Babylonian temples usually took place out of doors, in courtyards where there were fountains for washing before prayers and altars where sacrifices were offered. The private areas of a temple, the monopoly of the high priest, the clergy and royalty, were indoors. The occult tendency in Babylonian religion was fully represented among the clergy. They included astrologers, soothsayers, diviners, the interpreters of dreams, musicians and singers. Sacrifices took place daily. One Babylonian temple kept a stock of 7,000 head of cattle and 150,000 head of other animals for this purpose alone. Apart from animals, sacrifices consisted of vegetables, incense or libations of water, beer and wine. There were numerous festivals, including a feast for the new moon and the most important, *Akitu*, which lasted 11 days and involved lively processions. At *Akitu*, worshippers purified themselves, propitiated the gods, offered sacrifices, performed penance and obtained absolution.

🔄 see BELIEF p. 160

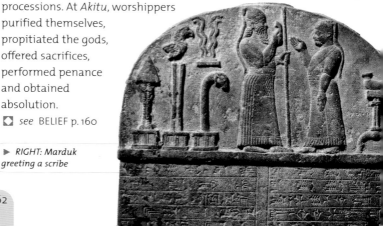

▶ RIGHT: Marduk greeting a scribe

THE ASSYRIANS

Religion had important political significance in Assyria. Kings were believed to derive their power from Assur, the chief god, and both divination and astrology were initially facilities for the use of the monarch. Underlying this though, was a popular religion based on fear and superstition.

▲ *ABOVE: A reconstruction of a wall painting found at Khorsabad*

ASSUR

Religion was a vital factor in unifying and strengthening the Assyrian Empire (746–612 BC). This was a state religion, with the king himself as chief priest and representative on earth of Assur, the chief Assyrian god.

163

Four of the six major Assyrian deities – Ishtar, Shamash, Adad and Sin – were identical in both name and function with those worshipped in Babylonia. However, Assur replaced Marduk as the chief deity and Ninurta, god of hunting and war, was Assur's eldest son. Assur was raised to prominence by King Sennacherib of Assyria (d. 681 BC). Originally, it was Marduk, chief god of Babylonia, who featured in the great ritual at the *Akitu* festival, which celebrated his victory over Tiamat. Tiamat was a primordial creature who had created monsters to avenge the death of her 'husband' Apsu at the hands of Ea, one of their children, the younger gods. In his role as champion of the younger gods, however, Marduk killed the monsters and Tiamat as well.

Sennacherib, however, ascribed the deed to Assur after he conquered and destroyed Babylon in 689 BC and so gave the god his central place in both the festival and the Assyrian pantheon. This was a political rather than a religious move. It was believed that Assyria had been granted its empire by Assur and that its armies were under his protection. Assyrian kings used to present Assur with reports on the campaigns they had conducted, virtually making the god a divine commander-in-chief.

■ see THE FOUR SECTORS p. 161

SUPERSTITION

Assyria was an extremely harsh land, with few natural advantages and much arid desert. The struggle for survival imposed on those who lived there produced a popular religion permeated with the power of the

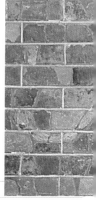

▶ *RIGHT: Ceramic art depicting a lion, the symbol of Ishtar*

supernatural and dominated by superstition. Devils and evil spirits lurked everywhere and charms and incantations were frequently used to exorcise them. To the Assyrians, devils and demons had the power to enter the human body and the clay and metal charms worn to fend them off included human heads and monstrous animals. Repeating seven times the seven magical words inscribed on stone tablets was another commonly used means of averting evil. The supernatural appeared so all-pervading in Assyria that a series of omens was developed, listing every conceivable piece of bad luck, with instructions on how to avoid them. A special class of priests – the *baru*, or seers – dealt with the science of omens and portents.

◆ *see* THE PENTECOSTAL MOVEMENT p. 207

THE CANAANITES

The Canaanites are the earliest recorded settlers of ancient Palestine, with a history in the region dating back to 3000 BC. Canaanite religion and Canaanite gods were synonymous with nature. For instance, the end of the rainy, fertile season was their sign that Mot, the god of death, had killed Baal in his guise as storm god.

93091

BAAL

Baal, who was worshipped not only in Canaan, but throughout the surrounding area, was not a name, but a title meaning 'lord' or 'master'. This did not describe a single god or divine function. Baal could be lord of trees, rocks, streams, mountains and other natural phenomena, but was most frequently identified with storms, rain and fertility. The fertility of an area frequently threatened by drought and desert was the main preoccupation of Canaanite religion and the gods were often associated with the manifestations of nature. Baal, for instance, was called 'rider of the clouds', 'god of lightning and thunder' or 'lord of the sky and the earth'. Likewise, Yarikh, the moon god, was called illuminator of myriads of stars, lamp of heaven or lord of the sickle. The Canaanite pantheon was based

◀ LEFT: The fertility goddess Astarte

around a family unit, with the gods envisaged as kings presiding over royal courts. The supreme god, and father of Baal, was El, creator of creatures. Shachar, the dawn, and Shalim, the dusk were his twin offspring. Apart from Baal, there were several fertility deities, such as Baalat, goddesses of conception and childbirth, sea-deities and hunter-deities.

During King Niqmad II's reign (c. 1360 BC), sacred texts were recorded on clay tablets at the king's request, using the cuneiform script invented by the Sumerians in the fourth century BC. Thirty-four deities were listed, beginning with the god residing in Tsafon, the sacred mountain. The deity of the cult of the dead came next, and thirdly El, the bull and source of creation, power, sagacity and virility. Dagan, a semitic god worshipped throughout the Near East, especially in the region of the middle Euphrates, was listed after that, then seven different Baals and the more minor deities.

◆ *see* BELIEFS p. 156

◀ *LEFT: A statuette of Baal*

THE CANAANITES OF THE BIBLE

For a long time, the Bible was the only source of information about the Canaanites and their religion. According to the Bible, the Canaanites' 'abominable' religious practices marked them for destruction. The Canaanites had many gods with sinister representations: death, sterility, destruction, chaos and the underworld. However, the worship of these and other gods as idols was not the only aspect of the Canaanite religion that earned such a pejorative image in the Bible. There is also the controversial assertion that many Canaanite religious practices were barbaric, together with what biblical scribes saw as abominations: incest, bestiality and human sacrifice. The practice of offering their children as sacrifices to Baal came under special censure. So did the essentially orgiastic, sensual atmosphere of Canaanite religion and its fertility cults and serpent symbols. The biblical view of God and worship was vastly different from that of the Canaanites. The Canaanites viewed worship as a means of controlling the gods, rather than serving them and the sexual nature of Canaanite deities was in complete contrast to the spiritual qualities of the biblical God who occupied a lofty place, far beyond such earthly temptations. The biblical representation certainly has elements of the polemic, and archeology and anthropology show a different side of the Canaanites.

see THE CHRISTIAN BIBLE p. 195

▶ *RIGHT: A figurine of El*

JUDAISM

Judaism was the first religion to profess faith in a single, omnipotent God, with a history dating back over 4,000 years. The Hebrew Bible consists of five books widely attributed to Moses, and which encapsulate the precursory elements of Judaism: the creation myths, Jewish law, and Israelite history. After the Biblical period, Jewish theology and practice were developed by the *rabbis*.

THE NATURE OF GOD

Worship of God is one of life's central activities for religious Jews. Maimonides, a twelfth-century Jewish philosopher and expert in Jewish law, defined 13 Principles of Faith, a brief codification of essential Jewish beliefs; nine deal with the nature of God. God is the creator and guide of the universe, is one, without bodily form, the first and the last, the only focus of prayer, the giver of the *Torah* (the first five books of the Bible), omniscient, who rewards those who keep the commandments and punishes those who break them and will resurrect the dead.

Some of God's Biblical names may originally have been associated with Canaanite pagan deities but have taken on a meaning appropriate to Jewish theology. For instance *YHVH*, the name of God considered too holy to pronounce, is derived from the Hebrew root 'to be' and is linked in later Jewish thought with God's mercy. *Shaddai* comes from a root meaning 'breast'; there are many breasted pagan goddess figurines which may the source of the name. It is translated 'Almighty' and used in the Bible to describe God as sustainer.

◪ *see* THE JEWISH BIBLE AND OTHER SACRED TEXTS p. 173

THE CHILDREN OF ISRAEL AND THE PROMISED LAND

Jews believe that Abraham (born c. 2000 BC) was the first to recognize the existence of God; God made a series of covenants with Abraham. Firstly, in return for leaving Ur in Babylon (now Iraq), his native land, Abraham and Sarah, his barren wife, were promised the land of Canaan (today Israel/Palestine) and many descendants. Later, God asked Abraham to circumcise himself, explaining that as a perpetual sign of the covenant between God and Abraham's descendants, they must circumcise their sons eight days after birth. Soon after he obeyed God's command, Abraham's son Isaac was born.

Abraham's descendants went down to Egypt c.1700 BC to avoid a famine. A few generations later they were regarded as hostile aliens, made into slaves and forced to do hard labour. When the pharaoh ordered their male babies to be killed, God acted upon the covenant he had made with Abraham, Isaac and Jacob and sent plagues upon Egypt when the pharaoh refused to let the people go out and worship their God.

◀ LEFT: A statue of Moses by Michaelangelo

When the Children of Israel (the Biblical phrase for what later became the Jewish people), led by Moses, left Egypt and reached Mount Sinai in the desert, God remade the covenant with the whole nation, giving them the Ten Commandments and many other instructions detailing how they were to serve God.

When the Children of Israel returned to the land under Joshua's leadership, they defeated the tribes living there and established themselves. David (who reigned 1006–965 BC), one of the first kings of Israel, erected a tent in Jerusalem to hold the ark containing the two stone tablets of the Ten Commandments. His son Solomon (who reigned 965–928 BC) built an impressive temple.

Jerusalem was captured by the Babylonians in 586 BC and many of the people were forced into exile. In 538 BC, the people were allowed to return to the land of Israel by Cyrus of Persia, who had crushed the Babylonian empire, and rebuild the Temple in Jerusalem. The Second Temple was built tall to combine maximum splendour with the dimensions given in the Bible for the portable shrine the Children of Israel carried in the wilderness.

By 44 BC the land was under the control of the Roman Empire. The Romans were normally tolerant of well-behaved local religions but the Zealots, an intemperate minority, refused to accept their rule and revolted. In response, the Romans successfully besieged Jerusalem, destroyed the Second Temple in AD 70 and martyred many leading *rabbis*. After a further unsuccessful rebellion against Rome in AD 135 by Simon bar Kochba, many Jews were exiled. A small number of Jews remained in the land of Israel but the majority of the Jewish people lived scattered across the world.

◆ *see* THE ROMANS p. 248

THE RABBIS

Yochanan ben Zakkai, a scholar who enabled Jewish teaching to survive and who can be regarded as the originator of *Rabbinic* Judaism, smuggled himself out of Jerusalem during the Roman siege in a coffin shortly before the destruction of the Temple in AD 70. The Romans permitted him to set up a school at Yavneh on Israel's Mediterranean coast. His students became rabbinical scholars; they expanded existing commentaries on the Bible and developed a framework of belief which enabled their generation, traumatised by the destruction of the Temple, to continue to live as Jews.

Judaism as it is practised now rests both on the Bible and on *rabbinic* development of Biblical ideas. The ancient *rabbis* in Israel and Babylon said their interpretations of the Bible represented its true meaning, even when these were not literal. For instance they said that 'an eye for an eye' meant paying compensation to the injured party, not seeking a similar revenge. Another innovation was their belief in the immortality of the soul.

◆ *see* SYNAGOGUES p. 182

THE JEWISH BIBLE AND OTHER SACRED TEXTS

Jews are called the 'people of the book' and a great deal of emphasis is placed on the study of the sacred texts in the Jewish faith. Jews believe that the nature of God is revealed through the events of history, and it is only through study that individuals can understand the essence of Judaism for themselves.

The Jewish Bible reached its present form soon after the Babylonian exile in the sixth century BC. It is divided into three sections. The first five books – Genesis, Exodus, Leviticus, Numbers and Deuteronomy – are called the *Torah* or *Pentateuch* (meaning 'written law'). The *Torah* records the revelation of God to Moses on Mount Sinai 3,000 years ago. They contain 613 commandments, as well as describing the early history of the Children of Israel. The second section, Prophets, includes the history of settling the Promised Land and the writings of prophets like Isaiah and Hosea. The third section, Writings, contains the Psalms, the short books read on festivals including Ruth and Song of Songs, wisdom literature (such as Proverbs and Job) and later historical books like Chronicles and Ezra.

◄ *LEFT: The destruction of the Second Temple*

◄ LEFT: *Tefillin, pouches holding sections of the Torah*

The *Mishnah* (Repetition) was written down around AD 200. This body of work defined the teachings and legal system intrinsic to the *Torah*. It is divided into six orders or subject areas: Prayer and Agriculture, Festivals, Women, Civil Law, Rituals and Purity. The *Mishnah* begins with prayer and its first chapter defines times of prayer; it also begins by referring to the Temple destroyed in AD 70 and ends by referring to the Messiah, whom Jews believe to be the messenger announcing the arrival of a future era of peace and perfection.

Once the *Mishnah* was written down, commentators started to analyze why Judah had preferred some existing oral laws to others. The Babylonian *Talmud* ('learning') was written down around AD 500; it contains the *Mishnah* and the *Gemara* (meaning 'completion' of the discussion on each topic). Its redactors also included aggadah, morally improving Bible interpretations and stories about the lives of the *rabbis*. The *Gemara* is written in Aramaic, the contemporary vernacular. There is also a Palestinian *Talmud* which is shorter and considered less authoritative.

◘ see THE CHRISTIAN BIBLE p. 195

JEWISH FESTIVALS

The cycle of the Jewish year includes festivals of joy and times of mourning, times of contemplation and times of dancing and happiness.

The prayer book calls *Rosh HaShanah* 'the birthday of the world', the anniversary of creation. Apples and honey are eaten at home to express the hope that the coming year will be sweet. As well as the new calendar year, *Rosh HaShanah* begins ten days of remembering all wrong-doings from the past year in order to rectify them before the Day of Atonement.

Yom Kippur, the Day of Atonement, is a spiritual cleansing enabling one to start the year afresh. Those physically able – not the young, or ill – abstain from all food and drink for 25 hours; services are held in the

▶ RIGHT: Purim *in Jerusalem*

175

evening and from early morning until dark. The synagogue vestments are white; once a year human beings aspire to be like angels who, white-clad, spend all day every day praising God.

Passover (from the Hebrew *Pesach*), commemorates the exodus from Egypt. It is celebrated by a *seder* (a sequence of readings and symbolic actions), described in a special prayer book, the *Haggadah* (recitation), when the events of the Exodus are explained to the children by their parents round their dining table and they eat unleavened bread to commemorate the Children of Israel's hasty departure from Egypt. Seven weeks after Passover, *Shavuot* (Pentecost) celebrates the giving of the Ten Commandments at Mount Sinai.

▲ *ABOVE: A female rabbi blows the shofar, a ceremonial horn*

► RIGHT: The festival of Passover

During *Sukkot* (Tabernacles) Jews remember living under God's protection during the 40 years in the wilderness. Each family builds a small open-roofed booth and, weather permitting, eats there; the lulav, palm fronds, myrtle and willow branches are shaken together with a citron. At the end of the festival, on *Simchat Torah* (the Rejoicing of the Law), the final chapter from Deuteronomy is read and immediately the cycle of reading the *Torah* recommences at the beginning of Genesis.

Purim commemorates the events of the book of Esther which tells how a decree stating that Jews should be killed on a certain date was averted. Jews read the book of Esther, thank God for averting the decree, give to the poor so they also can celebrate, send food gifts to friends and eat and drink. Children dress up, and in Israel there are carnival processions.

On *Chanukah* Jews light candles, starting with one and adding another daily throughout the eight days of the festival to remember the rededication of the temple in 164 BC after Judah the Maccabbee, his brothers and their small guerrilla forces drove out the Syrians.

The seven weeks between Passover and *Shavuot* are a time of

mourning when the deaths from plague of students of Rabbi Akiva, a
first century *rabbi*, are remembered; no weddings or parties are held. On
Lag b'Omer the plague lifted for a day so mourning restrictions stop.

On *Tisha b'Av*, the 9th of Av, Jews remember the destruction of the First

and Second Temples by fasting, reading the Book of Lamentations and singing dirges describing other episodes of persecution. Three minor fast days, 17th *Tammuz*, 10th *Tevet* and Fast of *Gedaliah* commemorate stages in the siege and defeat of Jerusalem.

Three significant events in twentieth-century Jewish history are now commemorated in the calendar: Holocaust Memorial Day (*Yom HaShoah*), 27th Nissan; the anniversary of the battle of the Warsaw Ghetto, Israel Independence Day (*Yom HaAtzmaut*) 5th Iyar; and Jerusalem Day, 28th Iyar, the anniversary of the reunification of Jerusalem in 1967.

■ *see* RITUALS p. 179

RITUALS

Judaism prescribes rituals for all stages of the life cycle and includes commandments to give charity and eat 'proper' or *kosher* food; all aspects of life connect to God and the commandments God gave to the Jewish people.

Eight days after birth, health permitting, Jewish boys have a *brit milah* ('covenant of circumcision') when they are circumcised and given a Hebrew name for use on religious occasions. Recently, new ceremonies have been written to welcome baby girls into the covenant – without circumcision. A month after birth, first-born baby boys from Orthodox families have a *Pidyon HaBen*, Redemption of the Firstborn; in Biblical times, the firstborn used to be dedicated to God's service.

Boys at 13 and girls at 12 are considered *Bar/Bat Mitzvah*, responsible for their own observance of the commandments and entitled to perform ceremonial roles in synagogue. To celebrate their new adult status, they

◀ *LEFT: The* menorah, *a twelve-branched candlestick, is lit at* Chanukah

say the blessings recited over the *Torah* in the Sabbath morning service and may also read from the Bible, lead the service or prepare a speech on the readings. A celebration follows the service.

Judaism believes that marriage is the happiest and holiest state for human beings. Jewish weddings take place under a canopy, symbolizing the couple's future home. To make the bride and groom happy on their wedding day is regarded as an important responsibility for all their guests. Traditionally the groom gave the bride a ring and a *ketubah* (marriage contract) was written, detailing his responsibilities to her and fixing the alimony to be paid in case of divorce. These days marriage is regarded as a more equal responsibility and many non-Orthodox couples exchange rings to symbolize this.

◀ *LEFT: The* Bar Mitzvah *ceremony*

Judaism teaches that the soul is immortal. There are many mourning rituals for the bereaved which at first protect them in their loss and then gradually help them return to daily life. At the funeral, the immediate family say the *kaddish*, a prayer praising God. After the funeral the mourners return home and should be brought food, visited and consoled throughout the next seven days. There follow 30 days in which some mourning restrictions still apply. One says the *kaddish* for a parent for 11 months and for 30 days for other close relatives. On the anniversary of a death, the family light a memorial candle and say the *kaddish*.

◆ *see* JEWISH FESTIVALS p. 175

KOSHER EATING

The laws for *kosher* eating are an important part of Jewish life and identity. The commandments listed in the Bible – do not eat blood, do not cook a kid in its mother's milk, do not eat shellfish, do not eat birds of prey, only eat meat from animals with split hooves who chew the cud – were further developed by the *rabbis*. They instituted *shechitah* (cutting across the arteries of the neck with a sharp knife), a method of slaughter which extracts the

▶ *RIGHT:* Kosher *foods for sale in a supermarket*

maximum amount of blood. They extended the prohibition of cooking a kid in its mother's milk to complete separation of all meat and milk, even prohibiting cooking them in the same vessels or serving them with the same plates and cutlery. Some have suggested that the biblical laws represent a rudimentary system of hygiene and are now an artificial barrier between Jews and others; others insist that eating is a vital part of life and so part of religious observance; blessing God before eating food prepared according to God's commands helps connect all daily life to the Almighty.

◘ *see* THE JEWISH HOME p. 182

SYNAGOGUES

There are three Hebrew names for the synagogue, illustrating its three main roles ('synagogue' means the same in Greek): *Beit HaKnesset* (House of Assembly), *Beit HaTefillah* (House of Prayer) and *Beit Hamidrash* (House of Study). Originally, when the Second Temple was still standing before AD 70, people would meet in the early synagogues to pray at the same times as when the sacrifices were offered. Once the Temple was destroyed in AD 70, the *rabbis* developed the synagogue as the place of Jewish community socializing, worship and study.

◘ *see* THE RABBIS p. 172

THE JEWISH HOME

Much of Jewish observance takes place in the home; a Jew with access to a synagogue but no facilities for home observance would find it harder to live a Jewish life than one with no synagogue available but with a well-equipped Jewish home with a *kosher* kitchen and all the books and

▶ *RIGHT: Jewish men studying in a synagogue*

artefacts needed for study and festival observance. Many festivals are observed entirely or mainly at home: the Sabbath meals, the Passover seder, the special foods associated with each festival, *Chanukah* candle-lighting. Ultra-Orthodox Jewish women who have no role in the synagogue beyond catering and perhaps special study sessions say that because they set the religious tone of their home, they have a religious position as influential as their husbands. The home is also the place of private prayer and study and children's early Jewish education.

◖ *see* KOSHER EATING p. 181

THE SABBATH

Shabbat ('rest') is a day on which no creative work is done, following God's example when he created the world. This frees time for prayer, singing, walking, eating, studying and enjoying oneself. This day is the crown of the week for a Jew; a day of blessing and happiness. Two candles are lit to usher in the Sabbath; and a cup of wine is blessed to declare the day holy. Best clothes are worn and especially good meals eaten. The main synagogue service of the week takes place on the Sabbath morning.

◖ *see* CHRISTIAN RITES p. 197

SHOAH

Six million Jews, including 1.5 million children were killed between 1942 and 1945 by Nazi Germany. In Israel this is called the *Shoah* ('catastrophe'). Holocaust, the term often used in English, means 'burnt-offering'; while many of the victims were cremated, surely no God would wish to be so served.

◖ *see* THE CHILDREN OF ISRAEL AND THE PROMISED LAND p. 170

▶ *RIGHT: Zoroaster's cube at the Achaemenid necropolis, built to house the sacred fire*

ZOROASTRIANISM

Like Judaism, Christianity and Islam, Zoroastrianism is a monotheistic religion that still survives today. It is thought by some to have been founded around 1200 BC; by others around 588 BC by Zarathustra, later known as Zoroaster. Its first adherents were the pastoral nomads of the ancient Afghanistan-Persian border areas. Zoroastrianism was the chief faith of Persia before the arrival of Islam.

AHURA MAZDA AND ZARATHUSTRA

The religions of India and Persia in Zarathustra's time were polytheistic. Zarathustra, who was probably a priest in what is now Iran, formulated a new religion that attempted to concentrate the many gods of these faiths into one, Ahura Mazda, meaning Wise One. Ahura Mazda, it seems, appeared to Zarathustra in a vision and appointed him to preach *asha*, the truth. Creator of the universe and the cosmic order, Ahura Mazda brought two spirits into being. One was the spirit of truth, light, life and good, Spenta Mainyu. The other was Angra Mainyu, the spirit of darkness, deceit, destruction and death. World history comprises the ongoing cosmic struggle between the two Mainyus. Ahura Mazda is therefore not omnipotent, but he and Angra Mainyu represent the contest between good and evil, or *asha* (truth) and *druj* (lies), which is weighted in favour of the former. Humans must join the cosmic struggle, bringing both body and soul to the great contest, but they must not debilitate themselves by fasting or celibacy, both of which are forbidden in Zoroastrianism. Zarathustra's monotheistic concept did not make Ahura Mazda the only focus of faith. There were also the souls known as Fravashis, which are venerated by Zoroastrians. The Fravashis also participate in the cosmic struggle as and when their aid is enlisted. In this, the Fravashis resemble the saints of Roman Catholicism.

◆ *see* THE CATHOLIC CHURCH p. 202

HEAVEN AND HELL

There is no belief in reincarnation or in *karma*, divine judgement of acts performed during life. Rather, humans are judged on the basis of whether good or evil predominated in their lives. After that, souls are consigned to Heaven, the best existence, or Hell, the worst existence. Zoroastrianism, a fundamentally optimistic faith, teaches that collectively, the good done by humanity will transform the world into a heavenly utopia, and when time ends, all souls, good or evil, will be purified.

◆ *see* SALVATION p. 191

▶ *RIGHT: A bas-relief from the Achaemenid necropolis*

SACRED FIRE

Ahura Mazda is represented by fire, which is believed to be a manifestation of the power of creation and God's divinity. Fire is a sacred element of Zoroastrianism, and is used in all religious ceremonies. The focal points of worship are the fire temples, which house a sacred fire that must never be allowed to go out. The architecture of the temples is designed to reflect this. The fire must also never be contaminated, and the Zoroastrian laity are forbidden to touch the fire. Priests are responsible for fuelling the fire, and must constantly purify themselves to avoid contamination. This includes wearing a mask or *Padan*, which covers the nose and mouth.

◆ *see* SYNAGOGUES p. 182

THE GATHAS AND THE ATTRIBUTES

The *Gathas* is a set of 17 hymns written by Zarathustra himself. Other texts were later added, but many were destroyed in the persecutions that followed invasions of Persia by the ancient Greeks, the Muslims and the Mongols. The language of the *Gathas* is a very ancient tongue, Avestan, which resembles Sanskrit, the language of the Aryans of India. It was in the *Gathas* that Zarathustra presented Ahura Mazda as the sole transcendent god who created the world through his divine Attributes. Zarathustra did not name a particular number of Attributes, but they have been specified as seven, known as Amesha Spentas, or Bounteous Immortals, all of which include an attribute of Ahura Mazda and human

virtue as well. The seven Attributes start with Vohu Manah, or good thought. Asha Vahishta represents justice and truth, Kshathra stands for dominion, Spenta Armaiti for devotion and serenity. Wholeness, or Haurvatat, is the fifth Attribute, followed by Ameretat, immortality, and the good spirit, Spenta Mainya, creative energy. In the *Gathas*, the Attributes are sometimes personified, or sometimes exist simply as ideas. The basic concept in Zoroastrianism is dedication to moral excellence and ethics, as expressed in the motto 'good thoughts, good words, good deeds'.

■ see THE CHRISTIAN BIBLE p. 195

◀ *LEFT: Zoroaster dying ritually in flames*

CHRISTIANITY

For Christianity the most important event in history has been, and will always be, the birth, life, death and resurrection of Jesus of Nazareth (6 BC–AD 32). Christians believe Jesus was the Son of God, that he was born on earth, lived the life of a human being, was crucified, died and then rose from the dead. His dying and rising revealed God's love for the world and offered all people the possibility of eternal life.

THE LIFE OF JESUS

Jesus was born in Bethlehem and grew up with his father, Joseph, and mother, Mary, in Nazareth, in Northern Galilee. Joseph is traditionally believed to have been a carpenter and would probably have taught the young Jesus something of his trade.

It is likely that Jesus' ministry began

▶ RIGHT: A mural depicting Jesus Christ

189

when he was about 30 years old. He probably taught for three years after being baptized in the River Jordan by John the Baptist (his cousin). Christians believe John was the forerunner of Jesus, preparing the way for him. Jesus travelled throughout Israel, teaching and healing. He gathered many men and women around him; key amongst them were 12 men called disciples. Jesus became involved in conflict with the religious authorities in Jerusalem. He was arrested, tried and nailed to a cross, crucified and died. Christians believe Jesus rose from the dead. He met his followers and ate with them. After a few weeks he was taken up into heaven promising to return at the end of the world. Jesus's followers believed he was the Messiah who had brought about the Kingdom of God. This was a dangerous idea to the Romans, who thought this might mean a challenge to their power, and equally disturbing to the Jewish authorities. Jesus taught in synagogues. The main concern of many Jews, however, was that he appeared to claim to forgive sins and only God could do that. Jesus was therefore claiming to be divine and that was not acceptable to the Jewish religious authorities.

Jesus used parables and healings to help people understand his teaching. He taught that the Kingdom of God (an acceptance of God as Ruler and King) had arrived and it was possible for everyone to enter that Kingdom. What was necessary was to see what Jesus did and hear and understand his teaching. His healings and miracles taught about God's power and authority. Jesus could do these things because he was carrying out God's will. He did remarkable things to challenge those around and to help people be more aware of the will of God and the nearness of God's Kingdom.

◆ see THE CHILDREN OF ISRAEL AND THE PROMISED LAND p. 170

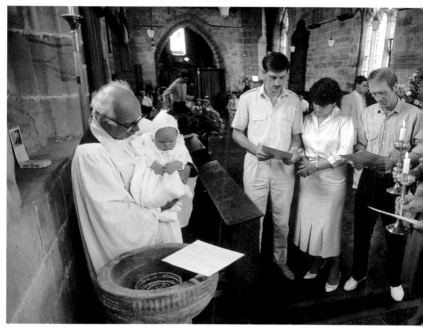

SALVATION

Christianity is a religion of salvation. Human beings have become separated from God through disobedience. Jesus' life and death renewed that relationship, giving an opportunity to enter into a special relationship with God. How this salvation occurs leads to the main beliefs of Christianity: the Trinity, the Incarnation and the Atonement.

The most mysterious and least understood of all Christian beliefs is

▲ *ABOVE: A priest baptises a baby at the font*

the Trinity. Christians believe there is, and always has been, only one God. Christians do, however, refer to God in three ways: as Father, the Creator; as Son, Jesus Christ; and as Holy Spirit, the power of God which people feel and experience in their lives. Thus God is expressed as Father, Son and Holy Spirit.

While Christians believe that God is Father, Son and Holy Spirit, the words used to describe this belief never fully capture the experience. Human language falls short when trying to express the nature of God. What the Trinity expresses is the personal nature of God and therefore the personal relationship that exists between God and creation.

Virtually every Christian believes that, in some mysterious way, Jesus was fully God and fully human and by becoming fully human, God is willing to share our pains and difficulties. Jesus knew pain and humiliation, was frightened, cried, and shared human experience. In becoming a human being, God revealed the extent of the love He felt for creation; to be born and live as a complete human being was the only way to save all people.

What were people to be saved from? Christians believe that sin is what separates people from God. It is not simply wrong-doing but a misuse of the free will given to humans by God. The sin of Adam in the Garden of Eden was disobedience – a failure to do God's will. Adam and Eve were given responsibilities in the garden but disobeyed God by eating from the forbidden tree. The cycle of sin could only be broken by God's son, Jesus, being born on earth and, through his life, death and resurrection, removing the stain of sin.

Jesus, therefore, atones for the sins of the world and recreates at-one-ment, the bringing together of God and human beings. At the heart of Christian belief is Jesus Christ who brought victory over evil and death.

see THE LIFE OF JESUS p. 189

THE APOSTLES AND THE CHRISTIAN CHURCH

After the events of Jesus' life, death and resurrection, his followers gathered to celebrate the Jewish festival of Pentecost. In the Acts of the Apostles, the coming of the Holy Spirit is recorded. The Holy Spirit of God arrived in the upper room of a house where the disciples were gathered, with the sound of a mighty wind, and it looked as if each of the disciples had a tongue of flame on his head. This powerful event gave the disciples power and courage to go out to preach in many different languages.

The disciples became known as 'apostles' – from a Greek word meaning 'sent as messengers'. They went out to preach the good news (the Gospel) of the risen Christ. There are many stories of where they went and what they said but Peter, who is considered to be the leading disciple, ended up in Rome, the centre of the Roman world. It is believed he was crucified there after he had founded a Church. He was the first Bishop of Rome.

The most significant apostle was not in the upper room at Pentecost. He is St Paul who, before his own conversion, when he was known as Saul, had persecuted the followers of Jesus. At his conversion on the road to Damascus he had a vision of Jesus that changed his life. He took the name Paul to show the change he had experienced and after a few years' quiet reflection set out to take the message of Jesus across the Mediterranean world. The extent of the Roman empire facilitated the spread of the Gospel.

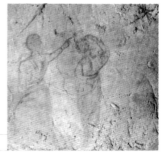

▶ RIGHT: The archangel Gabriel visits Mary

Paul wrote a number of letters contained in the Christian Bible. These were written before the Gospels and tell us a lot about Paul himself as well as about the growing groups of Christians. He was passionate, strong-willed and strong-minded and deeply committed to taking the message of Jesus Christ to the non-Jewish (Gentile) world. He probably died in Rome at about the same time as Peter, i.e. AD 60–65.

The early followers of Jesus believed the end of the world would come very soon with everyone living under God's rule. As the apostles died and the years passed the end did not arrive and each Christian group began to organize itself. Bishops, elders and deacons took a role in the organization and administration of the church with the bishops taking responsibility for the care of people within a larger area. The bishops of Rome, Jerusalem, Constantinople, Alexandria and Antioch became the most influential.

Persecution of the Christians in the Roman Empire largely finished when Constantine was Emperor in AD 312 although there were outbreaks during the next two centuries. During the fourth century Christianity became much more formalized, church building took place and by AD 381 Christianity was the official religion of the Roman Empire.

◘ see THE CHRISTIAN BIBLE p. 195

◀ LEFT: A church dating from AD 500 in the Taurus mountains, Turkey

▲ *ABOVE: A Catholic church in Calcutta*

THE CHRISTIAN BIBLE

The Christian Bible took nearly 400 years to reach its final form. It consists of two 'testaments' or 'promises'. The Old Testament is almost entirely made up of the Jewish scriptures and is written in Hebrew. The New Testament is written in Greek and tells of the new 'testament' made by God through the life, death and resurrection of Jesus. The New Testament was probably written by a variety of authors between AD 48–95. Christians believe the Old Testament shows how God had promised the coming of Jesus, the Messiah, to the Jews for centuries.

Jesus fulfilled those prophecies and writings so the Gospels and Epistles (letters) relate the story of a new promise – 'a new testament'.

The Epistles (the Greek word for 'letters') are the earliest known Christian writings. Paul wrote some of the epistles within 20 years of Jesus' death. He pays little attention to the detail of Jesus' life concentrating much more on what his life meant. There are other letters, some attributed to the apostles, written over a period of 50 years or so but little is known of most of their authors.

There are four Gospels (the word means 'good news'), Matthew, Mark, Luke and John. These are the only records of events in the life of Jesus but he wrote none of them. They all give a slightly different view of the meaning of Jesus' life and have different accounts of his death and resurrection. They were probably written between 30 to 70 years after Jesus' death.

The final collection of books in the Christian Bible was finally agreed at a Council in Carthage in AD 397. Even today however, there is no complete agreement as the Roman Catholic Bible includes a group of Jewish writings called the Apocrypha not normally found in other churches' Bibles.

The Bible is used in nearly every Christian service. Some Christians believe it to be

◀ LEFT: The Lindisfarne Gospels

literally true; others believe it uses symbols, metaphors and stories to express a truth. All Christians believe that in some way the Bible is inspired by God and it should be studied. It provides knowledge about God and the meaning of Jesus' life, who Jesus was and what he taught, and is the basis and major source of the churches' teachings.

The strength of the Bible for Christians is that it reveals God's continuing part in creation: the gradual unfolding of sacred history. There are many different writers, writing hundreds of years apart, yet Christians see in the Bible a collection of insights, understandings and revelations about God and God's purpose for the world. This ultimate revelation is found in the person of Jesus and Christians read about Jesus in the Christian Bible in order to understand more clearly what God's purpose is for the world and how Jesus' life reveals God's love.

◆ *see* THE JEWISH BIBLE AND OTHER SACRED TEXTS p. 173

CHRISTIAN RITES

There are two major practices in which most Christians participate. These are: baptism, universally agreed as the way in which one is received into the Christian church; and celebrating Holy Communion (the Mass, the Eucharist or whatever name churches give to the way in which Jesus' last meal with his disciples is commemorated).

Most Christians regard baptism

▶ *RIGHT: A nun prays in a convent*

as a sign of re-birth. It washes away their old life and starts a new life following Jesus Christ. Jesus' baptism at the hands of John the Baptist in the River Jordan acts as a model for Christians.

Churches use a variety of names for the ceremony recalling Jesus' Last Supper with his disciples the night before his death. They shared bread and wine with Jesus, who asked his disciples to remember him in the breaking of bread and the drinking of wine.

There are other rites of passage: marriage and funeral rites, and, in some churches, confirmation where the promises made at baptism are confirmed by a bishop laying hands on the person being confirmed. All churches find ways to express how the Christian faith affects the lives of each believer.

◆ *see* CHRISTIAN FESTIVALS p. 198

CHRISTIAN FESTIVALS

Christian festivals can be grouped into three sections. The most important group surrounds Easter and follows the cycle of the moon, so Lent, Easter, Ascension Day and Pentecost fall on different days each year. Christmas follows the solar calendar so the dates connected with the birth of Jesus occur on the same day each year. The third group is the celebration of the lives of individual saints and martyrs; these occur on the same day each year.

Easter rather than Christmas is the major Christian festival. It is the time when the central belief of Christians – that Jesus died and rose again – is celebrated. Easter Day, the day of resurrection, is always a Sunday in March or April; the Friday before, when Christians remember Jesus' death, is called 'Good Friday'. 'Good' because of the good deed Jesus

▶ *RIGHT: Catholics celebrate Easter*

performed – taking all the sins of the world on himself and enabling people to enter into eternal life.

Christians prepare for Easter Day, a time of delight and exhilaration, by undertaking a period of discipline and self-denial. This season of Lent lasts for 40 days. 'Lent' comes from an old word for spring because Easter is a springtime festival in the northern hemisphere. It used to be a time when prospective Christians were prepared for baptism but now it usually commemorates Jesus' 40 days in the wilderness. Lent is heralded by Ash Wednesday when some Christians have a cross of ash drawn on their forehead as a sign of sorrow for their sins. In some Orthodox

churches Lent is called the Great Fast and many Christians of all denominations fast or go without favourite foods as well as preparing themselves for the coming events of Easter. Some churches remove or cover images or icons during Lent and do not decorate the building with flowers; other churches do not hold marriages.

The week before Easter (Holy Week) re-enacts the last week of Jesus' life. Palm Sunday is the first day of Holy Week and commemorates the entry of Jesus into Jerusalem when people welcomed him by waving palms. As the week continues the end of the penitential period draws near. On Maundy Thursday, the day before Good Friday, many church leaders re-enact the occasion of Jesus' washing his disciples feet by washing the feet of ordinary people. It is a reminder that at their last meal together Jesus commanded his followers to serve others before eating bread and drinking wine.

The Easter cycle continues with the festival of the Ascension where Christians remember Jesus being taken up into heaven watched by his followers; and is completed at Pentecost when, Christians believe, the Holy Spirit settled upon the apostles giving them power to go out and preach the Gospel to the world.

The second cycle of festivals surround Christmas and celebrate the birth of Jesus. As with Easter, there is a period of preparation, Advent (coming), when Christians remember their sins and prepare for the 'gift' of Jesus' birth. Today Christmas in most Christian traditions is celebrated on 25 December. Some Orthodox churches celebrate it on 6 or 7 January (the difference is caused by changes to the calendar system). The date of Christmas was decided upon by the Emperor Constantine, during the third century AD, who chose the date of a Roman sun festival and by doing so he changed a non-Christian celebration into a Christian one.

▶ *RIGHT: A Sri Lankan Christ figure*

Epiphany – the 'showing forth' of Jesus to the world – comes 12 days after Christmas. The festival marks the arrival of the *Magi* (wise men or astrologers who had 'seen' news of this birth in the stars) from the East. The Christmas cycle finishes with Candlemas (2 February) when Christians remember Jesus' presentation by his parents in the temple, giving thanks to God for the safe birth of their son.

Saints are individuals believed to have possessed miraculous powers, and to have lead exemplary lives. Not all churches uphold the importance of saints but the Roman Catholic Church, Anglican and the Orthodox Churches continue to recognize the unique contribution of some Christians. For a saint to be recognized as such, they must be canonized by the church. This involves proof that they performed miracles, and of their virtuous life. The New Testament calls all believers 'saints'.

Many saints have a special day on which thanks is given for their lives and Mary, the mother of Jesus, has a number of days devoted to events in her life. One of these days, the Annunciation (25 March), remembers the obedience and acceptance of Mary receiving the news from the angel Gabriel that she was to bear the child Jesus.

◆ *see* CHRISTIAN RITES p. 197

THE CATHOLIC CHURCH

About half the Christians in the world are Catholic (approximately one billion people), and nearly half of these live in Latin America. The Pope, who lives in the Vatican City, Rome, is the head of the Catholic Church and is elected by a college of senior clerics called cardinals. The Church is strongly sacramental. It places great importance on rites and ceremonies marking the life of each Catholic.

The Catholic Church traces its origins back to Peter, one of the original disciples. The Gospel of Matthew records Jesus telling Peter, his leading disciple, that he would have the Keys of the Kingdom of Heaven – in other words, to life after death. Peter is also referred to as the 'rock' on which Jesus would build his Church. The word 'Catholic' means 'universal' and reflects a worldwide church.

◆ see THE APOSTLES AND THE CHRISTIAN CHURCH p. 193

▲ ABOVE: A Catholic priest gives communion to his congregation

THE ORTHODOX CHURCHES

The Orthodox churches each have their own distinctive history but are a group of churches based on an historic tradition. This tradition arose in the East and the churches of Constantinople, Antioch, Alexandria and Jerusalem grew at the same time as the Western (Catholic) Church expanded in Rome. The leaders of the churches are called patriarchs and they work together ecumenically. At the heart of all Orthodox churches lies the Divine Liturgy, the worship of God, continually celebrated regardless of social environment and political pressure.

The word 'orthodox' means 'right' or 'true worship' and the Orthodox churches trace their origins back to the very beginning of the early Christian church. Rome was then the capital of the Roman Empire but the four eastern churches of Jerusalem, Constantinople, Alexandria and Antioch remained in a strong relationship with each other. The authority of the Bishop of Rome was a growing problem for the bishops in the Orthodox churches who believed Church government should lie within an ecumenical group of bishops, rather than with one bishop alone.

◆ see THE CATHOLIC CHURCH p. 202

▲ *ABOVE: A Greek Orthodox priest in his church in Rhodes, Greece*

THE ANGLICAN COMMUNION

The 'Anglican Communion' is the name given to the collection of Anglican churches worldwide. They all derive from the Church of England, which moved away from Rome in the sixteenth century, but each has their own system of government with their own archbishops and bishops. They may have very different views from each other; some ordain women priests and bishops, others have women priests but no women bishops, and some have neither.

▲ *ABOVE: The choir of Winchester Cathedral sing during a service*

The Anglican Communion is neither Roman Catholic nor Protestant, though, in its variety, it has elements of both. Anglicanism is understood by Anglicans to be a bridge born out of an historical situation that continues to be a link between two of the great divisions within Christianity.

◆ *see* THE REFORMATION AND PROTESTANT CHURCHES p. 205

THE REFORMATION AND THE PROTESTANT CHURCHES

During the Renaissance in Europe, many scholars returned to the study of Classical literature. Theologians such as Erasmus (1466–1536) began to question the disparity between the practices of the Catholic church and the teachings of the early Christians. The worldliness and extreme wealth of the church were criticized and a movement for reform, inspired by Martin Luther in 1517 and taken up by other leading figures like Jean Calvin, began and came to be called the Reformation.

On 31 October 1517 Martin Luther, a monk and professor of biblical studies, pinned his '95 Theses' to the north door of the Castle Church in Wittenberg. The document, which would be read by worshippers coming to church on 1 November (All Saints' Day), attacked the Church policy on indulgences (the Church sold indulgences to the people to take away their sins). Luther believed this practice was not present in the Bible and that it encouraged people to turn their mind away from Jesus Christ and God's forgiveness. One of Martin Luther's key beliefs was that of the importance of the individual within the church. It is the responsibility of each person in the community of the Church to work towards their own salvation guided by scripture. Luther was shortly excommunicated and outlawed by the Catholic church, but his ideas spread throughout Europe and were taken up by kings and princes who stood up in 'protest' and opposed the Pope. Lutheranism spread across Germany, the Baltic

States and into Scandinavia to break Papal power and authority.

John Calvin, a contemporary of Luther and also a reformer, continued and developed Luther's ideas, creating Protestantism as a credible alternative to Catholicism. In his book *Institutes* (1536) he produced a clear defence of Reformation beliefs and ideas. In his later edition (1559) he argued forcefully how Protestant beliefs can sustain (and undermine) the state. He wove a fabric of Protestant ideas into the political, social and economic framework of the state. Calvin created a virtual theocracy (a society ruled by God) in Geneva.

Calvin taught that knowledge of God could only be found in the Word of God, that only God could pardon and save, and that only baptism and communion were sacraments. He gave great importance to the external organization of the Church, with the Church in Geneva being, in effect, a theocracy, a church and state ruled by God

◀ *LEFT: Salisbury Cathedral, UK*

as interpreted by Calvin. Calvin argued that if God is all-knowing and all-powerful then God knows who will be saved and who won't. This doctrine, called predestination, became a feature of the reformed churches that followed Calvin's teaching. It was his way of teaching that humans are saved by God's power alone; it has nothing to do with good works or good behaviour.

Today the variety found within Protestantism illustrates how strongly individualism, the ethos of the Reformation, has grown since the time of Luther and Calvin. The various Protestant churches include the Presbyterian Church, which arose out of Calvinism; the Methodists who broke from the Church of England; the Quakers, a movement founded by George Fox and the Baptists, the strongest Protestant tradition in the USA. The movements have their differences but at the heart of each is the individual's search for God and acceptance of the Lordship of God.

◆ see THE CATHOLIC CHURCH p. 202

THE PENTECOSTAL MOVEMENT

The Pentecostal movement began in the USA at the turn of the twentieth century, partly as a reaction against very formal styles of worship and partly, as Pentecostalists would say, as a result of the actions of the Holy Spirit. This led to many churches being established, all involved with innovation, experimentation and a rejection of formal, ordered worship.

Pentecostalists believe in prophecy, speaking in tongues, visions and, like many other Christians, the power of healing. Their worship is informal and uses powerful preaching, rhythmic singing and chanting. Pentecostalists believe that Jesus Christ will return to this world, literally, in person and in the near future. There is a vivid understanding of the afterlife, with Heaven and Hell being real places of rewards and punishments usually depicted in stark word pictures. In the early days they drew their huge congregations from the poor and the outcast – often a mixture of black and white people – but while there are some very large black Pentecostal churches it is by no means a black religious phenomenon.

Important features of the Pentecostal movement have been incorporated into the worship of the more traditional and mainstream churches. The term usually used to describe the movement is 'charismatic'. The word means 'gift' (of the Holy Spirit) and some charismatic mainstream Christian services have much the same power and force as the Pentecostal services. Pentecostalism touches the emotions, allowing people to forget about their everyday life and to lose themselves in the power of the Holy Spirit. The Devil can possess people to drive them away from the knowledge of Jesus or can cause illness and 'demonic possession'. In the Pentecostal movement the power of the Spirit lies very close to everyday life. The minister can exorcise the Devil

and cure sickness by calling on the Devil (or devils) to leave the person – but always in the name of Jesus. In a world where people can suffer great poverty and oppression, the vigour, vitality and sheer force of communal expression creates a situation where people believe they can feel God's presence.

◆ see SUPERSTITION p. 164

◀ LEFT: A service at an American Pentecostal church

ISLAM

'There is no God but God,
Muhammad is the Messenger of God'.

This is the Muslim profession of faith, the *shahada*, the first of
the five pillars of Islam. There is no single authoritative creed
in Islam, meaning 'submission', but it is the sincere repetition
of these two statements together that makes one a Muslim,
'one who submits'. The *shahada* is usually the first thing that a
Muslim child hears on entering this life and the last thing
heard on departing it. It is also recited every time Muslims
perform their five obligatory daily prayers.

The emphasis on one God (*Allah* in Arabic) connects Islam to its
monotheistic heritage in Judaism and Christianity. However,
Muslims believe that Islam, as communicated to the Prophet
Muhammad in the *Qur'an* (literally the 'recitation'), is the final
revealed religion. Muhammad is a prophet just like Abraham,
Moses and Jesus before him and yet his scripture is the
fulfilment and completion of these other prophets' messages.
God will send no other prophets after him.

ISLAM IN THE WORLD TODAY

While the origins of Islam are in the Near East, today it is a universal
faith which has adapted itself to local circumstances from Morocco in
the West to Indonesia in the East. Indeed, it is actually in South and
South-East Asia that the most populous Muslim countries are to be

found. Islam is the second largest religion in the world after Christianity and has the fastest growing body of believers.

Islam is also 'news' for other reasons. Long before the events of 11 September 2001 it was suggested that there is a 'clash of civilizations' between Islam and the West. No one can deny that religion is a vehicle for politics, especially in today's highly polarised, globalising world. However, Muslims are not, and never have been, a single homogenous constituency. An 'open' view of Islam does not generalise about all Muslims everywhere, yet it remains committed to a critical analysis of the political uses and abuses of all religions.

◻ *see* REVIVAL AND REFORM: FROM MEDIEVAL TO MODERN ISLAM p. 228

ARABIA BEFORE ISLAM

The rise and rapid spread of Islam in the seventh century is one of most significant developments in history. It was to be a religious ideology which would unite the Arabs, see them expand their control into the Fertile Crescent and eventually replace the much older civilizations of the Eastern Christian Byzantine and the Persian Zoroastrian Sassanid empires.

Arabia itself is a huge area of desert with scattered oases, 1300 miles long and 750 wide. In the seventh century AD, it was a politically fragmented pastoral society, the home of camps and oases. Nevertheless, Arabia was connected to the rest of the Near East by merchants and agents associated with the Byzantine and Persian powers.

Muslim tradition speaks of pre-Islamic Arabia as a period of *jahiliyya*, a time dominated by ignorance of God and immorality. While we have few independent sources to corroborate this, Arabia was certainly dominated by more or less sophisticated forms of polytheism. At the same time,

◀ *LEFT: A child studies the* Qur'an

some 'non-believers' were said to be familiar with monotheism and there were settlements of Jews and some (Monophysite) Christians in the region.

THE PROPHET MUHAMMAD: REVELATIONS AT MECCA

Muslim tradition relates that Muhammad was born in Mecca around AD 570. Mecca is said to have been a prosperous trading centre with a polytheistic sanctuary called the *ka'ba* which attracted pilgrims from all over Arabia. Muhammad was orphaned early in his life and raised by Abu Talib, a poor but generous uncle. While illiterate, Muhammad became a successful trader and many later stories relate that he was uniquely wise, just and trustworthy.

Muhammad is said to have been in the habit of meditating on Mount Hira', a few miles from Mecca. He was concerned about the materialism, injustice and spiritual malaise of the city. In AD 610, aged 40, Muhammad was asleep in a cave when he was commanded thus by a voice:

▶ *RIGHT: Rocky landscape surrounds Mecca*

◄ *LEFT: The desert landscape*

Recite in the name of your Lord who created,
Who created man from a clot of blood.
Recite! For your Lord is most generous,
Who taught by the Pen,
He taught man what he did not know.
Nay, man is, indeed, rebellious,
For he deems himself not responsible.
But to your Lord is the Return.

Later Muslim tradition understands that this instruction to Muhammad was the first in a series of revelations from God, conveyed through the Angel Jibril (Gabriel). Although just one chapter (96:1–8), it summarises the essential message of the *Qur'an*:

- The one true God is the Creator of the all the world
- He is most generous, sending humankind prophets with written messages (scriptures) to teach them what is required for salvation
- Humans are rebellious; they reject or ignore this message and are a law unto themselves
- Humankind should be mindful for, at the end of time, all will return to God for the Day of Judgement
- Elsewhere, the *Qur'an* narrates the pleasures of paradise for those who remain on the straight path and the punishments of hell for those who do not

Muhammad was initially disturbed by his experiences and did not know how to interpret them until a local Christian pronounced that he must be 'the prophet of his people'. The revelations were to continue in this fragmentary form for the rest of the Prophet's life, a period of about 22 years.

Until AD 613, the emerging religion of Islam was a largely private affair with converts confined to Muhammad's immediate family. However, in that year, God commanded Muhammad to go public with His message. Muhammad attacked the Meccans for compromising God's essential oneness with their pagan gods. This threatened the economic benefits of the polytheistic pilgrimage and in AD 615 the Meccan leadership began to persecute the Muslims. Muhammad initially had the protection of Abu Talib and his influential wife, Khadija, but both died in AD 619. Therefore the Muslims were forced to seek a home elsewhere.

A MUSLIM COMMUNITY: MUHAMMAD AT MEDINA

AD 622 is seen as a turning point in Islamic history. It is the date of the *hijra* (migration) of Muslims to Yathrib (later renamed Medina) and the starting point of the Muslim calendar. A delegation from the city, an agriculturally rich oasis north of Mecca, had been impressed by Muhammad's preaching and invited him to unite their divided population. Therefore Muhammad and around 200 migrants from Mecca, joined with the 'helpers' in Yathrib to form the first Muslim *umma* (community). The *umma* would become the vehicle for realising God's will on earth based not on the narrow divisions of tribe but on alliances born of a new religion.

Muhammad's revelations continued at Medina where there was increasing attention to prescriptions for the life of the *umma*. The *Qur'an* is not a compendium of laws. Rather, it is a text of principles and exhortations which had to be elaborated by Muslim jurists. Nevertheless, the Medinan revelations contain many injunctions of a legal nature. Topics covered include ritual (see below) but also such wide-ranging matters as marriage, adultery, divorce, inheritance, food-laws, usury, slaves and theft.

It was the custom of the day that any wronged party could take goods by force from an aggressor. Thus *razzias* (raids) on Meccan caravans were initiated given that the latter had forced the Muslims to leave their homes. These raids also helped the Muslims at Medina to gain economic independence. However, tradition relates that Muhammad was a reluctant combatant. He had received *Qur'anic* sanction for Muslims to fight and protect their persecuted community. Nevertheless, he never sought to rout his opponents and a truce with the Meccans was finally agreed in AD 628.

Muhammad took Mecca with little resistance in AD 630. The Meccans converted to Islam and the *ka'ba* sanctuary was rededicated to the one true God of Abraham. In AD 632 Muhammad sent out a mission to the foreign rulers of Persia, Byzantium, Ethiopia and beyond to proclaim God's final message. In June of this, the eleventh year of the *hijra*, Muhammad died.

'THE MOST BEAUTIFUL MODEL': FOLLOWING THE CUSTOM OF MUHAMM

This traditional account of Muhammad's life is told in a genre of literature called *sira* (biography). The *sira* of the Prophet, together with the *hadith* – traditions of Muhammad's sayings and practice collected and authenticated after his death – together represent the *sunna* (custom) of the Prophet. This is an authority second only to the *Qur'an* in Islamic law (see below); it helps contextualise the *Qur'an*, which is not a chronological narrative.

For ordinary Muslims the *sunna* represents 'the most beautiful model' of how they should live their lives. Nevertheless, Muhammad was a human being who did not claim divinity or knowledge of the unseen (*Qur'an* 7:188). However, some Muslims do see him as a sinless intercessor. Others would go so far as to venerate Muhammad – at his tomb in Medina, in devotional poetry or during the popular festival of '*id milad al-nabi* (festival of the Prophet's birthday). Despite such debates about the status of Muhammad in Islam, all pious Muslims who speak his name will respectfully add the salutation 'peace be upon him'.

◖ *see* THE PROPHET MUHAMMAD: REVELATIONS AT MECCA p. 212

THE QUR'ANIC TEXT AND ITS FORMATION

By the time of Muhammad's death in AD 632. Muslims believe that the entire content of the *Qur'an* had been revealed. The *Qur'an* was recited

▶ RIGHT: Medina Mosque of the Prophet, which houses the tomb of Muhammad

and memorised as part of an oral tradition until scribes began to write it down. Eventually, the *Caliph* (deputy) 'Uthman (see below) is understood to have appointed five Muslim scholars to copy the 'leaves' of a collection held by one of the Prophet's wives into a single volume. Within 20 years, a parallel version of this final authoritative text is said to have been sent out to the new provinces of Islam as the religion expanded out of Arabia. The *Qur'an* as we have it today comprises 114 chapters called *suras* which are arranged longest to shortest, bar the first chapter, '*al-Fatiha*' (the Opening). Each *sura* is divided into over 6,000 *ayahs* or verses.

THE QUR'AN IN MUSLIM BELIEF AND PRACTICE

Muslims believe that the *Qur'an* is *kalam Allah* (the word of God) and that no one is capable of imitating its stylistic perfection in Arabic. The 'proof' of Muhammad's prophecy and the *Qur'an's* divine origin has become linked to this, the 'miracle' of Islam.

The *Qur'an* is a book intended to be heard as well as read in Arabic; translation is no substitute for the original. Most Muslim children learn to recite the *Qur'an* at their local mosque and some become *hafiz al-Qur'an* having committed the whole text

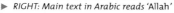

▶ RIGHT: Main text in Arabic reads 'Allah'

to memory. Like all good Muslims, they learn to treat copies of the *Qur'an* with respect; a copy of their scripture would never be placed directly on the floor. A small wooden *kursi* (literally 'chair') is often used instead.

The text of the *Qur'an* is put to a wide range of uses in Muslim society. Arabic calligraphy has become perhaps the highest form of art in Islam. At the same time, some Muslims believe that the *Qur'an* has therapeutic and magical qualities; reciting *al-Fatiha* is said by some to cure the bite of a scorpion.

◆ *see* THE JEWISH BIBLE AND OTHER SACRED TEXTS p. 173

THE 'FOUR RIGHTLY GUIDED' CALIPHS

The four 'rightly-guided' *Caliphs* (AD 632–661) were the immediate 'deputies' of the Prophet after his death. Their rule is often idealised by Muslims as an age of pious adherence to Islam coupled with many military conquests. All the *Caliphs* were 'Companions' of Muhammad.

- **Abu Bakr**, an early convert and the Prophet's father-in-law, became *Caliph* in AD 632. Today, a majority of Muslims, known as Sunnis (see below), believe that Muhammad did not appoint a successor. However, Shi'ites (see below) dispute this. In any case, Abu Bakr was elected the new head of the *umma*.
- **'Umar** (AD 634–44) initiated the great Arab expansion in the vacuum left by the warring Sassanians and Byzantines. Various cities in modern Syria, Iraq Palestine, Egypt and Iran fell to the Muslim armies during his rule, e.g. Damascus, Basra, Jerusalem, Cairo and Isfahan.
- **'Uthman ibn Affan** became the third *Caliph* in AD 644. Under his rule, the new Arab Empire expanded westwards towards modern Libya (as well as Cyprus, Rhodes and Crete) and eastwards towards modern Afghanistan and Pakistan. However, 'Uthman was assassinated by an early Muslim sect of 'secessionists' or Kharijites (see below) in AD 656.

- The fourth *Caliph*, **'Ali**, was cousin and son-in-law of Muhammad. His followers, the *Shi'at 'Ali* (party of 'Ali), argued that the first three C were interlopers who had denied 'Ali his rightful inheritance as leader of the Muslims. However, 'Ali's *Caliphate* was also beset by civil strife and he, too, was assassinated by the Kharijites in AD 661.

FROM ARAB KINGDOM TO ISLAMIC CIVILIZATION

Based in Damascus, the descendents of Caliph 'Uthman formed the first dynasty of Islam, the Umayyads (AD 661–750). Later Muslim tradition often accuses them of falling away from the 'rightly-guided' example of their predecessors. The second dynasty of Islam, the Abbasids (AD 750–1258), was descended from Muhammad's uncle, al-'Abbas. Based in Baghdad, the golden age of Islamic civilization emerged under their rule.

With the cessation of the Islamic conquests, the way was left open for a new social order based on a peace economy of agriculture and trade. Baghdad grew into the largest Near Eastern city of its day ruled by Abbasid *Caliphs* such as Harun al-Rashid, as mentioned in *A Thousand and One Nights*. The city also contained a cosmopolitan mixture of Jewish, Christian and Muslim scholars. Out of their exchanges grew a great knowledge industry which saw the works of the Greeks translated into Arabic.

◆ *see* THE 'FOUR RIGHTLY GUIDED' CALIPHS p. 219

ISLAMIC THEOLOGY AND THE EMERGENCE OF SUNNISM

The Abbasid period also gave rise to a professional class of religious scholars or *'ulama*. They gradually drew religious authority away from the *Caliphs*. Indeed, it is only really from the ninth century that we can speak of a Sunni 'orthodoxy'. As is generally true of religion, Islam simply took time to mature.

The earliest theological debates were often linked to the political troubles experienced by 'Uthman and 'Ali. The Kharijites, for example, believed in a simple equivalence between faith and works so much so that any sinners (including 'Uthman and 'Ali) were considered unbelievers and so liable to be killed.

While the absolutism of the Kharijites is often likened to militant and puritanical Islamic movements of today, it is a far cry from the position of a group known as the Murji'a (the 'postponers') and, indeed, later Sunni 'orthodoxy'. The Murji'a stressed that the judgement of sinners should be left to God alone on the Last Day.

In political terms such a position tended to support the status quo, suggesting that one should obey Muslim rulers, even if one questioned

◆ *LEFT: The Al-Aqsa Mosque in Jerusalem*

their character. Indeed, the *Caliphs* often encouraged the idea that their actions had been divinely ordained. However, some, such as the Mu'tazila (the 'Neutralists'), argued that people must have free will because a just God would not punish that which He had predestined. This, in turn, makes people, and rulers, responsible for their own actions. Therefore, unlike the Murji'a, the Mu'tazila were sometimes political rebels. However, unlike the Kharijites they believed that sinners were not 'unbelievers' but rather Muslim 'hypocrites'. They and others argued that there could be 'degrees' of faith in Islam.

The Mut'azila, in particular, were also known for adopting a rationalist style of argumentation adapted from Greek philosophy. While this influenced an emerging Sunni 'orthodoxy' in terms of methodology, in other respects their impact – and that of later Islamic philosophers – was fairly limited. For the traditionalist *'ulama*, the Mu'tazila were far too speculative and by the tenth century reason was becoming increasingly subordinated to revelation in Sunni thought.

ISLAMIC LAW: MUSLIM JURISTS AND JURISPRUDENCE

For all this early theological debate, it is law that is the queen of Islamic sciences. Islamic law or *shari'a* (literally 'the way' to the 'watering hole') seeks to articulate the way of life Muslims should rightfully practice, both to attain salvation and to maintain the good society.

As new situations have confronted Muslims at different times and in different places, it has been the jurist (*faqih*) who seeks to discern the will of God through the rules of jurisprudence (*fiqh*). Again, these rules were formalised only in the tenth century.

As the primary text of Islam, the *Qur'an* is always consulted first in reaching a legal decision. However, the scripture is not primarily a legal

▶ RIGHT: A school in Khartoum. The Qu'ran must be learned as it is the primary text of Is

work; therefore the *sunna* of Muhammad is often more crucial in reality. If a jurist fails to reach a decision on the basis of the *Qur'an* and *sunna* s/he can invoke *ijma'* (consensus of the scholarly community) or finally *qiyas* (analogy).

A ruling on any topic of Islamic law is called a *fatwa*. Any given action is classified as being either: obligatory; recommended; permissible; disapproved; forbidden. Contrary to popular belief in the West, Islamic law does not necessarily define a harsh dualism of 'right' and 'wrong'. With five possible rulings it recognises grey areas in human life. Indeed, any law may be broken under duress.

◆ *see* THE FOUR SUNNI SCHOOLS OF LAW p. 224

THE FOUR SUNNI SCHOOLS OF LAW

The relative flexibility of Islamic law is underlined by the fact that the Sunni community authenticates four legal schools. Each school (*madhab*) is named after an early legal figure in Islam:

- **Abu Hanifa** (d. AD 767) – school dominates in the Indian Subcontinent
- **Malik Ibn Anas** (d. AD 795) – school can be found in North Africa
- **al-Shafi'i** (d. AD 819) – school is prevalent in South-East Asia
- **Ahmad Ibn Hanbal** (d. AD 855) – school is associated with Saudi Arabia

While each school differs in its relative 'liberalism'/'conservatism', each is also considered by all of the others as an equally true implementation of the *sunna*. It is following one of the four schools that makes one a Sunni Muslim. Indeed no further schools of law emerged after the tenth century.

RITUAL PRACTICE: THE 'FIVE PILLARS' OF ISLAM

The five pillars of Islam are a set of obligatory practices which became the essence of Islamic law for Muslims from around the tenth century. None has its requirements fully expressed in the *Qur'an*. However, given their ritual character they represent a powerful vehicle for the expression of individual and communal Muslim identity.

- As we have seen, the **first** pillar is the *shahada* or confession of Islamic faith.
- The **second** is the *salat* or obligatory prayer. Prayer, which is preceded by ritual ablutions, is required of Muslims five times daily at dawn, noon, afternoon, sunset and night.
- The **third** pillar of Islam is the alms tax, *zakat*. This is levied on a Muslim's wealth at 2.5% over the *nisab* (minimum) although only a few countries, including Saudi Arabia, have maintained *zakat* along traditional lines.

- *Ramadan* is the month of the obligatory Muslim fast (*sawm*), the **fourth** pillar of Islam. For thirty days, between sunrise and sunset, Muslims should forgo food and drink, as well as smoking and sexual intercourse. The end of the fast is celebrated with the festival of *'Id al-fitr*.
- The **fifth** and final pillar of Islam is the *hajj* or pilgrimage to Mecca. Once in a lifetime, if finances allow, the Muslim must travel to the home of Islam. When various rituals have been completed each pilgrim offers an animal sacrifice commemorating the sheep that God accepted from Abraham in place of his son. All over the world Muslims join pilgrims in this, the festival of the sacrifice (*'Id al-adha*).

THE CHARISMA OF THE IMAMS: SHI'ITE ISLAM

Between 85% and 90% of Muslims today are Sunnis. The main alternative to the Sunni vision of Islam is Shi'ism. While the two groupings hold much in common, the essential difference is that the Shi'ites see infallible and sinless *imams* as a key source of religious authority.

Shi'ites argue that after the death of the Prophet, God, in His wisdom and justice, could not have left humankind without guidance. Therefore, they believe that there must be a spiritual

▶ *RIGHT: Ayatollah Khomeini*

225

guide or *imam* for every generation, someone who has inherited Muhammad's charisma. Shi'ites consider that the leadership of the Muslim community should rest with the Prophet's family and that 'Ali, the cousin and son-in-law of the Prophet, was the first of these.

The majority of Shi'ites are so-called 'Twelvers'. They hold that there were twelve *imams* until the last mysteriously disappeared in 941, perhaps to relieve his persecuted community of political pressures. Twelvers expect that at the end of time the so-called 'hidden *imam*' will lead the forces of good against evil in preparation for the Day of Judgement. In the absence of the hidden imam, the collective body of Shi'ite '*ulama* became caretakers of the *imam's* office. This idea of 'the trusteeship of the scholars' was key in the establishment of an Islamic Republic in Iran under Ayatollah Khomeini (d.1989). Indeed, nearly half of all Shi'ites worldwide are to be found in Iran.

◆ *see* ISLAMIC THEOLOGY AND THE EMERGENCE OF SUNNISM p. 221

THE INSIGHTS OF MYSTICAL KNOWLEDGE: SUFI ISLAM

Mystics seek direct experience of God and are aided in this by meditation, abstinence and, more controversially, poetry, dancing and music. In Islam mysticism is known as Sufism (*tasawwuf*). Sufis see mystical illumination as a supplement to the authority of the *Qur'an* and *sunna*. Most count themselves as Sunnis although some Sunnis are hostile to Sufism. Sufism and Shi'ism have much in common, especially the veneration of charismatic religious guides.

Sufism is thought to have developed as an otherworldly, ascetic reaction to the civil strife of early Islam. Two types of Sufi thinker can be distinguished: 'sober' and 'intoxicated'. An example of the former was

◀ *LEFT: Dancing dervishes of the Mevlevi Order, one of the numerous Sufi brotherhoods*

al-Junayd (d. AD 910), who argued that the goal of the mystic was *fana'* –
annihilation of the self and 'passing away' into God. A more intoxicated
Sufi, al-Hallaj (d. AD 922), was executed for suggesting that mystics could
actually feel themselves to be God incarnate. It was only when Sufism
was championed by al-Ghazali (d.1111), a leading scholar of Baghdad, that
its coexistence with classical Sunnism was secured. He maintained that
the learning of theology and law was uninspiring without restrained
Sufism.

In the medieval period, the emergence of numerous Sufi *tariqas*
(orders, brotherhoods) saw the institutionalisation of mystical Islam.
Those initiated into 'the Way' gathered at Sufi convents known as
khanaqas or *zawiyas*. Each order traces its origin to a Sufi master
(*shaykh*). For example, the Mevlevis – also known as the Whirling
Dervishes – are associated with Jalal al-din Rumi (d.1273). Today, living
shaykhs continue to guide pupils (*murids*) through the stages and states
of the mystical quest. Even after death their shrines remain a place of
pilgrimage, with many ordinary Muslims believing these saints to be a
continued source of blessing and intercession with God.

REVIVAL AND REFORM: FROM MEDIEVAL TO MODERN ISLAM

In 1258 Mongol armies from the east sacked Baghdad and brought the
Abbasid Empire to an end. Nevertheless, Islamic civilization still
prospered with important developments in astronomy, medicine and
other sciences, as well as a flowering of art, architecture and literature.
Three of the best-known medieval empires were:

- the Ottomans (1281–1924) of Turkey, the Balkans, the Fertile Crescent
  and beyond
- the Safavids (1501–1722) of Persia
- the Mughals (1526–1858) of the Indian-subcontinent

Of these, the Ottomans were the most powerful and it was their Sultans that assumed the title of *Caliph*, laying symbolic claim to the leadership of the Muslim world. However, by the end of the eighteenth century even the Ottomans were in decline and the technological superiority of Europe was increasingly evident.

For Muslim revivalists, political decline and crisis is often linked to a loss of Islamic 'purity'. In the pre-modern and modern periods they have advanced a critique of two key aspects of traditional Islam:

- popular Sufism, for 'corrupting' Islam with 'innovations' such as the cult of saints, belief in their miracles and rituals involving music and dance
- the '*ulama*, for allowing Islam to 'stagnate' by slavishly 'imitating' the interpretations of previous generations of scholars

Despite this critique, traditional Islam is probably still the most representative form of the religion today. Nevertheless, revivalism has grown in influence over the last two hundred years. It seeks to purge Islam of all 'un-Islamic innovations' and return to a direct reading of the *Qur'an* and *sunna*, using *ijtihad* (personal 'effort' in interpretation) in preference to the accumulated authority of the medieval scholars.

Some pre-modern revivalists such as Shah Wali Allah (d.1762) of India were actually working within Sufism to reform it. Others like Muhammad Ibn 'Abd al-Wahhab (d.1792) in Arabia were militant and uncompromising anti-Sufis who destroyed the tombs of saints. In the colonial period some Muslim elites, such as Sayyid Ahmad Khan (d.1898) of India were prepared to embrace Western ideas and revive the use of reason to reform and modernise Islamic thought. However, in the twentieth century, Islamists such as Pakistan's Mawdudi (d.1979) and Egypt's Sayyid Qutb (d.1965) have proven more influential. Both struggled

▲ ABOVE: Pages from a seventeenth century edition of the Qur'an

to assert Islam's independence from European economic, political and cultural domination, often reproducing a crude anti-Westernism. Both transformed Islam into a political ideology with the aim of establishing an Islamic state ruled by *shari'ah*. That said, like Muslims per se, Islamists are not a homogenous constituency. Into the twenty-first century, there are increasingly important differences in theory and method. Some, of course, advocate armed uprising.However, others accommodate to the political process and seek change gradually.

◻ *see* THE QUR'ANIC TEXT AND ITS FORMATION p. 216

BAHA'I

The Baha'i Faith is an independent monotheistic religion with a worldwide population of some seven million people. They come from more than 2,000 different tribal, racial and ethnic groups and live in 235 countries and dependent territories. It originated in Iran in 1844 and has its own sacred scriptures, laws, calendar and holy days.

BELIEF

The Baha'i Faith teaches that the Founders of the world's major religions, including Krishna, Buddha, Zoroaster, Abraham, Moses, Jesus Christ and Muhammad, are divine Teachers sent by one God to educate humanity through teachings and laws suited to its stage of development. The Baha'i Faith recognizes two additional Teachers for this age: the Bab and Baha'u'llah. Baha'is believe that religious revelation will continue in the future to provide guidance to 'an ever-advancing civilization'.

In 1844 the Bab ('the Gate')

▶ RIGHT: The shrine of the Bab, Israel

231

founded the Bábí Faith. His main purpose was to prepare humanity for the imminent appearance of another divine Teacher who would lead humanity into an age of universal peace. In 1863, Baha'u'llah ('the Glory of God') announced that He was the figure foretold by the Bab, and the Baha'i Faith was born. The Faith's unity has been preserved through the provisions of a written Covenant, which established the Faith's principles of succession and institutional authority. There are no clergy in the Baha'i Faith. The Baha'i community governs itself by elected councils at the local, national and international levels, and only Baha'is are permitted to contribute to the funds of their Faith. Baha'is in Iran have suffered persecution for their beliefs since the Faith's earliest days.

see THE LIFE OF THE BUDDHA p. 46

UNITY

The main theme of Baha'u'llah's revelation is unity. He taught that 'the earth is but one country, and mankind its citizens'. His writings contain principles, laws and institutions for a world civilization, including: abandonment of all forms of prejudice; equality between the sexes; recognition of the common source and essential oneness of the world's great religions; elimination of the extremes of poverty and wealth; universal compulsory education; responsibility of each individual to search independently for truth; establishment of a world federal system based on principles of collective security; and recognition that religion is in harmony with reason and scientific knowledge. Service to humanity is another central teaching of the Baha'i faith, which has led Baha'is to initiate thousands of social and economic development projects around the world. Most of these are modest, grassroots efforts such as schools, village healthcare campaigns and environmental projects.

The key points of Baha'u'llah's message can be summed up as global unity and justice. He taught that there is only one God who has revealed his will through a series of divine Teachers. While the social teachings of the great religions they founded differ according to the time and place they were delivered, the spiritual essence of all faiths is the same: that the purpose of all human beings is to know and worship their Creator. In this age, humanity is capable of recognizing the oneness of God, religion and the human family. Baha'u'llah called upon the world's secular and religious leaders to devote all their energies to the establishment of universal peace. He wrote: 'my object is none other than the betterment of the world and the tranquility of its peoples'.

◘ *see* BELIEF p. 231

◀ *LEFT: A Baha'i temple in Chicago, USA*

BAHA'U'LLAH

Baha'u'llah, which is Arabic for 'the Glory of God', is the title adopted by the Founder of the Baha'i Faith, Mirza Husayn-'Ali' (1817–92). Born into a noble family in nineteenth-century Iran, Baha'u'llah refused the political position offered to him when he was a young man and chose instead to spend his wealth caring for the poor and the sick. He became an early follower of the Bab, a young merchant from Shiraz who claimed to be the bearer of a new religion destined to renew Persian society.

In 1852, while imprisoned in Tehran for his belief as a follower of the Bab, Baha'u'llah received the first intimations of the mission foretold by the Bab. Upon his release from prison, Baha'u'llah was exiled to Baghdad and, in 1863, declared there that he was the long-awaited Messenger of God. The vast majority of the Bab's followers accepted this declaration and so the Baha'i community was born.

Before His death in 1892, Baha'u'llah provided for the succession of leadership of the Baha'i community, ensuring its unity and protecting it from schism. His eldest son, Abbas Effendi (who adopted the title Abdu'l-Baha, which means 'servant of the Glory'), was appointed the head of the Baha'i Faith and the sole authorized interpreter of Baha'u'llah's writings. This act enabled the Baha'i community to pass through the first century of its existence with its unity firmly intact, in the face of both external and internal challenges.

see BELIEF p. 231

◀ LEFT: Abdu'l-Baha, eldest son of Baha'u'llah, the Founder of the Baha'i faith

EUROPE

ANCIENT GREECE AND ROME

The civilization established by the ancient Greeks and subsequently built upon by Rome would in time be regarded as the foundation for 2,000 years of western history, though no-one could have forseen this imposing legacy. The story of classical religion, like that of classical culture more generally, is one of local practices and traditions being brought gradually to coherence through the evolution of ever more far-reaching states and empires.

THE MINOANS

Much speculation surrounds the religious beliefs of the early Greeks, as there are few religious artefacts and little written evidence to indicate what they were. One theory is that they honoured their own ancestors as guiding spirits and worshipped the deities of local springs, the weather and other life-sustaining forces.

The first significant civilization in the area seems to have evolved not in mainland Greece itself, but on the isle of Crete where what is known as the Minoan civilization had its capital at Knossos around 2000 BC. Minoan culture (its name derived from that of its great mythical ruler King Minos) was originally believed to have been a peace-loving culture of artistic accomplishment and nature-worship. The Minoans' elevated femininity over brute masculinity. However, more recent findings from impressive arsenals of weaponry to evidence of human sacrifice (and possibly even cannibalism) have questioned this idealized picture. Yet it seems that the Minoans were subject to a matriarchy, that the king was a mere figurehead beside the high priestess who really ruled.

The most vital role of the Minoan priesthood seems to have been in maintaining a highly centralized mercantile economy with contacts throughout the eastern Mediterranean; obviously sacred roles may well have been secondary to this. Inscriptions found at Knossos, dating from the fourteenth century BC and appearing to have been written in the hands of up to 70 different scribes, record agricultural output in the city's hinterland in great detail. Meanwhile, the priests seem to have supervised a large number of craftsmen working in the palace precincts. Pots, jewels and other luxuries from Knossos have been discovered throughout Asia Minor and Southeast Europe, while Egyptian tomb-paintings attest to the visits of Minoan merchants.

◪ see THE MYCENAEANS p. 240

▲ *ABOVE: A Minoan vase depicting an octopus*

THE MYCENAEANS

Records of Minoan culture disappear around 1400 BC, supplanted by
Mycenae, then emerging on the mainland. The Mycenaeans left an
archeological legacy of heavy bronze swords and helmets, and warlike
fortifications. Yet the Mycenaeans' most important force may well have
been their army of priestly scribes, for they were even more meticulous

than the Minoans in their administration of a trading empire. Their reign was brief: by about 1200 BC, Mycenean power itself was declining. By the beginning of the first millennium BC, the Mycenaeans had disappeared.

see THE MINOANS p. 238

▼ BELOW: A sixteenth century fresco found in the palace of Knossos, Crete

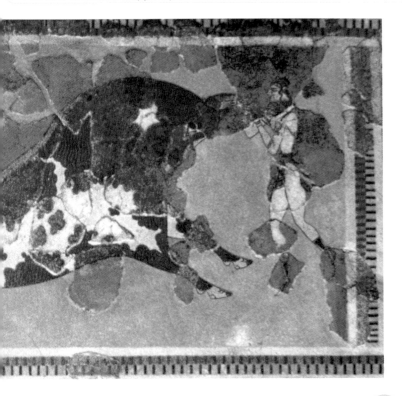

GREEK GODS

As recorded by Hesiod's Theogony (c. 700 BC), the world was once ruled by
the Titans (the children of Gaia, the earth) and Uranus (heaven, her son
and husband). To this point, the antique order corresponded with the
sort of matriarchy imagined by the Minoans, with their goddess Potnia,
but events took a different turn in the developing Greek tradition. The
story tells how Kronos, Gaia's youngest son, castrated his father and
usurped his throne; he then married his sister Rhea, but in order to
secure his position, he swallowed all their children as they were born.
One alone escaped: the infant Zeus was smuggled to safety in Crete,

where he grew to manhood plotting revenge against his unnatural sire. The god of open sky and mountain-top, Zeus was armed with flashing thunderbolts, and established his seat on the summit of Greece's highest peak, Mount Olympus, from where he led his own family in war against the Titans (now regurgitated so as to be able to help in their father's defence). The final victory of Zeus and his Olympians marked not only the end of the region's pre-Greek period, but also a significant break with a past in which mother earth had been at the spiritual centre of things.

THE TROJAN WARS

The epics of Homer (eighth century BC) did more than anything else to forge a common Greek identity. His famous tale of the battle for Troy, *Iliad*, and his account of the long and difficult homecoming of the trickster Odysseus, *The Odyssey*, both held up a set of Greek heroes for respect and emulation. These stories, and the values they enshrined, became part of the general Greek inheritance, uniting scattered communities which might otherwise have shared only mutual enmity.

The Homeric poems also mark the unforgettable mythic debut of the Olympians as rulers of the heavens, the often all-too human divinities presiding over the fortunes – and misfortunes – of mortal men and women. Hence, outraged at the slight they have received in being placed behind Aphrodite in terms of beauty, Hera, Zeus's sister and queen, and his daughter Athene, the goddess of wisdom, both side with the Greeks in the hostilities that follow Paris's theft of Helen. While the goddess of beauty and love herself may stand loyally by her supporter's city, Aphrodite cannot finally prevail over the other goddesses, despite the assistance of her lover Ares, the god of war. Poseidon the earth-shaker

◀ *LEFT: Dionysos, the god of wine, disguise and illusion*

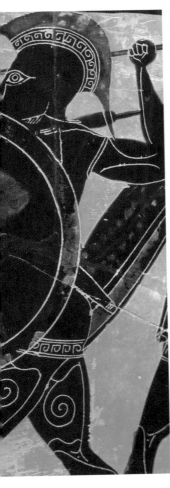

and god of the sea, sets himself against Troy from the very start, although he also does his best to hinder Odysseus' subsequent homeward journey. Fortunately, the hero has help from Hermes, the messenger of the gods. Even Apollo, the radiant sun-god, is not above intervening to bring about the death of the apparently invincible Achilles, while his sister the virgin-huntress Artemis, goddess of the moon, also takes the part of Troy.

▸ see GREEK GODS p. 242

GREEK TEMPLES

Religion in the Greek city state, or polis, was an inseparable part of civic life, its role being more than anything the celebration of the community's collective achievements. The temple, in these circumstances, was not so much a secret shrine for an initiated priesthood as a prestigious public building, proclaiming the pride and values of the state as a whole. The great constructions raised by the Athenian statesman Pericles on the city's

◄ LEFT: Pottery depicting the Trojan wars

Acropolis from 449 BC were only the most conspicuous, solid examples of this tendency. The Parthenon has endured as the ultimate symbol of 'classical' perfection; its lines assert the triumph of human skill and ingenuity, a disdainful reproach to the rough untidiness of nature. A temple to Athene, the Parthenon enshrines for ever the co-opting of an Olympian goddess as tutelary deity to a single city.

◆ see GREEK GODS p. 242

▲ ABOVE: The remains of the Parthenon on the Acropolis in Athens

GREEK FESTIVALS

The festival calendar in classical Greece placed a premium on mortal, rather than divine, accomplishment: so it was, for example, with the original Olympic Games. First held in 776 BC in the shadow of Mount Olympus, this gathering brought the youth of Greece together to compete in running, wrestling and other tests of speed, strength and skill. Although the athletes' achievements were offered up to Zeus (there were games in the name of Apollo and Athene elsewhere), such tournaments were first and foremost a showcase for the grace and strength of the human body. The importance of Dionysos, god of revelry, cannot be overestimated: there were seven Dionysiac festivals a year in Athens alone. The whole city processed to the theatre, where music and dancing set the scene for programmes of drama from farce to tragedy.

◆ *see* GREEK GODS p. 242

▶ RIGHT: *Statue of a Greek youth*

DEATH OF THE YEAR

The tradition that Kore (also known as Proserpine), the daughter of Demeter, goddess of the harvest, had been abducted by Hades, the ruler of the underworld, was commemorated by Athenian youths in an annual autumn pilgrimage to the scene of the crime at Eleusis, on the coast north-west of Athens. Enraged at her loss, the goddess of the harvest had struck down the crops where they were growing in the fields – they would not bear fruit again, she warned, until she once more had her daughter. Concerned that their human subjects would soon starve, the gods sent Hermes down into the earth to bring Kore back – if she had eaten nothing in her time below she would be free forever. Hades had tempted her to take a few pomegranate seeds, however, and she was thus deemed to have sealed her marriage with the infernal king. Although restored once more to her mother, Kore was from that time obliged to return to her husband's home for one season in every four. During that time Demeter's bitterness is marked by biting frosts and barren soil. The tradition of Kore's descent to the underworld each winter and her subsequent resurrection for the spring, clearly reflects an age-old concern with the continuation of the agricultural cycle (presided over, not by male Zeus, but by a female deity), as well as a more modern theological preoccupation with the question of life after death.

◆ see GREEK FESTIVALS p. 247

THE ROMANS

The origins of Rome were obscure and unpromising: through the earlier centuries of the first millennium BC another civilization dominated what is now central Italy – the Etruscans. Expanding downward from the

▶ RIGHT: Detail of a Roman shield showing the goddess Cybele in a chariot drawn by lions

surrounding hilltops, under the auspices of Etruscan rule, the settlement established by Latin shepherds in the mid-eighth century BC was slowly evolving and as it grew, so did its confidence and self-belief: by 509 BC, Rome had succeeded in expelling its Etruscan overlords; as a republic, it would bring all Italy under its control. By the second century AD, Rome's dominions spanned the known world, from Scotland to Syria, yet the civilization propagated there was recognizably Greek in origin.

◆ *see* RELIGIOUS DIVERSITY IN ROME p. 253

ROMAN GODS

The Romans took over the Greek gods along with much else, adapting more or less the entire Olympian pantheon to their own purposes. Thus father Zeus became thundering Jupiter, his wife Hera the imperious Roman Juno, while Aphrodite became the love goddess Venus and chaste Artemis Diana. Athene passed her wisdom on to Minerva, the messenger Hermes was reinvented as Mercury. Yet such apparently straightforward transformations may mask rather more complex origins: the most famous Roman god of all, for example, was the war-god Mars. Although in time he assumed the attributes of the Greek Ares, he had in fact started life among the early Latins as an agricultural deity. Only as Roman values shifted down the generations from agricultural to imperial did Mars by slow degrees take on his more warlike nature.

➤ see GREEK GODS p. 242

◀ LEFT: Bacchus, the Roman god of wine

JANUS AND MINOR DEITIES

One uniquely Roman deity was the double-faced Janus, god of gateways, entrances and exits, new ventures and fresh beginnings. Associated not only with daybreak but with the world's creation, he was honoured on the first day of every month, as well as throughout Januarius, the first month of every year. The Romans held innumerable other minor deities in awe: the Lares (household spirits) and Penates (guardians of the pantry) were only the best known of these. If Janus presided over doorways, there were separate spirits responsible for hinges, thresholds and the doors themselves. For the pious Roman any action, from pruning a vine to embarking on an overseas voyage, might require the performance of precise rituals, special prayers and propitiatory offerings.

◆ *see* ROMAN GODS p. 250

▲ *ABOVE: A Roman siver coin from 235 BC, depicting the double-headed god Janus*

DEIFICATIONS

As time went on, and power in what had once been a republic became concentrated more and more in the hands of individual leaders, Rome saw the development of what modern states would come to know as the 'cult of personality'. The adulation accorded to generals such as Julius Caesar led to their elevation to effective dictatorship, a role merely ratified when, in 27 BC, Octavian, Caesar's great-nephew and adoptive son, and final victor in the long years of faction-fighting that had followed the dictator's assassination in 44 BC, enthroned himself as 'Imperator' or Emperor Augustus (the name simply means 'splendid'). In

Egypt and the Asiatic provinces, where kings had long been venerated as gods, he was soon popularly regarded as a living divinity. After his death in AD 14, this became the official policy of Rome itself, and subsequent emperors were automatically promoted to the ranks of deities. So accepted a part of Roman life did such deifications become that, when the emperor Hadrian's young lover Antinous drowned during a visit to Egypt in AD 130, the emperor had the youth enrolled among the gods and worshipped at shrines throughout the Empire.

◆ see THE ROMANS p. 248

▲ ABOVE: A Roman coin showing Julius Caesar

RELIGIOUS DIVERSITY IN ROME

At its height in the second century AD the Roman Empire covered some five million sq km (2 million sq miles), occupying lands which now belong to over 30 different sovereign states. Around 100 million Roman subjects were drawn together into a single political entity, despite the enormous variety of their linguistic and cultural backgrounds. Yet, while their temporal authority was absolute, the Romans were much more relaxed about matters spiritual: under their iron rule a remarkable religious diversity was free to thrive. As the old gods had been subsumed into the official Roman pantheon, so indigenous cults came to be spliced together with Roman traditions.

In parts of Gaul the Roman war god was linked to a local god of light: Mars Loucetus, as he became known, was widely worshipped. At Bath the British spring goddess Sulis was associated so closely with the Roman Minerva that they became to all intents and purposes different facets of a single Romano-British deity. In North Africa, meanwhile, characteristics of the old Phoenician fertility god Baal-Hammon, renewer of all energies, were effectively grafted on to those of Jupiter, to produce a recognizably Roman deity, Jupiter-Ammon.

Some gods and goddesses in subject lands succeeded in maintaining their independent existence: the Egyptian Isis, and her husband Osiris, for example. At first an underground cult confined to slaves, the worship of Isis won a degree of official backing, and by the first century AD she had a prestigious temple in the heart of imperial Rome. By that time Mithras, the Persian god of light and truth, had won

▶ RIGHT: A Roman warrior advances

253

▲ ABOVE: Hadrian's Wall, running between England and Scotland

a wide unofficial following in the Roman army: a male-only cult, with tough initiation rites, it naturally appealed to battle-hardened legionaries. Wherever the legions went, Mithras went too, the soldiers' guardian and guide; signs of his worship have been found in the very shadow of Hadrian's Wall.

💠 see DEITIES p. 100

CELTIC RELIGION

The Celts emerged as a powerful force in central Europe, later expanding to occupy the north-west. Acknowledging the divine in all things, their religion was influenced by Roman practices. The Druids are the best-remembered ancient priesthood of northern Europe, although they suffered persecution first by the Romans, then by the Christian Church.

▲ ABOVE: *Druids celebrate the Summer Solstice at Stonehenge*

THE CELTS

The Celts emerged as a recognizable group around the seventh century BC in Austria. From the fifth century BC, the Greeks gave the name 'Keltoi' to the tribes of central Europe who raided their cities. During the late fifth century BC Celtic influences expanded westwards into what is now France and Spain, northwards to Britain and Ireland and eastwards through the Balkans into Asia Minor.

Early Celtic religion was aniconic (without images) and atectonic (without architectural settings). Celtic oral culture has left no ancient texts, and any information we have comes from contemporary Greek and Roman authors, in addition to archeology and later writings that put oral traditions in writing.

◻ see THE ROMANS p. 248

256

CELTIC DEITIES

From the late sixth century BC, the Celts began to make anthropomorphic images from stone which were set up on burial mounds. Under the influence of Mediterranean culture, the Celts in the areas of present-day France, Germany and Switzerland adopted human form for their deities. Sacred buildings were introduced as the result of the influence of Roman religion and some 70 Celtic deities are named in surviving inscriptions from the Roman period.

Julius Caesar stated that the Gauls considered Dis Pater, the lord of the underworld, to be their divine ancestor. In Ireland, the goddess Dana was the ancestress of certain tribes. The Celtic kings in Britain counted their descent from the divine couple Beli and Anna. Lugus, or Lugh, was the supreme god of the western Celts.

In Celtic regions under Roman rule, images and altars to Celtic deities bore inscriptions that reflected the interpretatio Romana. According to this, Lugus is equated with Mercury, Taranis, the Celtic god of thunder, with Jupiter, and Teutates, god of the tribe, with Mars. Gods of war, also assimilated with the Roman Mars, include Belutacadros, Cocidius, Corotiacus, Loucetius and Rigisamus. Ogmios, god of strength and eloquence, was equated with Hercules. Poeninus, god of mountain ranges, was also equated with Jupiter.

In common with other European traditions, the Celts acknowledged various gods of trades and crafts. Seafarers worshipped the sea-god called Manannan or Manawydden. Smiths had a god with a name close to the Irish Gobniu, Sucellos was god of vineyards and Rosmerta goddess of fruitfulness and financial gain.

◆ *see* ROMAN GODS p. 250

◀ LEFT: *A second or first century* BC *sandstone carving of a boar-god from eastern Gaul*

HOLY GROVES AND TEMENOI

Celtic holy groves (*nemetona*) were held in awe and approached only by members of the priesthood. The modern place-name element *nemet* or *nympton* denotes the former site of a holy grove. The goddesses

Nemetona and Rigonemetis are named as protectors of groves. The *temenos* was the central place of collective worship for the continental Celts; it was an enclosure, defined by ditches and generally square or rectangular, in which ceremonial gatherings took place. The *temenoi* contained aniconic or iconic images, sacred stones, ceremonial fireplaces, a tree or pole, wells and shafts for ritual offerings. Compressed earth at such places attests to ceremonial perambulation or dances around the central point.

see HOLY PLACES p. 261

CELTIC PRIESTHOOD

The Celtic priesthood comprised the Bards, Vates and Druids, all of whom were restricted to Ireland, Gaul and Britain. The Bards were the genealogists, keepers of myth and song. Vates performed sacred divinations, whilst the Druids performed religious rites.

According to classical writers, the Druids, whose name meant 'men of the oak tree', were keepers of astronomical knowledge and regulators of the Gallic calendar. Divided into 62 consecutive lunar months, this shows the main religious festivals of the Gallic year, with auspicious and inauspicious months. According to classical sources, the Druids taught the doctrine of transmigration of souls. In this belief, human souls at death enter into trees, rocks or animals, or newborn humans. Outside the Druidic order, each holy place had its own guardian, certain members of the family who owned the land. The office of dewar, keeper of sacred things, continued in Scotland and Ireland in a Christian context until the twentieth century.

see NORDIC PRIESTHOOD AND TEMPLES p. 262

◀ LEFT: *Lugh the sun-god is challenged to a chess contest*

GERMANIC RELIGION

Germanic religion spread to England in the sixth century AD; it was soon replaced by Christianity. In mainland Europe, it succumbed to the crusades of Charlemagne. It survived longer in Scandinavia, whence it was re-exported to the British Isles by the Vikings, who also took it to Iceland and Greenland.

DIVINE ANCESTOR

The polytheistic religion of the Germanic peoples was centred upon the cult of the divine ancestor. In early times, the king's ancestor was also the tribal god, and this principle was maintained until well into Christian times. Seven out of eight Anglo-Saxon royal genealogies begin with Woden, as does the Swedish royal line. Folk meetings were held on moot hills, the burial mounds of ancestors whose help was invoked in decision-making. Seeresses accompanied early Germanic rulers; they contacted the spirits of the ancestors by various divinatory techniques. From the fourth century AD, they used the runes – an alphabet derived from the Etruscans with religious significance, used in divination and sacred inscriptions – which were believed to come from Woden.

▶ see DIVINE ANCESTORS p. 134

THE GERMANIC GODS

Germanic religion continued in Scandinavia until the tenth century AD, long after it had died out in England and Germany. It was re-imported to parts of Britain (northern Scotland and eastern England) and to central Ireland by Viking and Danish settlers. In earlier times, the sky god Tîwaz was considered the chief deity. There is also evidence of an older, pre-agricultural pantheon, including the god Frey and the goddess Freyja,

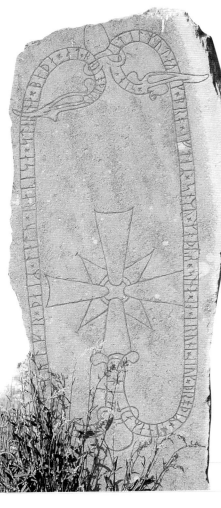

known in Scandinavia as the Vanir. In Anglo-Saxon England, Woden and Thunor were the major gods, whilst in Saxony their counterparts Wotan and Donar were venerated. Later, in Viking times, Odin (Woden) became pre-eminent, with the title Allfather. Thor (Thunor), god of the peasantry, was relegated to the status of son of Odin.

◆ *see* CELTIC DEITIES p. 257

HOLY PLACES

The Germanic religious landscape was filled with sacred places. The Anglo-Saxon *Wih* was a holy image standing in the open. In Scandinavian practice, unsheltered images were protected by a fence of hazel

◀ *LEFT: A rune stone, believed to have magical powers*

posts and ropes (the *Vébond*). More substantial was a shrine covered with a pavilion, the *Traef* or *Hørgr*. In Scandinavia and Scandinavian colonies, communal worship took place in the *Hof*, a hall-form farmhouse with a special extension, the *afhús*, where sacred objects and images were kept. Here, regular festivals were observed to mark the passing of the seasons.

◘ *see* HOLY GROVES AND TEMENOI p 258

NORDIC PRIESTHOOD AND TEMPLES

The office of *Godi* originated in the priest of a tribe or clan who held a certain sacred place in common. *Godar* were never full-time officials, but were rather hereditary landowners who had the duty to maintain ancestral holy places. In Iceland, the *Godi* in charge of the temple at Kialarnes, the direct descendent of the first settler, Ingulf Amarson, bore the title *Alsherjargodi*, or High Priest. In accordance with ancient tradition, Iceland was divided into four quarters each containing three jurisdictions further subdivided into three *Godord*, each with its ruling *Godi*. The Icelandic law-making assembly (*Lögrétta*) was originally composed largely of *Godar*.

Norse temples were the personal property of the hereditary keeper of the land on which they stood. In Iceland, the *Höfud-hof* or public temples were sometimes owned by women. During the settlement period (ninth to tenth centuries AD), whole temples were shipped to Iceland. *Erbyggja Saga* tells of the Norwegian *Godi* Thórolf Mostrarskegg transporting his timber temple of Thor, complete with the sacred earth on which it stood. Some Norse shrines were dedicated to particular gods, such as the temple of the Black Thor at Dublin. Others housed many deities. In the

▶ RIGHT: The two sacred volcanoes at Heimaey, Iceland

Viking age, important temples of the Nordic gods stood at Jellinge in Denmark; Sigtuna and Gamla Uppsala in Sweden; Mæri, Lade, Skiringssal, Trondenes and Vatnsdal in Norway; Kialarnes in Iceland and Dublin in Ireland. At Gamla Uppsala, the Swedish royal centre, which emerged as the most important temple, there were images of Thor, Odin and Frey – the three chief gods.

◆ see CELTIC PRIESTHOOD p. 259

SLAVIC AND BALTIC RELIGION

Slavic and Baltic religion followed the general pattern of the Celtic and Germanic traditions. Worship was conducted first in holy groves, and later in wooden temples served by priests and priestesses. In Lithuania, a state religion emerged in the thirteenth century whose remnants were still evident 300 years later.

THE SLAVS

The Slavs came into existence as a recognized ethnic group formed of the amalgamation of various tribes who came to occupy their territory in the sixth century AD. Their polytheistic religion continued long after the Christian church had taken over western and south-eastern Europe. In early times, the head of the family or clan officiated at religious ceremonies. From the eighth to ninth centuries onwards, a Slavic priesthood emerged. Rites formerly performed in open-air enclosures or groves were transferred to newly built temples. In Pomerania, there were three grades of priest. Central or provincial temples were officiated over by a high priest.

see THE APOSTLES AND THE CHRISTIAN CHURCH p. 193

THE SLAVIC GODS

Byzantine chronicles of the sixth century AD mention the Slavic god Svarog, a god of fire and light, equating him with the Greek Hephaistos.

◀ LEFT: A dvorovoi, a spirit which protected people and animals on a farm

His son, Dazbog, was paralleled with the sun-god Helios. Dazbog was brought into the pantheon of Kiev by Duke Vladimir in AD 980. As Svarozic (son of Svarog) the god Dazbog was worshipped by the Elbe Slavs. In 1008 Bruno von Querfurt described his cult centre at Retra. Inside a castle with nine towers was a timber temple adorned with aurochs – horns bedecked with gold and jewels. Among others, the main image was of Svarozic, dressed in armour, with weapons. The temple was destroyed in 1068.

The thunder god Perun (Lithuanian Perkunas) was venerated throughout the Slavic and Baltic lands, in association with the weather- and wind-gods Erisvorsh, Varpulis and Dogoda. Perun is first mentioned in the seventh century AD 'Life of St Demetrios of Salonika'. In AD 980, an image of Perun with a silver head and a golden beard was set up by the side of the River Volchov at Kiev. At Perynj, near Novgorod, an eternal fire of oak branches was maintained in honour of Perun. Oak trees were sacred to Perun. In Poland, a holy oak was venerated at Czestochowa. In the tenth century, Russian devotees sacrificed chickens, made offerings of meat and bread, and shot arrows in honour of the god at a sacred oak on the holy island of Chortice in the river Dnieper.

◆ see GREEK GODS p. 242

LITHUANIAN STATE RELIGION

Lithuanian religion was formulated by Sventaragis in the sixth century AD, when the cult of Perkunas was established. All over Lithuania, on tracts of land called *alkos* sacred to the god, eternal fires were maintained by priestesses known as *vaidilutes*. Sventaragis established an ancestral centre in an oak grove at Vilnius, where the ancestors of the ruling dynasty were venerated.

▶ RIGHT: Oak trees were sacred to Perun, the Slavic god of thunder, lightning and war

During the early thirteenth century, a polytheistic state religion was established by King Mindaugas. It amalgamated local cults, emphasized the worship of national heroes, practised cremation of the dead, and taught the doctrine of reincarnation. Until the early fifteenth century, Lithuanian royalty and noblemen were cremated in full regalia accompanied by their horses, dogs and falcons. As late as 1583, Jesuit monks visiting Lithuania reported that Perkunas was being worshipped at oak trees. Whilst Perkunas was the major god, the Lithuanian pantheon contained many other deities, including the goddesses Zemyna (earth), Saule (sun), Gabija (fire), and Laima, goddess of individual destinies.

⬥ *see* CELTIC PRIESTHOOD p. 259

OCEANIA/ PACIFIC

OCEANIA/POLYNESIA

The collection of islands in the Pacific Ocean and East Indies known as Oceania was colonized by hunters from Southeast Asia around 30,000 years ago. From this time a belief system developed that is still practised today. The belief in ghosts, as a projection of the life-force of a person, is central to spiritual thought throughout Oceania and has in fact become fused with Christianity rather than pushed away by it.

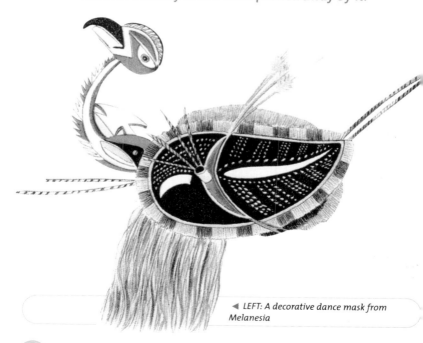

◄ LEFT: A decorative dance mask from Melanesia

GHOST AFTERLIFE

After life has departed the body, the spiritual residue of a person takes the form of a ghost – a *masalai* in the New Guinea Tokpisin language. These ghosts share the same life space with the community of living persons and constantly intrude, usually undesirably, in the affairs of the living. Men (it is only men who deal with ghosts in most of Melanesia) attempt both to placate the ghosts and to appropriate their special powers – to find lost objects; to foretell the future, to interpret dreams – for their own purposes.

◆ see GODS AND GHOSTS p. 157

THE FOI AND THE DARIBI

The Foi inhabit the Mubi River Valley in the Southern Highlands Province of Papua New Guinea, a long and somewhat narrow valley which runs from north-west to south-east. The Mubi River and all its smaller tributaries flow in this direction. The Foi do not speak of 'west' or 'east', but rather 'upstream' and 'downstream' as their main cardinal axis. The other dimensions they refer to are 'above', for places higher in altitude, and 'below', for places lower in altitude.

▶ *RIGHT: A Melanesian idol from a temple relief carving*

The afterworld in Foi is a place called *haisureri*, sometimes translated by the Foi as 'white sand'. It is conceived as a beautiful region with fine sandy banks that lies far downstream. They believe that when people die their souls travel downstream until they reach this place, and in *haisureri* they continue to live, eat the special ghosts' food that grows only there, and carry on in a caricature of living society.

Upstream, by contrast, is the source of all water and the source of all life. The distant west is sometimes referred to as *me ga kore*, (the 'place-source-upstream'), and it is the direction from which pearl shells are thought to have originated, as well as certain brightly coloured shrubs and flowers associated with pearl-shell magic.

The Daribi inhabit the southern part of Simbu Province around Mount Karimui. Their macrocosm is similarly oriented to the Foi by the flow of the Tua River, but in this case it flows from east to west, paralleling the movement of the sun. Thus, for the Foi, the sunset is associated with the origin and source of water and has connotations of vitality and life. For the Daribi the sunset means just the opposite to that of the Foi: it is associated with death and the place the ghosts go, for ghosts follow the direction of water in both the Foi and Daribi traditions.

◐ *see* GHOST AFTERLIFE p. 271

POLYNESIA AND MELANESIA

In island Melanesia, as in Polynesia, the institution of chieftainship is a central social and cultural institution. The chief has certain religious and ritual responsibilities and partakes of a certain divinity himself. He is the incarnation of certain deities, as in Hawai'i, or of the *totem*, as in New Caledonia.

▶ RIGHT: The Foi people believe the afterlife takes place in an idyllic location

Polynesian societies in general are hierarchical, usually with a chiefly ruling class, commoners, and a lower or slave class. As well as the king being of divine origin, the head of a family also mediates the divine realm. This function is increasingly taken over by a class of priests. There is much variation in the region as to how separate were the roles of chief and priest and the kinds of secular power they exerted.

The primary concern of religion is protection of the people – individual and group – from divine malevolence. Strict adherence to laws and procedures is necessary to keep the divine and physical worlds in harmony. The main functions of priests are the foretelling of events through divine intercession, and leading ceremonies to ensure the conventional stability of society.

All chiefly power in Polynesia is made possible by divine power. In the Marquesas, the birth of a firstborn is referred to as the epiphany of a god. It has also been reported that Marquesans believed that the firstborn was sired by an ancestral divinity.

In Tonga, the sacred king is known as the Tu'i Tonga. He was the main mediator between the realm of the human and that of the divine, and is said to have descended from the sky. In the myth, the first Tu'i Tonga is Aho'eitu. He is the son of the earth-mother Ilaheva, who was made pregnant by Eitumatupu'a, the sky god, who then went back to his heavenly realm. As a small boy the son goes to heaven to find his father. When the god sees his son, he falls to the ground, so overwhelmed is he by his son's beauty. Later, Aho'eitu defeats his older brothers, who in revenge, kill him and eat his body. The god father, however, forces them to regurgitate the body, which the god then brings back to life and sends to earth to be the first Tu'i Tonga.

◆ see DEIFICATIONS p. 251

HAWAI'IAN GODS

Humans and gods would compete over the power to reproduce themselves. La'ila'i is the older sister of both god and human and is also the firstborn. Her brothers, sometimes described as twins, are Ki'i (a man) and Kane (a god). She weds both of them, giving birth to both the line of humans and of gods, though the children of Kane are senior to those of Ki'i. As the generations succeed each other, the line of men repeatedly marry back into the line of gods, according to the Kumulipo chant.

In Hawai'i, the time of the god Lono begins with the winter rainy season, the period when all things planted bear fruit. Lono is the god of regeneration and fertility, while Ku is the god of war and sacrifice. This generative power is maintained at the expense of its opposite, the power of war, which is the province of the god Ku, whose temple rituals are suspended during this period. After Lono departs, the king has to re-sanctify the temples of Ku by means of human sacrifices.

It is said that Lono, as part of the general fertility he brings, descends from heaven to mate with a beautiful woman. Thus, when Captain Cook arrived, from the proper direction, at Hawai'i at the time of Lono, it was thought he was the god. The Hawai'ian women paddled out to meet him and his crew, eager to mate with the gods in the hope of bearing a sacred child who would be chief.

◆ *see* THE FOI AND THE DARIBI p. 271

HAWAI'IAN SHRINES

Stone petrolgyphs in Hawai'i were important ritual anchors between the surface world and the divine sky realm. Hawai'ian shrines, called *heiau*, were often built upon a sacred foundation of stones. One such place is Kukaniloko. When Kukaniloko was used as an ancient birthing place, there was a large stone that presumably held the mother up in a sitting position. A chief was required to stand before each woman. The child born would be called 'a chief divine; a burning fire'. The name Kukaniloko itself means 'an inland area from which great events are heralded'.

◆ *see* POLYNESIA AND MELANESIA p. 272

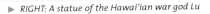

▶ RIGHT: *A statue of the Hawai'ian war god Lu*

AUSTRALIAN ABORIGINALS

The most distinctive concept of Australian Aboriginal religion is that of the 'dreaming' or, as it used to be called, the 'dreamtime'. This refers to a primordial creative period when ancestor beings roamed the land, in various human and animal forms, creating the landscape and the species of the earth as humans find them in the present day.

DJUGURBA

In the centre of Australia and the Great Victoria Desert, the term for the creative period when the earth and all its contents were first made by the ancestors, is *djugurba*. Not only was it the initial form-creating period of the world, but its creative powers exist to the present day. The ancestors continue to exert their form-making powers, and it is up to humans to detect this power and tap into it for their own purposes. The word 'dream' is highlighted, as many Aboriginal people say that ancestors and ancestral power often reveal themselves in dreams. There is much less discontinuity between the waking life and the dream life in terms of everyday meaning and significance for Aboriginal persons, although of course Aboriginal people know the difference between the real world and the dream world.

◆ *see* DREAMING TRACKS p. 278

◀ *LEFT: Carved Aborigine ancestor boards*

DREAMING TRACKS

Most of the major Australian creation myths detail the wanderings of mythical beings. They moved from place to place, creating waterholes, rocks, creatures, landscape features, and also giving these things their names. The pathway of a single creator being or a single route of travel is called a dreaming track. These can be very long and can connect dozens of groups literally across the breadth of the continent. The tracks criss-cross Australia and thus provide a network for religious and social communication between groups at very great distances from one another.

The dreaming track is a single thing and can be said to have a beginning and an end. But because different Aboriginal groups occupy only restricted portions of the route, they only 'own' part of the myth and its associated ritual. This creates the condition under which different groups come together to perform their own special segments of the total myth, although because of the length of the tracks, it could never be performed as a complete ritual performance. Thus, in a certain important sense, traditional Aboriginal groups of Australia were only parts of a larger mythological whole which they could infer but the extent of which they did not know.

◆ see 'ALL FATHER' AND THE RAINBOW SERPENT p. 280

THE WAWILAK MYTH

The *Wawilak* myth is central to the Australian Creation. At the beginning of time, it is said, the Wawilak sisters travelled north from their home in central Australia towards the sea. As they travelled they named places, animals and plants, and dug holes in the ground from which water

▶ RIGHT: Aboriginal women paint their bodies in Alice Springs, Northern Territory

▶ *RIGHT: Ayers Rock (Uluru)*

sprang. On their journey they stopped near a waterhole in which Yurlunggor, the great python, lived. It was here that one of the sisters (the eldest) polluted the waterhole with her menstrual blood. Yurlunggor was angry and emerged from the waterhole, commanding a great flood and heavy rains. The water covered the whole earth and everything on it. The flood receded as Yurlunggor descended back into the waterhole.

'ALL-FATHER' AND THE RAINBOW SERPENT

In south-east Australia, there is the widespread belief in a supreme being, a male 'All-Father'. He is called Ngurunderi among the Ngarrindjeri of the Lower Murray, South Australia; Baiami among the Wiradjuri of New South Wales and Victoria, and the Kamilaroi of New South Wales and Queensland. In the Lower Murray, Ngurunderi travelled along the south coast, creating the contours of the coastline and the mouth of the Murray River. Pursuing his two wives who had fled, he caught up with them around Cape Willoughby and caused the sea to rise, drowning them. They turned into the Pages Islands there.

The Rainbow Serpent is also a widespread figure across Aboriginal Australia. It is always associated with rain or water and is often said to inhabit deep water holes. Around Ayers Rock (Uluru) it is called *wanambi*; it is regarded as very dangerous and is treated with great circumspection by local Aboriginal people.

◼ *see* FERTILITY p. 281

FERTILITY

Among the Dalabon of the Northern Territory, *bolung* refers explicitly to the rainbow. The Dalabon believe that if a woman is to conceive, she must be entered by a rainbow snake, and that after death the performance of the proper ceremonies will transform a person's spirit back into its rainbow-snake form. Bolung as an adjective, however, means anything that had creative, transformative power in the dreaming period.

In Western Australia, a similar idea is contained in the notion of *ungud*. *Ungud* is a property of the *wandjina* paintings found in caves of Western Australia. These paintings show beings with no mouths and often no bodies. The *wandjina* are the creative spirits that made the land and its features. *Ungud* is the creative power that made the *wandjina* powerful. The *wandjina* have the power to make babies and ensure the coming of the wet season and the flourishing of edible plants and animals.

In the Pilbara region of Western Australia, south of Kimberley, early reporters mentioned the concept of tarlow – a pile of stones or a single stone set apart to mark some spot of particular fertile power, the power to make things increase and multiply. Among the Karadjieri of Western Australia, there are centres of ritual that belong to all-important plant and animal species, upon which increase rites are performed. The performance of these rites thus keeps dreaming power alive in the present.

◆ *see* DREAMING TRACKS p. 278

INITIATION

In the western desert, there are four main stages to initiation. First, the initiate is taken from the care of his female kinsmen. He is then painted with older men's blood and then with red ochre. After this, he is isolated with the other initiates for up to a year. In the second stage, fire is thrown over the heads of the novices. Older men take blood from their arms and use it to fasten bird feathers down in the shape of sacred *totemic* designs. In the third stage, the circumcision of the novices is performed and they are taken back into the seclusion camp to heal and

◀ *LEFT: The rainbow serpent*

to be shown the sacred bullroarers (oblong pieces of wood inscribed with sacred designs; the noise they make when swung over the head is believed to be the voice of the ancestor). Later on they are returned to the camp where their arrival is celebrated by their relatives. The novices are taken on to their country and instructed in their territorial mythology. After this, the novices may be sub-incised, a process whereby an incision is made in the underside of the urethra. In the last stage, the novices receive their cicatrizations – scars made on the initiate's back which leave a permanent raised weal of flesh on the body. At this point the young men are considered fully initiated and may participate in a range of rituals and ceremonies performed by men.

◆ see INITIATION p. 113

CIRCUMCISION AND SCARIFICATION

In eastern Arnhem Land, the boys who are being prepared for circumcision are told that the mythical python Yurlunggor has smelled their foreskins and is coming to swallow them, as he swallowed the mythical Wawilak sisters in the myth. The novices are also smeared with ochre during the djunggawon initiation cycle, which stands for the blood of the Wawilak sisters in the myth. In the Kunapipi (Gunabibi) initiation, men let blood from their arms fall upon the sacred trench dug in the ground – again, this is supposed to represent the Wawilak sisters' blood.

Sub-incision is practised in the Great Victoria Desert, northern South Australia and central Australia. In these areas, the wound is subsequently opened up in certain ritual contexts, so that blood may flow from the man's genitals on to his legs during dancing.

Scarification of the body was also practised extensively throughout

▶ RIGHT: An Australian Aboriginal elder

Australia, particularly in Queensland. Parallel scars were made on the chests of initiated men among the Butchulla and Kabi Kabi of the Wide Bay Coast of central Queensland as late as the twentieth century. Among the Dieri of Northern Australia cicatrizations are common.

➤ *see* THE WAWILAK MYTH p. 278

MAORI

Maori are the indigenous people of Aotearoa (New Zealand).
They name themselves *tangata whenua* ('people of the land' or
'locals'). Maori often say that they are very spiritual people.
Although many Maori identify themselves as Christians,
Baha'is, Rastafarians or as members of other religions, there is
a sense in which these religions are added to an omnipresent
and traditional Maori spirituality that informs much of
contemporary Maori culture.

MAORI RELATIONSHIPS

Maori spirituality is centrally concerned with relationships between
people, and between them and the land. It is about genealogy, family
and neighbourliness, and it is about the importance of particular
locations and what takes place there. These concerns underlie the highly
respected arts of oratory and carving that are especially evident in Maori
gatherings of various sorts. Such arts and encounters
engage the dynamics of *mana* and *tapu*, and involve a
wide community of human and other-than-human
persons. All of this (and much more) comes
together when Maori meet guests on *marae*
(sacred spaces) and their associated
wharenui (meeting-houses), and *wharekai*
(dining-halls).

Over the last 30 years there has been a
renaissance of Maori culture. Traditional

▶ *RIGHT: Nineteenth century Maori chiefs*

knowledge has been found to be rich and resonant and, importantly, well able to speak to contemporary concerns and issues. Even in an era when most Maori live in cities rather than small villages, when they participate in global forums like the internet and trade, and even when many are unemployed or impoverished, the knowledge of divine and ancestral deeds is increasingly valued. Maori cultural centres have been established in the cities, children are introduced to Maori language via traditional stories and elders again explore the wisdom handed down in powerful and evocative oratory. What may seem like myths of strange and miraculous events are rediscovered as resources for facing ordinary life and its concerns, whether everyday or overwhelming. Central to Maori knowledge and culture is the creation and maintenance of more respectful relationships and lifestyles.

◆ *see* MARAE p. 290

MANA AND TAPU

Traditionally, when a child is born its placenta is buried in the family's land, and establishes the child's rights in that place, its *turangawaewae* ('standing place'). Throughout life each person is encouraged to exercise their rights not only in living in a place, but also in acts that unfold inherent potential and increase the prestige of the family and place. Everything and everyone is understood to have an essence, *mauri*. As people develop their abilities and realise their potential, they increase in *mana* (charisma or the authoritative prestige of gifted people). Some people, places or things have more *mana* than others – they are more gifted, valued or powerful. Encounters between different strengths or kinds of *mana* are potentially fraught, if not dangerous: whose prestige

▶ *RIGHT: Carvings inside a Maori meeting-house*

is greater? How will one strength affect the other? Should one skilful ability come into contact with another? Especially difficult are encounters between different tribes, or between Maori and other peoples. These encounters are therefore controlled by social restrictions, *tapu*, a word widely known in its wider Polynesian form, *tabu*. Sometimes *tapu* involves keeping *mana*-full things or people separate, establishing a place and clear boundaries for every activity. However, when it is necessary to bring two mana together there are careful protocols and procedures that negotiate the boundaries and establish new relationships.

◆ *see* MAORI ORATORY p. 291

MARAE

When hosts receive visitors they typically do so on the *marae*, an open space in which potential becomes apparent as different *mana* encounter one another. The local hosts greet visitors, recognize their *mana* and that of their ancestors (who are ever-present with the current generation), but also insist on the pre-eminent *mana*, prestige, of local ancestors and community. By various ceremonies the visitors are brought into the *marae* space and their potential friendship is established rather than their potential hostility. The gifts of oratory are demonstrated in speeches made and received by hosts and guests. These refer to aspects of traditional knowledge (*korero tahito*) that demonstrate respect to both parties. Local ancestors are also present in the form of more-or-less elaborately carved meeting houses (*wharenui*): their arms outstretched in welcome of visitors, their spine supporting the roof that shelters those currently alive and making space for further talking and decision-making.

◆ *see* MAORI RELATIONSHIPS p. 287

IWI, HAPU AND WHANAU

Maori identify themselves not only as the indigenous people of the land, but also as members of particular tribes (*iwi*) which are further sub-divided into clans (*hapu*) and families (*whanau*). Around 1,000 years ago Maori migrated from elsewhere in the Pacific in a fleet (or series of fleets) of large canoes, *waka*. Each *iwi* descends from a common ancestor who captained one of those canoes and first settled a particular area in the new land, Aotearoa, Land of the Long White Cloud (or Long Twilight). Within each *iwi*, families trace their descent from more recent but also highly honoured ancestors. Thus *whanau* refers not just to a relationship between parents and their children, but includes the ancestors, all those alive today, and all those yet to be born. Each family community has strong ties to particular places where ancestors lived and are buried, where each generation is born, works, socializes and gives birth to the next generation. In speech-making (*korero*) people introduce themselves by referring to place and genealogy.

see RECLAIMING TRADITIONS p. 136

MAORI ORATORY

The following summary of a traditional Maori theme is not principally about 'how the world got to be as it is' but might establish a point about the constraints imposed by over-close relationships. It continues to demonstrate that space is needed if people are going to grow towards the fulfilment of their potential.

Some time ago in the evolution of all things, Father Sky and Mother Earth were so intimately devoted to one another that there was no space between them. The children born of their passion had neither light nor space in which to grow. The overwhelming closeness of the

parents caused a division in the affections of the children. Eventually, with considerable effort, Tanemahuta pushed his father up and away from his mother. With space and light to grow, the children took on the responsibilities of furthering the great unfolding of life's potential.

These acts engendered not only growth, but also further acts both of conflict and community. Tanemahuta's act is partly replicated every time someone skilfully makes space for life and potential. It is clear in the tall forest trees (Tanemahuta's domain), but also in the lifting of roofs above floors in *wharenui* and all other *whare* (houses). It does not encourage disrespect to parents, partly because it was only justified by the extreme conditions endured before the separation, and partly because traditional knowledge also speaks of the priority of peace despite the occasional necessity of conflict.

◆ *see* MANA AND TAPU p. 288

◀ *LEFT: Carving in a meeting-house*

▲ ABOVE: A Maori animal totem

MAUI

It is not only gods who contribute to the creative unfolding of potential; humanity is also implicated in the choices and constraints that arise in life. Maui, ancestor of all Maori, achieved many things that made life better for his relatives and descendants – and, indeed, for all humanity. Maui considered the day too brief to be useful. So, with the help of his brothers, he trapped the sun in a large net, and forced it to travel across the sky slowly enough to provide sufficient time and light to achieve great things. On another occasion Maui is said to have used New Zealand's South Island as a canoe from which to fish up the North Island out of the depths. However, in the end, Maui failed. Or maybe it is simply that he tried to go too far, and his failure must be counted a benefit to all. Had his attempt to gain immortality for humanity succeeded, there would be absolutely no room left on earth by now. In brief, an orator might draw out the following traditional knowledge to support a particular argument about restraint.

Maui hoped that immortality might be found by entering the body of the divine-ancestress. Transforming himself into a lizard, he warned his companions not to laugh. But the sight of Maui entering head-first into the vagina of the sleeping Hine-nui-te-po was far too funny. The twittering laughter woke the sleeper, who closed her legs and crushed Maui to death.

⬦ *see* DIVINE ANCESTOR p. 260

▶ *RIGHT: Carving from Rotorua, New Zealand*

TIMELINES

2000 BC	1500 BC	1000 BC	500 BC	0

BUDDHISM NEPAL
BC 586 (Birth of Gautama Buddha)

CHRISTIANITY BETHLEHEM
6-4 BC (Birth of Jesus Christ)

CONFUCIANISM CHINA
551 BC (Birth of K'ung Fu Tzu)

HINDUISM 1500 BC
INDIA

JAINISM INDIA
599 BC (Birth of Mahavira)

JUDAISM 1200 BC
MOUNT SINAI (Moses receives the laws)

TAOISM CHINA
500 BC (Lao Tzu believed to have lived)

ZOROASTRIANISM Between 1200 and 600 BC
PERSIA (Birth of Zoroaster)

o

| AD 500 | AD 1000 | AD 1500 | AD 2004 |

THE BAHÁ'Í FAITH PERSIA
AD 1844 (Birth of the Báb)

ISLAM AD 570
MAKKAH (Birth of Muhammad)

SIKHISM PUNJAB
AD 1469 (Birth of Guru Nanak)

WORLD RELIGIOUS BELIEFS

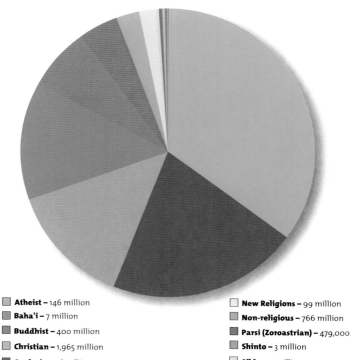

Atheist – 146 million

Baha'i – 7 million

Buddhist – 400 million

Christian – 1,965 million

Confucian – 6 million

Hindu – 740 million

Jain – 4 million

Jewish – 15 million

Muslim – 1,179 million

New Religions – 99 million

Non-religious – 766 million

Parsi (Zoroastrian) – 479,000

Shinto – 3 million

Sikh – 22 million

Taoist – 20 million

Tribal Religion – 244 million

Rastafari – 130,000

Please note that these figures are approximate and compiled from a number of sources

FESTIVALS

BAHA'I

Naw-Ruz
Following ancient Persian tradition, the Baha'i New Year and the end of a month of fasting. The Baha'i have a new calendar which begins on the spring equinox: March 21.

The Festival of Ridván (21 April to 2 May)
This festival commemorates the 12-day period when Baha'u'llah gathered the followers of Bab, announced to them the Revelation of Bab and revealed his identity as the Promised One. The followers of Bab then started calling themselves Baha'i. The first (21 April), the ninth (29 April) and twelfth (2 May) days of this period are Holy Days.

The Declaration of Bab (23 May)
On this date in 1844, Bab declared his mission.

Ascension of Baha'u'lla (29 May)

Martydom of Bab (9 July)
This took place in Tabriz in 1850.

Birth of Bab (20 October)

Birth of Baha'u'llah (12 November)
Celebration of the birth of the founder of the faith in 1817.

BUDDHISM
There are many special or holy days in the Buddhist calendar but the most important is Buddha Day. Buddhist festivals are joyous occasions; they usually consist of a visit to the local temple where food is offered to the monks and the Five Precepts are taken. This often consists of a *dharma* talk and food being given to the poor before, in the evening, a ceremony takes place which consists of walking round a *stupa* three times, as a sign of respect to the Buddha, Dhamma and Sangha.

Vesak (Wesak, Visaka and Visakha or Buddha Day)
Celebrates the birth, enlightenment and death of the Buddha. Vesak is named after the fifth month in the Indian calendar and is held on the first full moon day in May, except in a leap year when the festival is held in June. The Buddha is honoured through incense, flowers, candles and food. It is a joyful occasion as it celebrates the enlightenment of the Buddha and the potential for personal enlightenment, but Buddhists dress simply for the occasion, as if in mourning.

Dhammacakka (July)
Celebrates the Buddha's first sermon, in which he taught the principles of Buddhism.

CHRISTIANITY
Christian holidays celebrate the life of Jesus Christ.

Advent
The period of preparation for Christmas, and the start of the Church year.

Christmas (25 December)
The celebration of Jesus' birth.

The date of Easter changes each year according to a calculation connected with the full moon and therefore all holidays related to Easter (see below) also change.

Lent
A forty-day preparation for Easter, corresponding to the forty days Jesus spent in the wilderness before beginning his public ministry.

Palm Sunday
The first day of Holy Week, the week before Easter. It marks the day Jesus rode into Jerusalem on a donkey and was greeted by crowds throwing palm fronds in his path.

Good Friday
The solemn memorial of Jesus' death on the Cross.

Easter Sunday
The central Christian festival, celebrating the resurrection of Jesus.

Ascension Day
Celebration of Jesus' ascension to heaven, forty days after Easter.

Pentecost/Whitsun
The celebration of the day when God sent the Holy Spirit to the Apostles, ten days after Jesus' ascension.

Trinity Sunday
The first Sunday after Pentecost, honouring the Holy Trinity.

HINDUISM
Hinduism has many holidays, some celebrated by the majority of Hindus and others only by certain communities, or under special circumstances. Most of the holidays are based on the Hindu calendar, which originated in ancient India.

Diwali, 'The Festival of Light' (October to November)
Celebrating the New Year as well as Rama and Sita, the central figures of the Hindu epic *Ramayana*.

Dussehra (September/November)
This festival celebrates the triumph of good over evil, and frequently involves acting out the story told in the *Ramayana*. Held at the end of Navarati, nine nights in honour of Lakshmi.

Holi (March to April)
The harvest festival in honour of Krishna. It is a joyous occasion when people throw coloured water and bright powders at each other. In the evening visits are made to friends, and good wishes and sweetmeats are exchanged.

Mahashivaratri (February to March)
The festival of Shiva, the Hindu god who represents destruction before regeneration. A moveable festival, it is held on the fourteenth day of the dark fortnight during the lunar month of Phalguna.

ISLAM
Ramadan
Ramadan is the ninth month of the Islamic lunar calendar and its start depends on the sighting of the new moon. Ramadan was the month in which the first verses of the holy *Qur'an* were revealed to Prophet Muhammad. Muslims fast during daylight hours for all of the 29 or 30 days of this month. It is a time for Muslims to promote greater awareness of Allah and practice self-control and self-awareness. The festival of 'Id al-Fitr marks the end of Ramadan.

Hajj
This is the annual pilgrimage to Mecca undertaken from the eighth to the thirteenth day of Dhul-Hijjah, the twelfth month of the Islamic lunar calendar. As ordered by Allah, it is compulsory for every adult Muslim to complete Hajj once in a lifetime. The pilgrimage is from Mecca to Arafat, to Muzdalifah, to Mina and to Mecca again. Hajj is a journey of individual self-renewal, inspired by devotion to and consciousness of Allah Almighty. The festival of 'Id al-Adha marks the end of Hajj.

JAINISM
The birthday of Lord Mahavira (20 April)
The anniversary of his birth is celebrated with singing, music, praying and meditation.

Paryushana
The most important festival of the religion, Paryushana takes place in August and/or September depending upon the lunar calendar. Paryushana dates back to when the monks hibernated during the monsoon season. It is a time when Jains renew their faith and reflect on their spiritual journey. The holy week of Paryushana (ten days long for the Digambaras sect and eight days for the Svetambaras sect) concludes with a three-hour intensive prayer session.

JUDAISM
Purim (February to March) The carnival festival, which celebrates the story of Esther.

Passover or Pesach (March to April)
Commemorates the exodus of the Jews from Egypt. The major festival of the Jewish calendar, it lasts eight days, with the first and last days being holy days. The night when the Angel of Death passed over the house of the Jews is remembered and the Passover meal (*Seder*) represents the last meal the Jews ate in slavery.

Shavuot or Pentecost (May to June)
Celebrates the giving of the *Torah* by God to Moses on Mount Sinai.

Rosh HaShanah (September to October)
The Jewish New Year. This is usually spent in the synagogue. Each morning a *shofar* (ram's horn)

is blown as a call for renewed spiritual awareness and to remind everyone of the wrongs committed the previous year.

Yom Kippur (September to October)
The day of Atonement, which involves fasting and the deprivation of pleasure for a 25-hour period.

Sukkot (September to October)
A seven day festival which commemorates the forty years the Jews spent in the wilderness. Families build temporary shelters (*tabernacles*) symbolic of those used during this period and during harvest.

Chanukah (December)
Chanukah means dedication and the holiday is all about a Jew's dedication to the pursuit of religious and human ideals. There is historical meaning to the holiday too, as it commemorates the return of the Jerusalem Temple to the Jews after its desecration at the hands of foreign forces.

RASTAFARIANISM

Rastafarianism began with the coronation of Prince Ras Tafari Makonnen in 1930 as Emperor of Ethiopia. He later took the name Haile Selassie and is regarded as the true Messiah by Rastafarians. They celebrate important dates in his life:

Emperor Haile Selassie I's birthday (23 July)

Haile Selassie's coronation (2 November)

SIKHISM

Some major Sikh festivals are held on the same day as Hindu festivals, such as Holi and Diwali, but have different meanings for Sikhs. Sikh festivals commemorate special events in the lives of the Gurus. In addition, Sikhs celebrate festivals called *gurpurbs* where the *Guru Granth Sahib* is read in its entirety and may be carried through the streets in procession.

Baisakhi (13 April)
Celebrates the foundation of the Khalsa – the community of 'pure ones' – in 1699.

The Martyrdom of Guru Arjan Dev (May to June)
Anniversary of the martyrdom of the fifth *guru* of Sikhism.

The Birthday of Guru Nanak (11 November)
The celebration of the founder of Sikhism's birthday

The Martyrdom of Guru Tegh Bahadur (24 November)
Anniversary of the martyrdom of the ninth *guru* in 1675.

The Birthday of Guru Gobind Singh (5 January)
The celebration of the birth of the tenth *guru*.

SHINTO

Communal festivals are now voluntary affairs; the largest ones can be spectacular. They feature magnificent floats decked with lanterns, a retinue of priests and other costumed participants. Many small local festivals retain the character of solemn religious rites, followed by communal celebrations.

TAOISM

There are hundreds of local festivals but these are the main ones:

Chinese New Year (January to February)
The Chinese lunar calendar is a yearly one; the start of the year is based on the cycle of the moon and so the New Year can fall anywhere between late January and the middle of February.

Ching Ming Festival (March to April)
A form of ancestor worship that dates back thousands of years, Ching Ming is when Chinese families visit the graves of their ancestors. They show respect by clearing away weeds from the gravestones and offering wine and fruit.

The Hungry Ghost Festival
The Chinese believe that during the seventh month of the lunar New Year, the gates of hell open to allow the hungry ghosts to wander earth looking for food. It is thought that offering food appeases the ghosts and wards off bad luck. Other offerings are used to placate the ghosts, for example forms of entertainment such as concerts. Feasts are prepared for dead ancestors who, it is believed, can return to their families during this time.

ZOROASTRIANISM
Gahambars
These are the six seasonal festivals with the New Year festival, Navroz being the largest of the six. The spring festival is also important – it is in honour of Rapithwin, the personification of noonday and summer.

SACRED TEXTS

BAHA'I
Kitab-i-Aqdas
The title of this work, revealed by the prophet Baha'u'llah during his imprisonment in Acre (Akka) in the 1860s–1890s, means 'The Most Holy Book'.

BUDDHISM
Pali Canon
The Buddhist faith has a wide range of sacred texts, with different works having their own relevance to the various schools of Buddhism. One well-known sacred Buddhist text is the Pali Canon, which describes the teachings of Buddha and is divided into three sections called *pitaka* ('baskets'). Pali is an old Indian language which is similar to the one that the Buddha spoke.

CHRISTIANITY
Bible, Book of Common Prayer
The main text of Christianity is the Bible, the title of which comes from the ancient Greek word for 'books'. The Bible was written over a period of around 1000 years in a variety of styles and languages (based around Hebrew and Greek). The form we recognize today was reached in AD 397. There are two main sections: the Old Testament (similar to the Jewish Bible but interpreted differently by Christians) and the New Testament (which centres around the life and deeds of Jesus Christ and was probably written between AD 48–95). Some Christians believe that the Bible contains the literal word of God, while others maintain that it was written by prophets who were inspired by God, and that the work is therefore open to interpretation.

There are various other Christian texts, one of which is the Book of Common Prayer, an Anglican work reformed by Archbishop Thomas Cramner in 1549, which recasts many Roman Catholic texts.

CONFUCIANISM
The Analects of Confucius, The Book of Mencius, The Great Learning, The Doctrine of the Mean
Soon after his death in 479 BC, Confucius' teachings were compiled by his followers into a book entitled *Lun Yu*, or The Analects of Confucius, which became one of the most influential books of East Asia. Mencius (371–289 BC) developed Confucianism further

and wrote the Book of Mencius, another important Confucian text. The other key works are The Great Learning (written in 500–200 BC) and the mystical Doctrine of the Mean. These ancient texts were arranged into their present form in the late 12th century.

EGYPTIAN
The Book of the Dead
The Book of the Dead consists of a series of almost two hundred spells and magical writings, of which certain extracts would be copied out onto papyrus, cloth, a coffin or even a tomb wall, to facilitate a deceased person's entry into the afterlife.

EUROPEAN LANDSCAPE RELIGIONS
Pre-Christian indigenous Northern European religions were based upon the climate and landscape. Ancient texts preserving such landscape myths include the Irish *Dindsenchas*, and *Landnámabók*, a text written in response to the Icelandic landscape by the settlers who arrived there in the 9th and 10th centuries AD.

GREEK
The works of Homer (8th century BC) tell of the Olympian gods and goddesses of Greek mythology. The most important epics are the warlike *Iliad*, and the *Odyssey*, an account of the long and difficult homecoming of Odysseus.

HINDUISM
Vedas, Mahabharata, Ramayana, Upanishads
Hindu scriptures are divided into two main groups, the *Shruti* ('that which is heard') and *Smriti* ('that which is remembered').

The *Shruti* texts deal with the eternal principles of Hinduism and consist of the four *Vedas*, which are thought to be the oldest books in the world. *Rig Veda* ('Songs of Knowledge') is a cycle of around 1000 sacred songs, and is the longest *Veda*, as well as being the earliest and the most sacred to the Hindu faith. The other *Vedas* are *Sama Veda*, *Yajur Veda* and *Atharva Veda*.

The *Upanishads*, of which there are around 108, contain the philosophy known as the *Vedanta*, and were designed to facilitate the reading and understanding of the *Vedas*. The text contains a number of dialogues between students and their *gurus*, which explain clearly the principles laid down in the *Vedas*.

There are eighteen *Smritis*, which explain how to apply the principles of the *Vedas* to practical situations. The most famous texts from the *Smritis* are the two great epic poems, the *Mahabharata* and the *Ramayana*. The *Mahabharata* is a vast epic of over 100,000 couplets and was written around 300 BC– AD 300. The story tells of a civil war between two branches of a ruling family, and can be read as an allegory of the fight between the forces of good and evil. It includes the *Bhagavad Gita* ('The Song of the Lord'), a beautiful, spiritual poem telling the story of the god Krishna and Prince Arjuna, and their great battle for the kingdom of heaven. The discourse between the two develops a complete system of ethics, containing the essence of the *Vedas* and the *Upanishads*. The other great epic poem of the Smritis, the *Ramayana* (written around the same time as the *Mahabharata*), tells the story of Rama's rescue of his wife Sita from the demon king Ravana.

ISLAM
Qur'an
A literal translation of 'al-Qur'an', the name of Islam's sacred text, is 'the recitation'. Muslims believe that the Qur'an is *kalam Allah* (the word of God) as revealed to the Prophet Muhammad over 22 years through the medium of the Angel Jibril (Gabriel). By the time of Muhammad's death in 632 AD, Muslims believe that the entire content of the Qur'an had been revealed. The main themes of the Qur'an are: God and monotheism (*tawhid*); other 'spiritual' beings such as angels, Satan, *jinns*; the Prophets of God sent as 'warners' to humankind; the Last Judgement and the Afterlife; the life of the Muslim community, including liturgical, social and legal topics. The Qur'an is Islam's primary theological and legal authority.

JUDAISM
Torah, Talmud, Shulchan Aruch
The main sacred text in the Jewish religion is the written *Torah* ('teaching'). This consists of the Pentateuch ('written law') – the first five books of the Hebrew Bible (*Genesis, Exodus, Leviticus, Numbers* and *Deuteronomy*), which were said to have been revealed to Moses on Mount Sinai. The interpretations of the *Torah* by the *Rabbis* are gathered in the *Mishnah* ('repetition'), which was written around 200 AD and sets out the great structure of Judaism. This, together with its attendant commentary the *Gemara* ('completion' of the

discussion on each topic), comprises the *Talmud*, which is second only to the *Torah* in authority within the Jewish faith. The essence of this work was distilled into the *Shulchan Aruch* in the late 16th century, explaining the guidelines of Judaism in a more accessible form.

RASTAFARIANISM
The Bible, Kebra Negast, Fetha Negast
The main sacred text for followers of the Rastafarian faith is the Bible (*see* Christianity). There are also two important Ethiopian texts: the *Kebra Negast* ('glory of the kings') and the *Fetha Negast* (a book of royal laws).

SIKHISM
Guru Granth Sahib
The *Guru Granth Sahib* was compiled in the mid 16th century. Also known as the *Adi Granth* ('first book'), it contains hymns written by the *Gurus* as well as by writers of other faiths whose philosophies conformed to the Sikh school of thought. The work contains 5,894 hymns altogether, of which the founder of Sikhism, Guru Nanak, contributed 974. The *Guru Granth Sahib* serves to provide the teaching and guidance no longer available from a human *Guru* and is generally treated as if it were human; it is kept in a room of its own, resting on cushions upon a small table, and is covered by a special canopy and cloths.

SUMERIAN
The Epic of Gilgamesh
Gilgamesh was the fifth king of the first dynasty of Uruk (in present-day southern Iraq) and reigned in around 2600 BC. He was the subject of five Sumerian poems probably written six centuries later. The epic tells of how Gilgamesh sets out on a quest for immortality and how, after numerous adventures, he fails and is forced to accept the reality of death. His tale was also adopted by later peoples of the Ancient Near East.

ZOROASTRIANISM
Avesta
The *Avesta* comprises a number of texts including the *Gathas*, a series of hymns written in an ancient language called Avestan by Zoroaster, the prophet. According to Zoroastrian tradition, the holy book has been destroyed twice, firstly by Alexander the Great and then by the Arabs. The work survived in oral form and was written down in the late 18th century by the French philologist Anquetil du Perron. The texts are quite obscure and their meanings are not always clear, and so they have been subject to a variety of interpretations.

GLOSSARY

Abraham: One of the three Jewish Patriarchs who originally received God's promise and blessing.

absolution: (Christian) Pronouncement by priest of forgiveness of sins.

adhan: (Islam) Call to prayer.

Adi Granth: (Sikh) The 'first book'; the name given to the collection of hymns put together by Guru Arjun, and the basis of the Sikh holy book.

Adur: (Zoroastrian) Sacred fire.

Advent: 'Coming'; the period observed by Christians in preparation for Christmas.

Aesir: The race of great and proactive gods in Norse mythology.

ages of man: (Greek) In Greek mythology, the five races of humans created by Zeus. The first race, the Race of Gold, was succeeded by those of Silver, Bronze, Heroes and Iron (the current race).

agnosticism: Doubt as to the truth of the reality of God.

ahimsa: (Hindu/Jain) Non-violence to all living things.

Ahura Mazda: (Zoroastrian) The Wise Lord, the creator.

ajiva: (Jain) Everything which is not *jiva* (soul).

akhira: Islamic term for life after death.

Al-Fatiha: (Islam) 'The Opener'; the first *surah* of the *Qur'an*.

Allah: (Islam) 'The God'.

Amesha Spenta: (Zoroastrian) The seven Holy Immortals, offshoots of God.

Amish: (Christian) Protestant movement founded in Europe in the late 17th century. Followers, renowned for their austere, separatist lifestyle, later settled in the United States and Canada.

amrit: Sikh initiation by baptism in sweetened water stirred by a two-edged sword.

Anabaptists: (Christian) A persecuted radical Protestant group that arose during the Reformation in sixteenth-century Europe. Followers believed that only adults should be baptized and that they should live apart from the wider society.

Anand Sahib: A Sikh hymn sung at all services.

ancestor worship: The veneration of the dead by their relatives. It plays an important part in many religions including those of China and Africa.

angels: (Jewish/Christian) Spiritual beings, messengers of God.

Anglican: Christian churches in full communion with the Church of England.

Angra Mainyu: (Zoroastrian) The Hostile Spirit, source of all evil.

animism: Belief that spirits are present in the natural world.

Anubis: Jackal-headed god of ancient Egypt, the guardian of tombs.

Apocrypha: (Jewish/Christian) Greek for 'Hidden'. These are the books whose authority is accepted as part of the Bible by the Roman Catholic Church but not by all Christians.

Apollo: Major god of both Greeks and Romans, the sun-god and patron of the arts.

Apostle: (Christian) 'One who is sent'; name for the twelve original followers of Jesus.

Archbishop: Chief bishop. Britain has three – Canterbury, York and Wales.

Ardas: Sikh prayer.

Ares: Greek god of war.

Ark: (Jewish) Artefact, probably in the form of a miniature portable temple, containing the *Torah*.

Artemis: Greek goddess of hunting.

Ascension: (Christian) The ascent of Jesus Christ into Heaven after his resurrection.

asceticism: The practice of self-denial in order to reach a higher spiritual level. Found in many religions, it includes fasting, self-mortification and celibacy.

Asgard: In Norse mythology, the home of the gods.

Ashkenazim: Jews originating from central and Eastern European countries.

ashram: In Indian religion, a monastery or communal house of meditation.

atheism: Denial of the existence of God.

atman: (Hindu) An individual soul, but can refer to body, soul or mind.

atonement: (Christian) The bringing together of God and humankind through the death and resurrection of Christ.

atua: In Polynesian religions, a god or other supernatural being.

avatar: (Hindu) Incarnation of a god.

Baha'i: A faith arising out of the Persian Bab movement in the 19th century.

Baisakhi: (Sikh) Festival held in April, celebrating the founding of the Khalsa.

baptism: (Christian) Sacrament of initiation into the church involving immersion in, or sprinkling with, water.

Baptist Churches: Christian churches whose main distinguishing feature is believer's adult baptism by total immersion.

baraka: Islamic word for blessings.

Bar Mitzvah: Ceremony by which Jewish boys, aged 13, become adult members of the community.

Bat Mitzvah: Ceremony by which Jewish girls, aged 12, become adult members of the community.

Bhagavad Gita: (Hindu) The Song of the Lord: a section of the epic poem the *Mahabharata*, and to many Hindus the most important scripture.

bhajan: Hindu devotional song or hymn.

bhakti: (Hindu) Warm devotion to a single god.

Bible: The collection of books that Christians view as the revelation of God's word.

bimah: Jewish desk or lectern at which to lead services and to read the *Torah*.

bishop: The most senior order of ministry in the Christian Church.

Bismillah: (Islam) 'In the name of Allah'.

Blavatsky, Helena: Founder of the Theosophical Society in 1875 and one of the first to present Eastern philosophy as accessible to Westerners.

Bodh-Gaya: Place where Buddha received enlightenment; the tree under which the Buddha sat was called the *bodhi*-tree.

Bodhisattva: (Mahayana Buddhist) Buddha-to-be who defers his final liberation to work for others.

Book of Common Prayer: (Christian) Main traditional book of worship of the Anglican Church.

Book of Mormon: (Christian) Sacred book of Mormonism, as revealed to Joseph Smith, the story of the journey to America of early biblical peoples.

Book of the Dead: Name given to various collections of incantations buried with the dead of ancient Egypt to assist their souls through judgement.

Booths, Feast of: Jewish harvest festival also called *Sukkot* or Tabernacles.

Brahma: Hindu deity.

Brahman: (Hindu) The impersonal, absolute reality, the universal soul.

breviary: (Christian) Liturgical book containing correct instructions for daily church services.

Buddha: 'The Enlightened One'; applicable to any human who has reached enlightenment, especially Siddharta Gautama, who lived in India in the 6th century BC, the founder of Buddhism.

Buddhism: The religion which developed from the teaching of Siddharta Gautama, the Buddha.

Calvin, John: (Christian) Protestant church reformer and theologian.

caste: Sub-divisions within the *Varna* in Indian society.

catechism: Instruction on Christian faith.

cathedral: (Christian) The principal church in a Bishop's jurisdiction (Diocese), its size and splendour reflects its role as the location of the bishop's throne (*Cathedra*).

catholic: 'Universal'; the whole Christian Church throughout the world.

Cernunnos: 'The horned one'; Celtic horned god of fertility.

Ch'an: (Chinese) Meditation.

Charismatic: (Christian) Modern movement within the Church which emphasizes spiritual gifts.

ch'i: (Chinese) Material energy which combines with *li* to make up all things.

chanani: (Sikh) The canopy over the *Guru Granth Sahib*, used as a mark of respect.

Chanukah: (Jewish) Festival of Light, or Dedication, lasting eight days and celebrating the rededication of the temple in Jerusalem in 164 BC.

chela: (Indian) A follower of a *guru*.

Ching: (Chinese) Classical text.

Christ: see **Jesus Christ**

Christian: Follower of Jesus Christ.

Christian Science: Unorthodox Christian sect founded in the USA in 1866 by Mary Baker Eddy.

Christmas: Christian festival commemorating the birth of Jesus Christ, celebrated on 25 December.

Church/church: The community of Christians on earth and in heaven, or the building in which Christians worship.

communion: Christian rite, also known as Mass (Roman Catholic), Eucharist (Anglican), Liturgy (Russian Orthodox) and The Lord's Supper (non-Episcopal). The primary sacrament of sharing Christ's life by partaking of the bread and

wine as his body and blood.

confirmation: Christian rite (in Episcopalian churches) by which a person achieves full entry into the Church.

Confucius: Chinese administrator of the 5th century BC whose system of social ethics has greatly influenced Chinese society.

Coptic Church: The Christian Church of Egypt and Ethiopia.

corroboree: Australian Aboriginal festival or ceremony.

Counter-Reformation: (Christian) The revival of the Roman Catholic Church in response to the Reformation.

cosmology: Beliefs about the structure of the universe.

covenant: A bargain or agreement, particularly that struck between the Jews and Yahweh, with Yahweh promising his protection as long as the Jews adhered to the *Torah*.

Cranmer, Thomas: (Christian) Archbishop of Canterbury who helped King Henry VIII overthrow the Pope's authority in England, and created a new order of worship with his Prayer Books (1549 and 1552).

creed: Formal statement of Christian religious belief.

crucifixion: A death penalty widely used by the Romans which involved fastening the victim's arms and legs to a cross or stake and leaving him to die. In Christianity, Jesus was crucified by the Romans under Pontius Pilate.

cult: Traditionally, a style of worship and its associated rituals. More commonly used to describe a religious group characterized by relatively small size and existing in a state of tension with the host society. In popular usage, a dangerous or destructive religious movement.

Dalai Lama: Religious leader of Tibetan Buddhism.

David: (Jewish/Christian) King of the Israelites 1000 years BC, to whom authorship of many of the psalms is ascribed.

dawa: Inviting people to Islam, usually by good example.

deity: A god or goddess; a supernatural being.

dharma: (Hindu/Buddhist) Cosmic order, the truth of existence, universal law, religious duty.

dhul-hijjah: Last month of the Islamic year, the month of the *hajj*.

dhyana: (Hindu/Buddhist) Meditation.

diaspora: The Jewish people living scattered round the world, that is, not in Israel.

dietary laws: Rules about food and drink which are characteristic of a particular religion.

digambara: (Jain) 'Sky-clad' – Jains who adhere to the rule of nudity for monks.

disciple: Follower of a religious leader or teaching; also the name given to Jesus' 12 original companions.

divination: Any method of predicting future events whether through 'reading' the stars, runes or the entrails of animals.

Diwali: (Hindu/Sikh) Festival held in October. Hindu Festival of Lights marking the new year; Sikhs remember the release of Guru Har Gobind from prison.

doctrine: Religious teaching or belief.

dogma: A truth defined by a religious group and believed to be essential to its teachings.

Dreamtime (Australian Aboriginal) The period in which ancestral beings shaped the earth.

Druids: In Celtic society, the caste of priests, arbitrators and healers.

dualism: The belief that everything is divided into good and evil – whether beings, deities or concepts.

dukkha: (Buddhist) Suffering caused by the effects of bad *karma*: the nature of existence.

Dussehra: (Hindu) Festival, usually celebrating the victory of Rama over Ravana on the tenth day of the moon.

Easter: (Christian) The central festival of the Church, celebrating the resurrection of Jesus Christ from the dead.

Ecumenism: The promotion of understanding between traditions within a single religion. The term is used most commonly within Christianity.

Eddy, Mary Baker: American founder of Christian Science and founder of the *Christian Science Monitor* newspaper.

Enlightenment: Movement emphasizing human reason and rational scientific enquiry which arose in the 18th century across much of western Europe and North America. In France, many of the enlightenment philosophers attacked established religion.

Epic of Gilgamesh: Babylonian poem dating from the 7th century BC, telling the story of Gilgamesh's search for immortality.

Epistle: Letter in the New Testament, usually from one of the Apostles to an early Christian community.

ethics: The study of human values and moral conduct.

Eucharist: (Christian) 'Thanksgiving'; the central act of Christian worship as instituted by Christ the night before his death, involving sharing bread and wine to symbolize sharing in Christ's life and death.

Evangelicals: (Christian) Christians of any denomination who emphasize the importance of the Bible and the need for personal conversion.

Evangelism: Preaching the Christian Gospel to the unconverted.

Exodus: The flight from Egypt of the Jewish people, led by Moses.

faith: An attitude of trust and certainty relating the worshipper to his or her God or religion. While central to, for example, Islam and Christianity, in Hinduism correct behaviour is more important.

fasting: Forgoing food and/or water for a period of time in order to advance spiritually. Muslims are expected to fast completely between sunrise and sunset during *Ramadan*.

fatwa: In Islamic jurisprudence, a legal opinion.

festivals: Originally religious celebrations which included sacred communal feasts, hence their name. Many festivals are connected with rites of passage or seasonal celebrations.

Five Ks: The five symbols every initiated Sikh wears.

Five Pillars of Islam: Five duties every Muslim must undertake in daily life.

Five Precepts: Five ethical restraints on the lives of Buddhists.

font: (Christian) Large basin holding the water used in baptism by sprinkling.

Four Noble Truths: Buddha's summary of his teaching.

Four Stages of Life: (Hindu) Outline of a man's ideal spiritual journey through life.

Fox, George: (Christian) Founder of the Society of Friends (Quakers).

Francis of Assisi: (Christian) Founder of the Franciscan Order, embracing a simple life and especially concerned with Nature.

Free Churches: (Christian) Protestant churches in England which are non-Episcopalian and independent of the Church of England.

Frey: Norse god of fertility.

Freya: Norse goddess, patron of sorcery and sister of Frey.

Friends, Society of: see Quakers.

Fundamentalism: (Christian) Originally, a Christian movement which arose in the United States in the early 20th century. Followers abided by The Fundamentals, tracts which laid down the 'fundamentals' of Christianity and insisted on strict rather than metaphorical interpretations of the Bible. More generally, the term refers to the conservative wing of religions. Amongst non-fundamentalists the term can be used to imply intolerance and anti-intellectualism.

Gandhi: Indian spiritual and political leader, 1869–1948.

Ganesh: (Hindu) Elephant-headed deity of luck and wealth.

Ganges: India's holy river, sacred to Hindus, in which pilgrims may wash away evil.

Gautama: Family name of the Buddha.

Gemara: Jewish commentary on *Mishnah*, included in the *Talmud*.

Gentile: Person who is not a Jew.

ghost dance: North American Indian dance believed to lead

to the resurrection of all dead Indians.

ghusl: Islamic ablution carried out before prayer (see *wudu*).

God: Deity, Divinity, creator of the world and sustainer of life.

Good Friday: (Christian) The Friday before Easter, the day on which Jesus Christ was crucified; kept as a holy day.

Gospel: (Christian) 'Good News'; The teachings of Jesus. Also one of the four books of the New Testament written by Matthew, Mark, Luke and John.

grace: Central concept of Christianity through which salvation occurs not on merit but only by the power of God.

Granth: Sikh sacred scriptures.

granthi: (Sikh) Person who reads from the *Guru Granth Sahib* at services.

gurdwara: Sikh place of worship and meeting house, housing a copy of the *Granth*.

Gurmukhi: Language in which the Sikh scriptures are written

gurpurb: Sikh festival.

Guru: 'Teacher'; i) spiritual guide; ii) (Sikh) one of the ten teachers who ruled the Sikh community from Nanak to Gobind Singh.

Guru Amar Das: Third Sikh Guru, who set up the institution of the *langar*.

Guru Angad: Second Sikh Guru, who chose Gurmukhi as the script in which the Sikh hymns should be written.

Guru Arjun: Fifth Sikh Guru, who built the Golden Temple at Amritsar and collected together the Sikh hymns, with others, to form the *Adi Granth*.

Guru Gobind Singh: Tenth and last Sikh Guru, who instituted the Khalsa.

Guru Granth Sahib: The Sikh scripture; the final version of the *Adi Granth* and the teacher of the Sikhs in place of a human *guru*.

Guru Har Gobind: Sixth Sikh Guru, who encouraged the military aspect of Sikhism.

Guru Har Krishnan: Eighth Sikh Guru.

Guru Nanak: First Sikh Guru.

Guru Ram Das: Fourth Sikh Guru, who founded the holy city of Amritsar.

Hadith: (Islam) A record of something said or done by Muhammad.

hafiz: (Islam) A person who knows the *Qur'an* by heart.

hagadah: (Jewish) A moral precept or teaching, many of which are to be found in the *Talmud*.

hajj: (Islam) Pilgrimage to Mecca.

hajji: (Islam) Muslim man who has completed a pilgrimage to Mecca.

hajjah: (Islam) Muslim woman who has completed a pilgrimage to Mecca.

halal: (Islam) Action which is permitted. Referring to meat, that which is slaughtered according to Islamic requirements.

Hanuman: (Hindu) Monkey-god who in the *Ramayana* led an army of monkeys to victory for Rama against a host of demons.

Hare Krishna: (Hindu) Mantra used by followers of Krishna or, in the most popular version, to invoke both Krishna and Rama.

Hasidim: (Jewish) Movement founded in Eastern Europe in the late 18th century with an emphasis on mysticism.

Hathor: Ancient Egyptian goddess of the sky.

Heaven: Realm of the gods; in Christianity the ultimate destination of the saved.

Hebrew: Language of the Jewish people and of the modern state of Israel.

Hell: The region where the evil are punished after death; in Christianity, total separation from God.

heresy: The denial of or deviation from a religious doctrine (esp. Christian).

hijra: (Islam) Muhammad's departure from Mecca to Medina; an exodus.

Hindu: Indian religion and those who practise it.

Holi: (Hindu) Spring festival dedicated to Krishna, marked by boisterous games and the throwing of coloured water and powders.

Holocaust: The name given to the murder of six million Jews in Nazi concentration camps during the Second World War.

Holy Communion: (Christian) Name usually given to the Eucharist by the Anglican and some Protestant Churches.

Holy Spirit/Holy Ghost: (Christian) The third person of the Trinity, the source of faith and holiness, often

portrayed as fire or wind, or as a dove.

Horus: Ancient Egyptian hawk-headed god, associated with the pharaoh.

huppah: Four-poster canopy used at Jewish wedding ceremonies.

hymn: Sacred song, usually sung as part of an act of worship.

ibada: (Islam) Acts of worship.

icon: An object of devotion, an image of a saint or divine figure, usually painted or in mosaic, used in devotions especially in Greek or Russian Orthodox Churches.

Id al-Adha: (Islam) Festival of sacrifice, coinciding with the end of the *hajj*.

Id al-Fitr: (Islam) Festival marking the end of *Ramadan*.

ijma: (Islam) The consensus of opinion in the Muslim community; lawmaking.

imam: (Islam) Prayer leader in a Sunni Muslim community; for Shi'ites a more charismatic and authoritative religious leader

immortality: The continued spiritual existence of individuals after death.

Inca: The divine king of the Inca people of South America, whose empire lasted from AD 1100 to the Spanish conquest in 1532.

incarnation: i) Christian doctrine that God became human in Jesus Christ; ii) Hindu doctrine of *avatar*.

incense: Aromatic smoke given off by burning special resins or spices, used during worship.

indigenous religion: A 'home-grown' religion, one originating in and associated with a particular region, such as the Shinto religion of Japan.

Indra: Early Hindu god of war and storm.

ISKCON: International Society for Krishna Consciousness, modern cult based on Hinduism, founded in 1965 by Swami Prabhupada.

Isaac: One of the three main Jewish patriarchs, son of Abraham and father of Jacob, who lived in the 18th century BC and originally received God's promise and blessing.

Ishtar: Babylonian goddess associated with fertility rites. Known as Astarte to the Phoenicians and Ashtoreth to the Hebrews.

Isis: Ancient Egyptian goddess of fertility.

Islam: Literally 'submission'; religion based on God's revelation to the Prophet Muhammad in the 7th century AD.

Israel: i) Name given by God to Jacob the patriarch and hence to his descendants, 'the people of Israel'; ii) The modern state of Israel founded in 1948.

Jacob: One of the three main Jewish patriarchs, son of Isaac, and later given the name *Israel* by God.

Jahannam: (Islam) Muslim term for Hell.

Jain: A devotee of Jainism.

Jainism: Ascetic Indian religion which arose in 6th century BC.

Janamsakhi: (Sikh) Punjabi writings celebrating the life of Guru Nanak.

jati: Hindu group also called a caste, a sub-division within a *Varna*.

Jehovah's Witnesses: Unorthodox Christian sect founded in the USA in 1884 by Charles Taze Russell, whose followers believe in a literal interpretation of the Bible.

jenoi: (Hindu) Sacred thread worn by Indian men of the 'twice-born' castes.

Jerusalem: Principal city of the early Jewish people, remaining the focus for Jewish religious ideals. It is also a holy city for Christians and Muslims.

Jesus Christ: (Christian) Teacher, believed to be the Son of God, who lived in first-century Palestine and who is believed to have risen from the dead. Christians believe him to be the Messiah and await his Second Coming and the fulfilment of the Kingdom of God.

Jew: i) A person who is a member of the Jewish race; ii) A person who worships according to the Jewish faith.

jihad: (Islam) literally 'struggle'; the 'greater *jihad*' is an inner spiritual struggle for righteousness; the 'lesser' *jihad* is external and often associated with the idea of 'holy war'.

jinja: A Shinto shrine.

jinn: (Islam) Fire spirits, capable of good but usually portrayed as wicked.

jiva: (Jain) 'Soul', capable of liberation from *karma*.

John the Baptist: (Christian) Cousin of Jesus and his forerunner; he baptized Jesus.

Joseph: (Christian) Earthly father of Jesus, and husband of Mary.

Judaism: The religion of the Jewish people, deriving from the religion of the people of ancient Israel. It is one of the great monotheistic religions.

judgement: The assessment of, and conclusion to the destiny of, human souls by the divinity.

Ka'ba: (Islam) The sanctuary in the grand mosque at Mecca towards which Muslims face in prayer.

kach: (Sikh) Type of shorts; one of the Five Ks.

kachina: Ceremonial masks used among the Pueblo Indians of the American south-west.

Kali: (Hindu) Goddess, consort of Shiva, who is both destroyer and giver of life.

Kami: (Shinto) Traditional nature spirit.

kangha: (Sikh) Comb worn in the hair; one of the Five Ks.

kara: (Sikh) Steel bracelet; one of the Five Ks.

karma: (Hindu/Buddhist) Natural law which governs the effect of deeds in this life and in subsequent lives.

kashrut: Jewish dietary requirements, setting out what is '*kosher*', or pure.

Kaur: 'Princess'; name given to all Sikh women who have joined the Khalsa.

kesh: (Sikh) Uncut hair; one of the Five Ks.

Khadija: (Islam) First wife of Muhammad.

Khalsa: Special Sikh group, entry to which is voluntary and by initiation.

kirpan: (Sikh) Sword; one of the Five Ks.

Kitab-i-Aqdas: Holy Book of the Baha'i Faith.

koan: (Zen Buddhist) Enigmatic or paradoxical questions used to develop intuition.

Kojiko: Shinto scripture, the oldest book in the Japanese language, but written in Chinese characters.

kosher: 'Fit, proper'; used of food permitted by Jewish dietary laws.

Krishna: (Hindu) An *avatar* of Vishnu and one of the best-loved gods in the Hindu pantheon.

laity: The non-ordained members of a religious community.

Laksmi: (Hindu) Goddess of fortune.

lama: Tibetan religious leader, some of whom have been credited with magical powers attained after long ascetic training.

langar: (Sikh) 'Guru's kitchen' – meal served in the dining hall of the *gurdwara*.

Lao-Tzu: Chinese author of *Tao Te Ching* and a contemporary of Confucius.

lares: Roman household gods.

Latter-day Saints: *see* Mormons.

Lent: (Christian) A forty-day preparation for Easter, corresponding to the forty days Jesus spent in the wilderness before beginning his public ministry.

li: Central concept of Confucianism; rituals, rules of good behaviour, spiritual substance or energy which, correctly applied, guarantee social harmony.

Limbo: (Christian) According to Roman Catholic doctrine, the place for souls which go neither to Heaven nor to Hell (e.g. souls of unbaptized babies).

liturgy: (Christian) Divine service according to a prescribed ritual.

Loki: Norse god associated with mischief.

Lord's Supper: (Christian) Alternative name for the Eucharist, generally used by Evangelical Christians.

lotus position: Seated position considered by Hindus and Buddhists to be an aid to meditation.

love: Reverence for other humans; the primary Christian virtue.

Luther, Martin: (Christian) Founder of the German Reformation within the Church.

Magi: Priests or wise men from Persia; the wise men who came to see the baby Jesus Christ in Bethlehem. Followers of Zoroastrianism.

Mahabharata: (Hindu) Great epic scripture, compiled in 2nd or 3rd century BC.

Maharishi Mahesh Yogi: Guru of the Transcendental Meditation movement.

Mahavira: Great Jain leader of 6th century BC.

Mahayana: 'Greater Vehicle' – form of Buddhism practised in Nepal, Tibet, Korea, China and Japan.

Mahdi: (Islam) 'The guided one' – the one who, according to Shi'a teaching, will come at the end of the world.

Makkah: *see* Mecca

Mecca (Makkah): Holy city of Islam, birthplace of Muhammad. Pilgrimage to Mecca is one of the Five Pillars of Islam, and all Muslims face Mecca to pray.

mana: Sacred power associated with gods or with natural forces in primal religions.

mandala: (Tibetan Buddhist) A visual aid to concentration in meditation in the form of a series of concentric circles.

mandir: Hindu temple.

Manji Sahib: (Sikh) The cushion on which the *Guru Granth Sahib* rests while being read.

mantra: In Eastern religions, word or phrase of power with special resonance and an aid to meditation.

marae: (Polynesian) Sacred area with shrine.

Mary: (Christian) Mother of Jesus Christ, honoured by all Christians and venerated by Roman Catholics and Eastern Orthodox Christians.

Mass: Standard Roman Catholic term for a service with the Eucharist as its main focus.

matsuri: Shinto festivals or ceremonies.

matzoh: (Jewish) Unleavened bread.

Maya: i) Ancient Middle American civilization at its height 300–900 AD; ii) In Hindu thought: illusion or deception; iii) Mother of Buddha.

meditation: Deep contemplation, often assisted by breathing exercises, mantras or special posture, intended to attain either self-knowledge or union with the divine.

menorah: (Jewish) Seven- or eight-branched candelabrum used in synagogues.

Messiah: Hebrew word for 'Anointed One', referring to the person chosen by God to be

king; to Christians this means Jesus Christ of Nazareth.

Methodist Churches: (Christian) Churches which developed from the preaching of John Wesley, answerable to the Methodist Conference, first established by John Wesley in 1784.

mezuzah: Box containing scriptures fixed to the doorpost of a Jewish household.

Middle Way: The Buddha's description of his moderate teaching, designed to lead to *nirvana*.

Midrash: Jewish tradition of interpretation and discussion intended to reveal inner meaning of the *Torah*.

mihrab: (Islam) Semi-circular recess in the wall of a mosque which indicates the direction of Mecca.

miko: Shinto priestesses dedicated to the cult of the local *kami*.

minaret: (Islam) Tower attached to a mosque from which the call to prayer is broadcast.

minbar: (Islam) Dais in a mosque from which the *imam* speaks.

miracle: Marvellous event, apparently impossible to explain by the normal laws of nature and therefore attributed to divine intervention.

Mishnah: A collection of Jewish oral teachings compiled by Rabbi Judah Ha Nasi around AD 200, the basis for the *Talmud*.

missal: (Christian) Roman Catholic liturgical book giving the order of service for Mass.

missionary: A general term for someone who aims to spread their religion. More specifically, those who strive to win converts to Christianity.

Mithraism: A religion of Ancient Rome of which the chief element was the killing of a bull by Mithras.

mitzvah: (Jewish) Commandment. There are 613 in all, with ten main ones.

mizimu: (Bantu) Spirits of the dead; ancestors.

Moderator: (Christian) Chairman of the General Assembly of the Church of Scotland, elected annually. Also of the Free Church Federal Council and the United Reformed Church.

moksha: (Hindu) Liberation from *karma* and from the cycle of death and rebirth.

monastery: The residence of a religious order, particularly one of monks.

monk: A member of a male religious community living under certain rules, which often include poverty and chastity.

monotheism: The belief that there is only one God. The three great monotheistic religions are Judaism, Christianity and Islam.

Moon, Sun Myung: (Christian) Korean founder, in 1954, of the unorthodox Unification Church.

Mormonism: Unorthodox Christian sect founded in 1830 by Joseph Smith in the USA, and later led by Brigham Young to found a community at Salt Lake City in Utah.

Moses: Father of Judaism, who received the Ten Commandments and other legislation from God on Mount Sinai, having led the people of Israel out of captivity in Egypt.

mosque: (Islam) Muslim place of worship.

mudra: Buddhist ritual gesture, as in the different hand positions of Buddhist statues.

muezzin: (Islam) Person who calls Muslims to prayer.

Muhammad: Founder and prophet of Islam.

mulla: Scholar and exponent of the laws of Islam.

muslim: 'One who submits' – a follower of Islam.

mystery religions: Term for a group of religions from the ancient Mediterranean world all of which emphasized a central 'mystery' (often concerning fertility and immortality), for example the Dionysian mysteries.

myth: Sacred story – within this context there is no suggestion that the story is untrue.

Nanak, Guru: Indian religious teacher and founder of the Sikh religion.

New Testament: Collection of 27 books forming the central canon of Christian scriptures.

nganga: African specialist in dealing with illness and evil, erroneously called a witch doctor.

nirvana: Final release from the laws of *karma*, when *dukkha* ceases: a state beyond any form of known existence.

Noble Eightfold Path: (Buddhist) The eight precepts to follow in order to extinguish desire and suffering.

Nonconformist Churches: (Christian) Protestant denominations generally known as the Free Churches.

nun: A member of a female Christian or Buddhist religious community living under certain rules, which often include poverty and chastity.

obeah: Magic and religious practices found in the West Indies, usually of West African origin.

Odin: Chief of the Norse gods and god of war. Variants of his name include Woden (Anglo-Saxon) and Wotan (Germanic).

Old Testament: (Jewish/Christian) Collection of 39 books of Jewish scriptures, included in the canon of Christian scriptures.

om: Most sacred Hindu word; the sound represents the ultimate.

oral tradition: The verbal dissemination, from one generation to the next, of a people's ancestry and cultural history, including religious beliefs.

ordination: (Christian) Rite by which individuals are authorized as ministers or consecrated as priests.

original sin: (Christian) The concept which teaches that sin and evil came into the world when Adam and Eve ate the forbidden fruit and lost their innocence, becoming estranged from God.

Orthodox Church: Term used for the eastern Christian churches after they split from the Roman Catholic Church in AD 1054. Most Orthodox Churches are related to a particular country, such as the Russian Orthodox and Greek Orthodox.

pagan: A person who is neither a Christian, a Jew nor a Muslim.

pagoda: Tower found in Buddhist temple enclosures in China, India and Japan, usually shrines, or memorials, and often shaped as a spire.

Pali Canon: Buddhist scriptures, containing

the collected teachings of Buddha and fixed in form in the 3rd century BC.

panj kakkar: Five Ks: the symbols of the initiated Sikh.

panth: The community of Sikhs.

pantheism: Belief that divinity resides in all aspects of reality.

pantheon: Term which has come to mean a particular people's group of deities, for example, the ancient Egyptian pantheon included Isis and Osiris.

Paradise: Usually, a beautiful enchanted garden brimming with life and symbolizing a time of bliss and plenty. Paradise is found in many traditions including the Sumerian Dilmun, the Bible's Garden of Eden (also mentioned in the *Qur'an*), and China's Isles of the Blessed.

Parsees: Descendants, living in India and the Indian diaspora, of the ancient Persian Zoroastrians.

Passover: (Jewish) Spring festival lasting seven days, marking the deliverance of the Jews from Egypt.

Patriarch: i) An early Israelite leader such as Abraham and Jacob; ii) (Christian) Title for Eastern Orthodox bishops.

Paul: (Previously called Saul) Christian Apostle converted, while travelling on the road to Damascus, by a vision of Christ resurrected. Paul is the author of several New Testament Epistles to Christian communities throughout the Middle East.

penates: Roman household gods.

Pentecost: i) (Jewish) Festival (*Shavuot* or Weeks), celebrated 52 days after Passover; ii) (Christian) Festival commemorating the coming of the Holy Spirit to the Apostles fifty days after Easter, the second most important Christian festival; also called Whitsun.

Pentecostalists: (Christian) A movement which began in the United States in the early 20th century and teaches that, following conversion, Christians can be baptized in the Holy Spirit, a phenomenon characterized by *glossolalia* or speaking in tongues.

Peter: (Christian) Apostle and leader of the early Christians, to whom, according to Matthew, Jesus gave the keys to heaven.

pilgrimage: A journey to a holy place usually undertaken as penance or celebration.

pluralism: A situation in which no single group holds a monopoly in the definition of beliefs, values and practices.

polytheism: Belief in a variety of gods, each with its own area of rule.

Pontius Pilate: Roman governor of Judea on whose authority Jesus Christ was crucified.

Pope: (Christian) Head of the Roman Catholic Church, Bishop of Rome, regarded as the successor of St Peter.

prayer: Private or public communication with God.

prayer wheels: Buddhist cylinders or wheels used mainly in Tibet, inscribed with a *mantra*, the effect of which is increased as the wheel turns.

Presbyter: (Christian) Term for a Protestant minister.

Presbyterian Churches: (Christian) Reformed Churches whose form of worship follows Calvinism.

priest: A Christian minister, or a person authorized to perform religious ritual (in many religions).

primal religion: The religion of tribal people, having no written tradition, usually characterized by reverence for ancestors and nature spirits.

prophecy: Broadly, a prediction of the future. In ancient times the oracle at Delphi was particularly famous for its prophecies. Moses is regarded by the Jews as the greatest prophet whereas in Islam both Jesus and Muhammad are seen as prophets. Today, prophecy plays an important part in Pentecostal and Charismatic Christianity.

prophet: One through whom God is believed to speak.

Protestantism: Forms of Christian faith resulting from the Reformation, emphasizing justification by faith and the priesthood of all believers.

psalm: Sacred song, the basis of much Jewish and Christian worship.

puja: Hindu worship, particularly at temple or household shrines.

Purgatory: (Roman Catholic) A state where the dead may be punished for their sins before entering Heaven.

Purim: (Jewish) Festival celebrating the foiling of a plan to destroy all the Jews in Persia 2500 years ago.

pyramid: Egyptian royal tomb constructed between about 2600 and 1600 BC.

qi: (Tao) The vital energy or life force which pervades the universe and in the body, centred near the navel.

Quakers: Members of the Society of Friends, a Protestant movement distrustful of tradition which stressed instead the possibility of direct inward address by God deriving from that founded by George Fox in c. 1650.

Quetzlcoatl: Mythical figure in Maya and Aztec religion, often symbolized by a feathered serpent.

qibla: Direction of Mecca to which Muslims turn when praying.

Qur'an: (Islam) The Word of God, 'recitation', as revealed to the prophet Muhammad; the sacred book of Islam.

Ra: Sun-god of ancient Egypt.

rabbi: Jewish teacher of the *Torah*, spiritual leader of the community.

Radhakrishnan, Sarvepalli: Indian philosopher who became President of India. He taught the basic unity of all religions.

Ragnarok: In Norse mythology, the end of the world.

Rahit: The code of ethics and rituals laid down for Sikhs.

Rama: (Hindu) In Indian mythology, an incarnation of Vishnu whose exploits are described in the *Ramayana*.

Ramadan: (Islam) Month in which Muslims are obliged to fast between sunrise and sunset.

Ramayana: (Hindu) One of the two epic scriptures, compiled in the first or second century BC, telling the story of Rama and Sita.

Rastafarianism: Religious movement arising in the Caribbean, a cult of Ras Tafari (Haile Selassie I, Emperor of Ethiopia).

'Recite': (Islam) The beginning of the passage in the *Qur'an* in which God's revelations to Muhammad are found.

Reformation: Movement of reform within the Roman Catholic Church in the 16th century which led to the formation of the Protestant Church.

Reformed Churches: Christian churches in the Calvinist tradition, including Presbyterian and Congregationalist churches.

reincarnation: The belief that an individual soul survives the death of the body and is reborn in a different body.

ren: (Confucian) Loving benevolence towards humans; a central concept in Confucian ethics.

resurrection: i) (Christian) Belief that Jesus Christ was raised from the dead by God; ii) The raising of the dead for judgement as taught by Judaism, Islam and Christianity.

Rig Veda: The first and most sacred Hindu scripture.

ritual: Religious ceremony performed according to prescribed pattern.

Roman Catholic: Christians who recognize the authority of the Pope and who view themselves as orthodox.

Rosh HaShanah: Jewish New Year, celebrating the anniversary of the creation of the world.

Rosicrucianism: Mystical brotherhood based on fictitious secret society in 17th-century Germany.

rumala: (Sikh) The cloth which is wrapped round the *Guru Granth Sahib*.

Russell, Charles Taze: American founder of Jehovah's Witnesses.

Russian Orthodox Church: (Christian) Main church of Russia since 10th century AD. Suppressed under Communism, it is now undergoing a revival.

sacrament: (Christian) 'An outward and visible sign of an inward and spiritual grace', as described in the Book of Common Prayer.

sacrifice: A ritual offering as a means of communicating with God.

sadhu: A Hindu holy man or ascetic.

saint: (Christian) A holy person. Sainthood is established by canonization, a process requiring formal approval by the Pope. The New Testament uses the word for all Christians.

Saktism: (Hindu) The worship of Sakti, the supreme female creative energy, often as personified in the goddess Devi.

Sala: (Islam) Ritual prayer, carried out five times a day, facing Mecca.

salvation: i) Christian belief in forgiveness by God; ii) In Eastern religions, attainment of *nirvana*.

samsara: (Hindu/Buddhist) The cycle of life, death and rebirth.

Sanskrit: Ancient Aryan language; also the sacred language of the Hindu scriptures.

Sat Guru: The name given to God in Sikhism.

satori: 'Awakening'; a Zen Buddhist term.

sawm: (Islam) Fasting, especially during the month of *Ramadan*.

scripture: Text revered by a community as the basis of its faith.

seder: Jewish Passover supper.

Seventh Day Adventists: Christian sect accepting the Bible as infallible and leading lives of strict temperance. Their holy day is Saturday.

shabbat: Jewish day of rest and worship, lasting from sunset on Friday to sunset on Saturday.

shahada: Islamic declaration of faith.

shakti: Energy or power, particularly of a Hindu god.

shaman: Among the Tungu people of Siberia, a visionary, an intermediary between the people and the spirit world who also practises healing; a similar figure among other primal religions.

Shari'a: Islamic law.

Shavuot: *see* Weeks.

shema: (Jewish) Recitation of faith, made morning and evening.

Shi'ites: (Islam) One of the two great branches of Islam (the other being the Sunnis). Shi'ites disagree with Sunnis over who should have succeeded Muhammad as the leader of the Muslim community. They insist that true authority lies with the Prophet's family and that 'Ali, the Prophet's cousin and son-in-law, should have been the first Caliph (deputy).

Shinto: The way of the *kami*. For a short period in modern times Shinto expressed Japanese nationalism.

Shiva: Hindu god, Lord of the Dance, associated with both good and evil, creation and destruction.

shrine: A building or place considered holy by a religious group, sometimes because it houses a religious object.

shruti: (Hindu) 'That which is heard' – term applied to the *Vedas* and the *Upanishads*

Sikh: 'Disciple'; member of the Sikh religion.

sin: An action which breaks divine law; in Christianity, the estrangement of humans from God.

Singh: 'Lion' – surname taken by all male Sikhs who have joined the Khalsa, representing the militant stance of the Sikh community.

Sita: Hindu goddess, the consort of Rama.

Smith, Joseph: Founder of the Mormon religion.

smriti: (Hindu) 'That which is remembered'; includes the *Ramayana* and *Mahabharata*.

stupa: A mound containing Buddhist holy relics, later to become the central feature of temples and pagodas.

sufi: A mystic within Islam.

Sukkot: *see* Booths.

Sunna: 'Custom' of the Prophet Muhammad; second only to the *Qur'an* as an authority in Islamic law.

Sunni: The majority grouping of Muslims (around 85–90%); those who subscribe to one of four authoritative schools of law.

surah: Division of the *Qur'an*, there are 114 in all.

Sutra: i) Text of the word of the Buddha; ii) Short sayings of profound philosophical meaning.

svetambara: (Jain) 'White-clad', that is Jains who do not practise monastic nudity.

swastika: 'Well-being', an emblem of good luck, an Aryan and Buddhist mystic sign; misused by the Nazis.

synagogue: Meeting house for Jewish worship.

syncretism: A religion or belief system created from concepts from two or more religions.

Tabernacles: *see* Booths.

tabu: (Polynesian) That which is forbidden.

Talmud: A major text of Jewish tradition, binding in its legal and ethical provisions on all orthodox Jews.

tanha: (Buddhist) 'Craving' or 'desire'; the main cause of suffering.

Tao: (Chinese) 'The Way', or the principle through which nature works.

Taoism: Chinese philosophy as outlined in the *Tao Te Ching*, whose aim is to live in harmony with natural laws.

tapas: (Jain/Hindu) Austerity (lit. 'heat') which creates heat and with it, power.

Ten Gurus: Ten Sikh teachers believed to share an insight into the nature of God.

Theology: The systematic study of God, and more generally, religion.

Theosophy: Mystical principles of Theosophical Society, founded by Madame Blavatsky in 1875, comprising a mixture of ideas from Eastern and Western religions, with stress on the idea of 'unexplained laws of nature and the powers latent in man' to achieve direct experience of the divine.

Theravada: 'Doctrine of the Elders'; the form of Buddhism practised in Sri Lanka, Burma, Thailand, Cambodia and Laos.

Thor: Norse god of thunder and lightning.

Torah: Jewish teaching or law as handed down to Moses on Mount Sinai; the first five books of the Bible.

torii: Gateway to a Shinto shrine, whose shape echoes that of a bird's perch.

totem: (North American) An animal or plant associated with a clan; '*totem* poles' were erected as clan emblems.

towers of silence: Areas where Parsees place their dead to be consumed by vultures.

Transcendental Meditation (TM): Meditation technique taught since the early 1960s by Maharishi Mahesh Yogi.

Trinity: (Christian) God as three in one: God the Father, God the Son and God the Holy Spirit (Holy Ghost).

umma: Community of Islam.

Unification Church: Unorthodox and controversial Christian sect founded by the Korean Sun Myung Moon in 1954.

Unitarianism: Form of Christianity which denies the existence of the Trinity, believing in the existence of God in one form.

Upanishad: (Hindu) Sacred text. Means 'to sit down near', as it would have been explained to students sitting at the feet of a teacher.

Vajrayana: 'Diamond vehicle'; expression for Tibetan Buddhism.

Valhalla: In Norse mythology, the great hall in the sky where dead heroes' days were spent in battle and nights in feasting.

Vanir: The race of lesser and reactive gods in Norse mythology.

varna: 'Colour'; the four main divisions of Hindu society.

Vatican: (Christian) Residence of the Pope in Rome; the administrative centre of the Roman Catholic Church.

Vedanta: (Hindu) The *Upanishas*, or the end of the *Veda*: the *Upanishads* are the texts, and the *Vedanta* is the philosophy expounded therein.

Vedas: Scriptures of the Aryan peoples of India, whose religion became classical Hinduism.

Vishnu: Hindu god, creator of the cosmos.

Voodoo: Religion of Haiti and Jamaica, with roots on the slave coast of Africa.

Wailing Wall: Site in Jerusalem believed to be part of the original temple of Solomon and used by Jews to lament the fall of Jerusalem.

Weeks: (Jewish) Feast celebrated seven weeks after Passover, also known as Pentecost or *Shavuot*, celebrating the giving of the *Torah* on Mount Sinai.

Wesley, John: (Christian) Founder of the Methodist movement.

wudu: (Islam) Ablution performed before prayer (see **ghusl**).

Wycliffe, John: (Christian) English religious reformer and translator of the Bible into English.

Xipe Totec: (Aztec) The god of agriculture, represented wearing the flayed skin of a sacrificial victim.

Yahweh: (Jewish) The Hebrew name for God; Jehovah.

Yang: (Chinese) The male principle in the world, whose interplay with *Yin* forms the basis of much Chinese thinking.

yasasna: (Zoroastrianism) Worship.

Yin: (Chinese) The female principle in the world.

yoga: (Hindu/Buddhist) Method of meditation, involving physical as well as spiritual discipline, and leading to union with God.

yogi: (Hindu/Buddhist) Indian holy man.

Yom Kippur: (Jewish) Day of Atonement, a solemn day of fasting.

zakat: (Islam) The obligatory giving by Muslims of alms to the poor.

za-zen: (Zen Buddhist) The practice of meditation.

Zen: 'Meditation'; the name of a Japanese form of *yogic* Buddhism.

Zeus: Supreme ruler of the Greek gods.

ziggurat: Ancient Babylonian temple, built like a stepped pyramid.

Zionism: (Jewish) Movement formally established in 1897 for founding a Jewish national home in Palestine. Since the establishment of Israel in 1948 it has continued to seek support for the state.

Zoroaster: Another name for Zarathustra: prophet and founder of Zoroastrianism.

Zoroastrianism: Religion of ancient Persia, founded by Zoroaster.

BIBLIOGRAPHY

AFRICAN TRADITIONAL RELIGIONS

Achebe, Chinua, *Things Fall Apart*, Heinemann, London, 1958

Iliffe, John, *Africans: The History of a Continent*, Cambridge University Press, Cambridge, 1995

Mbiti, John, *Introduction to African Religion*, Heinemann, London, 1991

Ray, Benjamin, *African Religions: Symbol, Ritual and Community*, Prentice-Hall, New Jersey, 1999 (second edition)

Samkange, Stanlake, *The Mourned One*, Heinemann, London, 1975

Thiong'o, Ngugi wa, *The River Between*, Heinemann, London, 1965

Visona, Monica B. et al, *A History of Art in Africa*, Thames and Hudson, London, 2000

Zuesse, Evan M., *Ritual Cosmos: The Sanctification of Life in African Religions*, Ohio University Press, Ohio, 1979

ANCIENT EGYPT

Hart, George, *A Dictionary of Egyptian Gods and Goddesses*, Routledge and Kegan Paul, 1986

Hart, George, *Egyptian Myths*, British Museum Publications, London, 1990

Hornung, Erik, trans. by John Baines, *Conceptions of God in Ancient Egypt: the One and the Many*, Routledge and Kegan Paul, London, 1983

Meeks, Dimitri and Favard-Meeks, Christine, translated by G. M. Goshgarian, *Daily Life of the Egyptian Gods*, John Murray, London, 1997

Quirke, Stephen, *Ancient Egyptian Religion*, British Museum Press, London, 1992

ANCIENT NEAR EAST

Crawford, Harriet, *Sumer and the Sumerians*, Cambridge University Press, Cambridge, 1991

Gibson, John C. L. and Driver, Geoffrey Rolles, *Canaanite Myths and Legends*, Continuum International, 1978

Hardy, Friedhelm (ed.), *The World's Religions: the Religions of Asia*, Routledge, London, 1990

Holloway, Steven W., *Assur is King! Assur is King!*, Brill Academic Club, 2001

King, L. W. (ed.), *The Tablets of Creation*, Book Tree, 1998

Kramer, Samuel Noel, *Sumerian Mythology*, University of Pennsylvania Press, 1998

Oppenheim, A. Leo, *Ancient Mesopotamia*, University of Chicago Press, Chicago, 1977

Postgate, N., *The First Empires*, Phaidon, 1977

Smart, Ninian (ed.), *Atlas of World Religions*, Oxford University Press, Oxford, 1999

AUSTRALIA

Berndt, R., *Kunapipi*, Cheshire, Melbourne, 1951

Berndt, R., and Berndt, C., *The World of the First Australians*, Rigby, Adelaide, 1985

Durkheim, E., *The Elementary Forms of the Religious Life*, Allen and Unwin, 1915

Eliade, M., *Australian Religions An Introduction*, Cornell University Press, Ithaca, 1973

Howitt, A. W., *Native Tribes of South East Australia*, Macmillan, London, 1904

Maddock, K., *The Australian Aborigines: A Portrait of Their Society*, Penguin, 1972

Munn, N., *Walbiri Iconography*, Cornell University Press, Ithaca, 1973

Stanner, W. E. H., 'The Dreaming', in *Reader in Comparative Religion*, Vogt, E. and Lessa, W. (eds.), Peterson, Evanston, 1958

Strehlow, T., *Aranda Traditions*, Melbourne University Press, Melbourne, 1947

Warner, L., *A Black Civilization*, Harper, New York, 1958

BAHA'ISM

Abd ul-Baha ibn Baha Ullah, *The Baha'i Revelation*, Baha'i Publishing Trust, London, 1970

Baha Ullah, *Writings of Baha Ullah: a Compilation*, Baha'i Publishing Trust, New Dehli, 2001

Cooper, R., *The Baha'is of Iran,*: Minority Rights Group, London, 1982

Momen, M. (1981) *The Babi and Baha'i Religions, 1844-1944: Some Contemporary Western Accounts,*: Ronald, Oxford

Perkins, M. and Hainsworth, P., *The Baha'i Faith*, Ward Lock Educational, 1980

Smith, P. (1987) *The Babi and Baha'i Religions: From Messianic Shi'ism to a World Religion*, Cambridge University Press, , Cambridge

Smith, P., *The Baha'i Faith: A Short History*, Oneworld, Oxford, 1996

BUDDHISM

Austin, Jack, (trans), *The Dhammapada*, The Buddhist Society, London, 1988

Besserman, Perle and Steger, Manfred, *Crazy Clouds; Zen Radicals, Rebels and Reformers*, Shambhala, Boston, 1991

Blofeld, John, *The Way of Power, A Practical Guide to the Tantric Mysticism of Tibet*, George Allen and Unwin, London, 1970

Conze, E., *Buddhist Scriptures*, Penguin, 1995

Fowler, Merv, *Buddhism, Beliefs and Practices*, Sussex Academic Press, Brighton and Portland, Oregon, 1999

Gethin, Rupert, *The Foundations of Buddhism*, Oxford University Press, 1998

Jayatilleke, K. N., *The Message of the Buddha*, Allen & Unwin, 1975

McConnell, John A., *Mindful Mediation, A Handbook for Buddhist Peacemakers*, Buddhist Research Institute, Mahachula Buddhist University et al., Bangkok, 1995

Pym, Jim, *You Don't have to Sit on the Floor; Bringing the Insights and Tools of Buddhism into Everyday Life*, Riders, London, 2001

Radhakrishnan, S., *The Dhammapada*, Oxford University Press, 1992

Reps, Paul, *Zen Flesh, Zen Bones*, Pelican Books, Harmondsworth, 1971

Sprung, M., *Lucid Exposition of the Middle Way*, Routledge, 1979

Suzuki, Shunryu, *Zen Mind, Beginner's Mind, Informal Talks on Zen Meditation and Practice*, Weatherhill, New York and Tokyo, 1996

Unno, Taitetsu, *River of Fire, River of Water; An Introduction to the Pure Land Tradition of Shin Buddhism*, Doubleday, New York, 1998

CENTRAL AND SOUTH AMERICA (ANCIENT RELIGIONS)

Clendinnen, I., *The Aztecs*, Cambridge University Press, Cambridge, 1991

Cobo, Father B., (ed. & trans. Hamilton) *Inca Religion and Customs*, University of Texas Press, Austin, 1990

Howland, J. (ed.), 'Inca Culture at the Time of the Spanish Conquest', *Handbook of South American Indians*, Vol. 2, 1946

Katz, F., *The Ancient American Civilisations*, Weidenfeld, 1989

Miller, M. and Taube K., *The Gods and Symbols of Ancient Mexico and the Maya*, Thames and Hudson, London, 1993

Pasztory, E, *Pre-Columbian Art*, Weidenfeld & Nicolson, London, 1998

Sahagun, Fray B de, (trans. by Anderson, J.O. & Dibble, C.), *Florentine Codex: General History of the Things of New Spain*, (13 vols.), School of American Research, Santa Fe, New Mexico, 1950–82.

Schele, L and Miller, M. E., *The Blood of Kings*, Thames and Hudson, London, 1992

Tedlock, D. (trans), *Popol Vue: the Mayan Book of the Dawn of Life*, Simon and Schuster, New York, 1985

CENTRAL AND SOUTH AMERICA (INDIGENOUS RELIGIONS)

Hugh-Jones, C., *From the Milk River: Spatial and Temporal Processes in Northwest Amazonia*, Cambridge University Press, Cambridge, 1979

Hugh-Jones, S., *The Palm and Pleiades: Initiation and Cosmology in Northwest Amazonia*, Cambridge University Press, Cambridge, 1979

Myerhoff, B., *Peyote Hunt: the Sacred Journey of the Huichol Indians*, Cornell University Press, London, 1974

Reichel-Dolmatoff, G, *Amazonian Cosmos: the Sexual and Religious Symbolism of the Tukano Indians*, Chicago University Press, Chicago, 1971

Rostas, S, 'A Grass Roots View of Religious Change Amongst Women in an Indigenous Community in Chiapas, Mexico', *Bulletin of Latin American Studies*, Vol. 18, No 3, pp. 327–341, 1999

Tedlock, D, *Time and the Highland Maya*, University of New Mexico Press, Albuquerque, 1982

Watanabe, J., *Maya Saints and Souls in a Changing World*, University of Texas, Austin, 1992

CHRISTIANITY

Bowker, John (ed.), *The Oxford Dictionary of World Religions*, Oxford University Press, Oxford, 1997

Brown, Alan, *The Christian World*, Simon and Schuster, 1994

Burridge, Richard, *Four Gospels, One Jesus?*, SPCK, London, 1994

Cohn-Sherlock, Lavinia, *Who's Who in Christianity*, Routledge, London, 1998

Dowley, T., *A History of Christianity*, Lion, 1996

Heyendorff, J., *Christ in Eastern Christian Thought*, Corpus, 1975

Hinnells, John, *Who's Who in World Religions*, Penguin, London, 1996

Hollenweger, W. J., *The Pentecostals*, SCM, 1972

Lenman, Bruce P., *Chambers Dictionary of World History*, Chambers, London, 2000

McManners, John (ed.), *The Oxford Illustrated History of Christianity*, Oxford University Press, Oxford, 1990

Porter, J. R., *Jesus Christ. The Jesus of History, The Christ of Faith*, Duncan Baird Publishers, London, 1999

Pritchard, James, *The Times Atlas of the Bible*, Times Books, London, 1987

Sykes, S. W., & Clayton, J. P., *Christ, Faith and History*, Cambridge University Press, 1995

Ware, Timothy, *The Orthodox Church*, Penguin, 1995

CONFLICT OF IDEOLOGIES

Armstrong, Karen, *The Battle for God: Fundamentalism in Judaism, Christianity and Islam*, HarperCollins, London, 2000

Bowker, John (ed.), *The Oxford Dictionary of World Religions*, Oxford University Press, Oxford, 1997

CONFUCIANISM

Chu His, *Learning to be a Sage*, University of California Press, Berkeley, 1990

Confucius, *The Analects*, (trans. D.C. Lau), Penguin Books, Harmondsworth, 1979

De Bary, William Theodore (ed.), *Sources of the Chinese Tradition*, Columbia University Press, New York, 1950

Fung Yulan, *A Short History of Chinese Philosophy*, The Macmillan Company, New York, 1948

Hsun-tzu (Xun Zi), *Basic Writings*, Watson, Burton (trans.), Columbia University Press, New York, 1961

Lau, D. C. (trans.), *The Analects by Confucius*, Penguin, 1996

Mencius, *The Book of Mencius*. (trans. D.C. Lau), Penguin Books, Harmondsworth, 1970

Smith, D. H., *Confucius*, Paladin, 1973

The Book of Songs, Houghton Miflin, Boston/New York, 1937

Three Ways of Thought in Ancient China, George Allen and Unwin, London, 1939

Waley, Arthur, *The Analects of Confucius*, George Allen and Unwin, London, 1938

Yang, C. K., *Religion in Chinese Society*, University of California Press, Berkeley and Los Angeles, 1961

CONTEMPORARY PAGANISM

Adler, M., *Drawing Down the Moon*, Boston, Beacon Press, 1986 (1979)

Harvey, G., *Listening People, Speaking Earth*, Hurst & Co., London, 1997

EAST MEETS WEST

Basham, A. L., *The Wonder That Was India*, Sidgwick & Jackson, London, 1967

Eck, D., *Encountering God*, Penguin, London, 1985

Gombrich, R., *Mahayana Buddhism*, Routledge, London

Gombrich, R., *Theravada Buddhism*, Routledge, London

Grifiths, B., *A New Vision of Reality: Western Science, Eastern Mysticism and Christian Faith*, Collins, London, 1989

Grifiths, B., *The Marriage of East and West*, Collins, London, 1983

Krishnan, R., *The Hindu View of Life*, Allen & Unwin, 1927 (HarperCollins, India, 1993)

Ling, T., *A History of Religion East and West*, Macmillan, 1969

Lipner, J., *Hindus*, Routledge, London, 1994

Panikkar, R., *The Unknown Christ of Hinduism*, Darton, Longman & Todd, 1964

Zaehrer, R. C., *Hinduism*, Oxford University Press, Oxford, 1966

GREEK

Austin, M. M. and Vidal-Naquet, P. (eds.), *The Economic and Social History of Ancient Greece: An Introduction*, Batsford, London, 1977

Boardman, John, *The Greeks Overseas: Their Early Colonies and Trade*, Thames and Hudson, London, 2nd edn., 1980

Boardman, John, *The Oxford History of Classical Art*, Oxford University Press, Oxford, 1993

Carpenter, T. H., *Art and Myth in Ancient Greece*, Thames and Hudson, London, 1996

Castleden, Rodney, *Minoans: Life in Bronze-Age Crete*, Routledge, London, 1990

Graves, Robert, *New Larousse Encyclopedia of Mythology*, Hamlyn, 1968

Green, Peter, *Alexander to Actium: The Hellenistic Age*, Thames and Hudson, London, 1990

Guthrie, W. K. C., *The Greeks and Their Gods*, Methuen, 1950

Murray, Oswyn, *Early Greece*, Fontana, London, 1980

Nock, A. D., *Essays on Religion and the Ancient World*, Clarendon Press, 1996

Renfrew, Colin, *The Emergence of Civilization: The Cyclades and the Aegean in the Third Millennium bc*, Methuen, London, 1972

Scarre, Christopher and Fagan, Brian M., *Ancient Civilizations*, Longman, Harlow, 1997

HINDUISM

Brockington, J.L., *The Sacred Thread*, Edinburgh University Press, Edinburgh, 1981

Flood, G., *An Introduction to Hinduism*, Cambridge University Press, Cambridge, 1996

Fuller, C., *The Camphor Flame*, Princeton University Press, Princeton, 1992

Hinnells, J.R. and Sharpe, E.J., *Hinduism*, Oriel Press, Newcastle upon Tyne 1972

Kinsley, D.R., *Hinduism: A Cultural Perspective*, Prentice-Hall, London, 1982

Klostermaier, K.K., *A Survey of Hinduism*, State University of New York Press, New York, 1994

Knott, K., *Hinduism: A Very Short Introduction*, Oxford University Press, Oxford, 1998

Zaehner, R.C., *Hinduism*, Oxford University Press, London, 1966

ISLAM

Al-Ghazali, *Inner Dimensions of Islamic Worship*, (trans. Holland, M.), Leicester: Islamic Foundation, 1983

Cook, M., *Muhammad*, Oxford University Press, Oxford, 1983

Cook, M., The Koran: *A Very Short Introduction*, Oxford University Press, Oxford, 2000

Ernst, C.W., *The Shambala Guide to Sufism*, Shambala Publications, Boston, 1997

Lapidus, I., *A History of Islamic Societies*, Cambridge University Press, Cambridge, 1990 (2001)

Halliday, F. *Two Hours That Shook The World: September 11, 2001*, Saqi, London, 2001

Momen, M., *An Introduction to Shi'i Islam: The History and Doctrine of Twelver Shi'ism*, Yale University Press, New Haven and London, 1985

Rahman, F., *Islam*, The University of Chicago Press, Chicago, 1966 (1979)

Rippin, A., *Muslims: Their Religious Beliefs and Practices*, Routledge, London, 2001

Roald, A., *Women in Islam*, Taylor and Francis, London, 2001

Robinson, N., *Discovering the Qur'an: A Contemporary Approach To a Veiled Text*, SCM Press Ltd., London, 1996

Ruthven, M., *A Very Short Introduction to Islam*, Oxford University Press, Oxford, 1997 (2000)

Schimmel, A., *And Muhammad is His Messenger: The Veneration of the Prophet in Islamic Piety*, The University of North Carolina Press, Chapel Hill, NC, 1985

Sirriyeh, E., *Sufis and Anti-Sufis*, Curzon Press, Richmond, 1998

Watt, W.M., *Bell's Introduction to the Qur'an*, Edinburgh University Press, Edinburgh, 1970 (1990)

JAINISM

Dundas, P., *The Jains*, Routledge, London, 1992

Jain, K., *Lord Mahavira and His Times*, Motilal Banarsidass, Delhi, 1974

Jaini, P., *The Jaina Path of Purification*, University of California, Berkeley, 1979

Sangave, V. *Jaina Community, a Social Survey*, Popular Prakashan, Bombay, 1980

Schubring, Walther, *The Doctrine of the Jainas*, Motilal Banarsidass, Delhi, 1962

Shah, Natubhai, *Jainism: The World of Conquerors* (2 vols.), Sussex Academic Press, Brighton, 1998

JUDAISM

Babylonian Talmud, (Hebrew and English edition), Soncino Press

Epstein, Isidore, *Judaism*, Penguin, 1995

Gilbert, Martin, *The Dent Atlas of Jewish History*, Dent, 1993

Greenberg, Irving, *The Jewish Way: Living the Holidays*, Simon and Schuster, London, 1993

Guttman, J., *The Philosophies of Judaism*, Holt Rinehart & Winston, 1983

Jacobs, Louis, *The Jewish Religion: A Companion*, Oxford University Press, Oxford, 1995

Kaufmann, Y., *The Religion of Israel*, Allen & Unwin, 1961

Kedourie, E. (ed.), *The Jewish World*, Thames and Hudson, 1979

Landau, Ronnie S. and Tauris, I. B., *The Nazi Holocaust*, London, 1992

Mendes-Flohr, Paul and Reinharz, Jehuda, *The Jew in the Modern World: A Documentary History*, Oxford University Press, Oxford, 1980

Plaut, Gunther, *Torah, A Modern Commentary*, UAHC Press, 1981

Polaikov, Leon, *The History of Anti-Semitism* (3 vols), Littman Library, 1955

Roden, Claudia, *The Book of Jewish Food: An Odyssey from Samarkand and Vilna to the Present Day*, Penguin, London, 1996

Roth, Cecil (ed.), *Encyclopedia Judaica*, Keter Publishing, Jerusalem, 1972

MAORI

Barlow, C., *Tikanga Whakaaro: Key Concepts in Maori Culture*, Oxford University Press, Auckland, 1991

Grace, Patricia, *Potiki*, Women's Press, London, 1987

Harvey, Graham (ed.), 'Art Works in Aotearoa' and 'Mana and Tapu: Sacred Knowledge, Sacred Boundaries', *Indigenous Religions: a Companion*, Cassell, London/New York, 2000

Harvey, Graham (ed.), 'Maori Religion' (by Tawhai, T. P.), *Readings in Indigenous Religions*, Continuum, London/New York, 2002

Reedy, Anaru (ed.), *Nga Korero a Mohi Ruatapu (The Writings of Mohi Ruatapu)*, Canterbury University Press, Christchurch, 1993

Sutherland, Stewart and Clarke, Peter (eds.), 'Maori Religion', *The Study of Religion, Traditional and New Religion*, Routledge, London, 1988

MULTI-FAITH SOCIETIES

Bellah, R., *Beyond Belief: Essays on Religion in a Past Traditional World*

Hart, D., *One Faith: Non-Realism & The World Faiths*, Mowbray, 1995

Hinnells, J. R., *A Handbook of Living Religions*, Viking, 1984 (Penguin, 1985)

Kung, H. et al, *Christianity and the World Religions*, Collins, London, 1987

Smart, N., *The World's Religions*, Cambridge University Press, Cambridge, 1989

NATIVE NORTH AMERICANS

Bordewich, Fergus M., *Killing the White Man's Indian: Reinventing Native Americans at the End of the Twentieth Century*, Anchor Books/Doubleday, New York/London, 1997

Rajotte, Freda, *First Nations Faith and Ecology*, Cassell, Anglican Book Centre, United Church Publishing House, 1998

Underhill, R. M., *Red Man's Religion*, University of Chicago Press, 1972

Versluis, Arthur, *Native American Traditions*, Element, 1994

Wright, Ronald, *Stolen Continents: The New World Through Indian Eyes*, Penguin Books, London, 1993

NEW RELIGIOUS MOVEMENTS; WOMEN AND RELIGION

Barrett, David, *The New Believers*, Cassell, London, 2001

Bloom, William, *The Penguin Book of New Age and Holistic Writing*, Penguin, London, 2001

Christ, Carol and Plaskow, Judith, *Womanspirit Rising:*

A Feminist Reader in Religion, HarperCollins, New York, 1992

Daly, Mary, *Beyond God the Father: Toward a Philosophy of Women's Liberation*, Beacon Press, Boston, 1985

Gallagher, Ann-Marie, *The Way of the Goddess*, HarperCollins, London, 2002

King, Ursula, *Women and Spirituality*, Macmillan, London, 1995

Orr, Emma Restall, *Druid Priestess*, HarperCollins, London, 2000

Osho, *Autobiography of a Spiritually Incorrect Mystic*, St Martin's Press, New York, 2001

Puttick, Elizabeth, *Women in New Religions*, Macmillan, London, 1997

Starhawk, *The Spiral Dance*, HarperCollins, San Francisco, 1989

NORTHERN EUROPE

Davidson, H. R. E., *Gods and Myths of Northern Europe*, Penguin, 1996

Davidson, H. R. E., *Pagan Scandinavia*, Thames and Hudson, 1977

Davidson, H. R. E., *The Lost Beliefs of Northern Europe*, Routledge, London, 1993

Jones, Prudence and Pennick, Nigel, *A History of Pagan Europe*, Routledge, London, 1995

Pennick, Nigel, *Celtic Sacred Landscapes*, Thames and Hudson, London, 2000

Trinkunas, Jonas (ed.), *Of Gods and Holidays: The Baltic Heritage*, Hverme, Vilnius, 1999

Vana, Zdenek, *Mythologie und Götterwelt der slawischen Völker. Die geistigen Impulse Ost-Europas*, Urachhaus Johannes M. Mayer, Stuttgart, 1992

OCEANIA

Bonnemaison, J., *The Tree and the Canoe*, University of Hawaii Press, Honolulu, 1994.

Damon, F. and Wagner, R. (eds.), *Death Rituals and Life in the Societies of the Kula Ring*, Northern Illinois University Press, 1989.

Goldman, I., *Ancient Polynesian Society*, University of Chicago Press, Chicago, 1970

Hocart, A. M., *Kings and Councillors*, University of Chicago Press, Chicago, 1970

Lawrence P., *Road Belong Cargo*, Manchester University Press, Manchester, 1956

Lawrence, P. and Meggitt, M. (eds.), *Gods, Ghosts and Men in Melanesia*, Oxford University Press, Melbourne, 1965

Sahlins, M., *Historical Metaphors and Mythical Realities*, University of Michigan Press, 1976

Thomas, N., *Planets around the Sun. Oceania Monographs no. 31*, Oceania Publications, Sydney, 1986

Wagner, R., *Asiwinorong*, Princeton University Press, 1986

Wagner R., *Habu*, University of Chicago Press, Chicago, 1972

RASTAFARIANISM

Anbessa-Ebanks, Ras Kwende B., *Health and Nutrition: A Rastafari Perspective*, Kwemarabak Publications, 1995

Barrett, L., *Rastafarians: Sounds of Cultural Dissonance*, Beacon Press, Boston, 1988

Campbell, H., *Rasta and Resistance: From Marcus Garvey to Walter Rodney*, Africa World Press, Trenton NJ, 1987

Cashmore, E., *The Rastafarians*, Minority Rights Group London, 1984

Cashmore, E., *Rastaman: The Rastafarian Movement in England*, G. Allen and Unwin, London, 1979

Chevannes, B., *Rastafari: Roots and Ideology*, Syracuse University Press, Syracuse, 1994

Clark, P., *Black Paradise: The Rastafarian Movement*, Borgo Press, San Bernadino, 1994

Simpson, G. E., *Black Religions in the New World*, Columbia University Press, 1978

Williams, K. M., *The Rastafarians*, Ward Lock Educational, 1985

ROME

Boardman, John, *The Oxford History of Classical Art*, Oxford University Press, Oxford, 1993

Carcopino, Jacerome (tr. Lorimer, E. O.), *Daily Life in Ancient Rome: The People and the City at the Height of the Empire*, Penguin, London, 1991

Graves, Robert, *New Larousse Encyclopedia of Mythology*, Hamlyn, 1968

Liberati, Anna Maria and Bourbon, Fabio, *Splendours of the Roman World*, Thames and Hudson, London, 1996

Scarre, Christopher and Fagan, Brian M., *Ancient Civilizations*, Longman, Harlow, 1997

ROOTS OF RELIGION

Burl, Aubrey, *A Guide to the Stone Circles of Britain, Ireland and Brittany*, Yale University Press, New Haven, 1995

Chauvet, Jean-Marie, Deschamps, Eliette Brunel and Hillaire, Christian, *Chauvet Cave*, Thames and Hudson, London, 1996

Hutton, Ronald, *Pagan Religions of the Ancient British Isles*, Blackwell, Oxford, 1991

Levy, G.R., *The Gate of Horn*, Faber, London, 1963

O'Brien, Joanne and Palmer, Martin, *State of Religion Atlas*, Simon and Schuster, London, 1993

O'Shea, Stephen, *Perfect Heresy*, Profile Books, London, 2000s

SCIENTIFIC RELIGIONS

Barbour, I. G., *When Science Meets Religion*, HarperSanFrancisco, San Francisco, 2000

Brooke, J. H. and G. N., Cantor *Reconstructing Nature: The Engagement of Science and Religion*, T & T Clark, Edinburgh, 1998.

Fraser, Caroline, *God's Perfect Child: Living and Dying in the Christian Science Church*, Metropolitan Books/Henry Holt & Company, New York, 1999

Gilbert, J. B., *Redeeming Culture: American Religion in an Age of Science*, University of Chicago Press, Chicago, 1997

Gould, S. J., *Rocks of Ages: Science and Religion in the Fullness of Life*, Ballantine, New York, 1999

Haught, J. F., *Science and Religion: From Conflict to Conversation*, Paulist Press, New York, 1995

Lindberg, D. C. and Numbers, R. L. (eds.), *God and Nature: Historical Essays on the Encounter between Christianity and Science*, University of California Press, Berkeley, 1986

Ward, K. God, *Chance and Necessity*, Oneworld Publications, Oxford, 1996

SHINTO

Bocking, B., *A Popular Dictionary of Shinto*, Curzon Press, London, 1997

Breen, J. (ed.), *Shinto in History: Ways of the Kami*, Curzon Press, London, 2000

Harris, V. (ed.), *Shinto: The Sacred Art of Ancient Japan*, British Museum, London, 2001

Herbert, J., *Shinto: At the Fountainhead of Japan*, Allen & Unwin, 1967

Nelson, J.K., *A Year in the Life of a Shinto Shrine*, University of Washington Press, Washington, 1996

Ono, S., *Shinto, the Kami Way*, Charles Tuttle, Boston, 1962

Reader, Andreasen & Stefansson (eds.), *Japanese Religions Past and Present*, Japan Library, Japan, 1993

Reader, I., *Religion in Contemporary Japan*, Macmillan, London, 1990/University of Hawaii Press, Hawaii, 1991

SIKHISM

Cole, W. Owen, & Sambhi, Piara Singh, *Sikhism*, Ward Lock Educational, 1984

Joshi, L.M. (ed.) *Sikhism*, Punjabi University, 1990

Kalsi, S.S., *Simple Guide to Sikhism*, Global, Folkestone, 1999

Kaur, Sahib, *Sikh Thought*, Sundar Printers, 1986

McLeod, W.H., *Sikhism*, Penguin, London, 1997

Sambhi, Piara Singh and Cole, W. O., *The Sikhs*, Vikas Publishing House, 1978

Singh, D., & Smith, A., *The Sikh World*, Simon and Schuster, 1994

Singh, Dr S., *Philosophical Foundations of the Sikh Value System*, Gurmat Publishers, 1982

Singh, Kapur, *Guru Nanak's Life And Thought*, Guru Nanak Dev University, 1991

WESTERN CULTURE

Bowker, John (ed.), *The Oxford Dictionary of World Religions*, Oxford University Press, Oxford, 1997

Bruce, S., 'Religion in Britain at the close of the 20th century', *Journal of Contemporary Religion*, vol. 11, no 3, p. 264, 1996

Kerkhofs, Jan (ed.), *European Values Survey*, Louvain, 1990

MacIntyre, Alasdair, *After Virtue*, second edition, Duckworth, London, 1985

Vallely, Paul (ed.), *The New Politics: Catholic Social Teaching for the 21st century*, SCM Press, London

ZOROASTRIANISM

Boyce, M., *Zoroastrians: Their Religious Beliefs and Practices*, Routledge, 1984

Clark, Peter, *Zoroastrianism*, Sussex Academic Press, 1998

Hardy, Friedhelm (ed.), *The World's Religions: the Religions of Asia*, Routledge, London, 1990

Hinnells, J. R., *Zoroastrianism and the Parsis*, Ward Lock Educational, 1981

Kapadia, S. A., *Teachings of Zoroaster and the Philosophy of the Parsi Religion*, R. A. Kessinger Publishing Company, 1998

Oppenheim, A. Leo, *Ancient Mesopotamia*, University of Chicago Press, Chicago, 1977

Smart, Ninian (ed.), *Atlas of World Religions*, Oxford University Press, Oxford, 1999

Zaehner, R. C., *The Dawn and Twilight of Zoroastrianism*, Weidenfeld, 1975

BIOGRAPHIES & CREDITS

Seán McLoughlin (Introduction and Near East) is a lecturer in Theology and Religious Studies at the University of Leeds. While his research to date has focused on Muslim communities in Britain, he has experience of teaching across a wide range of themes and traditions in the study of religion. His first book, *Representing Muslims: Religion, Ethnicity and the Politics of Identity* (Pluto Press, London) will be published in 2004.

CONTRIBUTORS

Alan Brown (Near East) is director of the National Society's Kensington R. E. Centre and R. E. (Schools) Officer of the General Synod Board of Education. He has written numerous books, articles and reviews about the Christian faith and world religions.

Dr John Chinnery (Asia) formerly headed the Department of East Asian Studies at the University of Edinburgh. He is currently Honorary President of the Scotland China Association.

Susan Greenwood (Europe) is lecturer in the School of Cultural and Community Studies at the University of Sussex, an Open University Associate Lecturer and Visiting Fellow at Goldsmiths College, University of London.

Graham Harvey (Oceania/Pacific) is Reader in Religious Studies at King Alfred's College, Winchester. He is particularly interested in Maori and Ojibwe spirituality, but has also

published books about contemporary Paganism and ancient Judaism.

Michael Kerrigan (Europe) is a freelance writer specializing in the civilizations of ancient times . He has written on almost every aspect of archaeology, ancient history and culture.

Tara Lewis (Asia). Having obtained a joint Honours degree in Comparative Religions and History of Art, she went on to work for the Alliance of Religions and Conservation and established ARC Asia.

Rameshchandra Majithia (Asia) has co-ordinated Hindu religious education for children aged five to 16 for the last seven years at his local temple in Leicester.

Rabbi Rachel Montagu (Near East) is Assistant Education Officer for the Council of Christians and Jews and teaches Judaism and Biblical Hebrew at Birkbeck College and Allen Hall.

Robert Morkot (Africa) is an ancient historian specialising in North-East Africa. He currently teaches at Exeter University.

Martin Palmer (Asia) is the Director of the International Consultancy on Religion, Education and Culture (ICOREC). He is the author of many books, and frequently appears on television and radio.

Nigel Pennick (Europe) initially trained in biology before moving on to become a writer and illustrator. He is author of over 40 books on European spiritual traditions, arts and landscapes.

Dr Elizabeth Puttick (Europe) is a sociologist of religion. She teaches religious studies at the British American College, London.

Jim Pym (Asia) is the author of You Don't Have to Sit on the Floor; a book on practical Buddhism in Western culture, editor of Pure Land Notes, a Buddhist journal, and a member of the Council of the Buddhist Society, London.

Rev Dr Freda Rajotte (Americas) has always been dedicated to both justice issues and to preserving the integrity of creation. As a Geography professor she focused upon the related issues of economic development and environmental conservation.

Brenda Ralph-Lewis (Near East) is a freelance author specializing in history, with particular reference to ancient civilizations. Her publications include a history of ritual sacrifice.

Susanna Rostas (Americas) has a D.Phil in Social Anthropology and has taught at both Goldsmiths' College and Durham University. She is currently a Research Associate in the Department of Social Anthropology in Cambridge.

Michael Shackleton (Asia) is Associate Professor of Social Anthropology at Osaka Gakuin University in Japan with a special interest in Japanese Religion.

Professor Natubhai Shah (Asia) teaches Jainism at numerous universities. He represents Jainism at the highest level and was responsible for the creation of the beautiful Jain temple in Leicester, and for establishing Jain Academy.

Dr Rajwant Singh (Asia) helped initiate the Sikh Association of America, and he is a founding member of the Guru Gobind Singh Foundation. He has been a special advisor to Jathedar Manjit Singh, one of the spiritual heads of the worldwide Sikh community.

Rachel Storm (Americas) has studied and written about mythology and religion since the 1980s. She is the author of three books in the area and has contributed to a number of encyclopedias magazines and newspapers.

Mark Tully (Asia) has an MA in History and Theology from Cambridge University. For 22 years he worked as the Delhi correspondent for the BBC.

Paul Vallely (Asia) writes on religion for *The Independent* newspaper, of which he is associate editor. He is chair of the Catholic Institute for International Relations.

Dr Kevin Ward (Africa) teaches African Religious Studies in the Department of Theology and Religious Studies at the University of Leeds. He worked for over 20 years in East Africa, as a teacher in Kenya and as a lecturer at a seminary in Uganda. He is ordained in the Church of Uganda.

Dr James F. Weiner (Oceania/Pacific) has held teaching and research positions in anthropology in Australia and Britain. He worked in Papua New Guinea with the Foi people and has published two books on New Guinea mythology.

PICTURE CREDITS

The Art Archive: 68, 135, 139, 188, 270, 271, 286, 287; Album/Joseph Martin: 246; Archaeological Museum Aleppo Syria/Dagli Orti: 156; Archaeological Museum Milan: 236-237, 249, 253; Bibliothèque de l'Arsenal Paris: 177; British Library: 17, 196; British Museum: 62, 71, 73, 251; Dagli Orti (A): 6, 151, 154-155, 170, 187, 193, 194; Egyptian Museum Cairo/Dagli Orti (A): 101, 102, 106; Galleria d'Arte Moderna Venice/Dagli Orti (A): 172; Galleria Uffizi Florence/Dagli Orti (A): 250; Heraklion Museum/Dagli Orti: 240-241; Jan Vinchon Numismatist Paris/Dagli Orti (A): 252; Mireille Vautier:127 t, 141, 142-143; Musée des Antiquites St Germain en Laye: 256; Musée des Arts Africains et Océaniens/Dagli Orti:110, 112; Musée du Louvre Paris/Dagli Orti: 162; Musée Guimet Paris/Dagli Orti (A):

57; National Anthropological Museum Mexico/Dagli Orti: 130; National Archaeological Museum Athens/Dagli Orti: 244-245; National Museum Damascus Syria/Dagli Orti (A):167; Private Collection/Dagli Orti (A):115; Victoria and Albert Museum London/Eileen Tweedy: 82 t

Baha'i World Centre: 232

Barnaby's Picture Library: 185

Bridgeman Art Library: Gripsholms Castle Collection,Sweden: 261; Private Collection: 264

Chloë Sayer: 148, 149

Christie's Images: 276

Dipak Joshi: 21, 22, 26, 32, 33

Foundry Arts: 18, 38, 100, 105, 107, 126, 231, 234

Graham Stride: 44, 47, 48, 51, 53, 54, 55, 289

Hutchison Library: 124

Image Select: 129, 273

Impact Photos: 19, 24, 28, 30, 31, 34, 36, 37, 41, 45, 50, 61, 66, 69, 74, 78, 81, 82 b, 83, 84, 85, 86, 88, 90, 92, 93, 94, 95, 96-97, 109, 111, 114, 116-117, 123, 144, 181, 189, 191, 195, 197, 199, 201, 202, 208, 254, 255, 279, 285, 294, 295

Jak Kilby: 210, 212, 213, 217, 218, 220, 223

MacQuitty International: 131

Mary Evans Picture Library: 63, 64, 127 b, 242, 258

N J Saunders: 120, 122

Susanna Rostas: 146

Tara Lewis: 13

Topham Picturepoint: 10-11, 14 t, 14-15, 23, 42-43, 56, 59, 76, 98, 103, 118-119, 133, 137, 150, 152, 157, 158, 161, 163, 165, 166, 168, 174, 175, 176, 178, 180, 183, 203, 204, 206, 225, 226, 230, 239, 247, 263, 267, 268-269, 281, 282, 292-293

INDEX